PUNISHED
for
DREAMING

Also by Bettina L. Love

We Want to Do More Than Survive

Hip Hop's Li'l Sistas Speak

PUNISHED
for
DREAMING

HOW SCHOOL REFORM
HARMS BLACK CHILDREN
AND HOW WE HEAL

Bettina L. Love

ST. MARTIN'S PRESS
NEW YORK

First published in the United States by St. Martin's Press, an imprint of St. Martin's Publishing Group

www.stmartins.com

Design by Meryl Sussman Levavi

Chart on page 280 by Shanyce Campbell, M. Billye Sankofa Waters, Hope Wollensack, Nzinga Broussard, and Bettina L. Love

Library of Congress Cataloging-in-Publication Data

Names: Love, Bettina L., 1979– author.
Title: Punished for dreaming: how school reform harms Black children and how we heal / Bettina L. Love.
Description: First edition. | New York: St. Martin's Press, 2023. | Includes bibliographical references and index.
Identifiers: LCCN 2023019663 | ISBN 9781250280381 (hardcover) | ISBN 9781250280398 (ebook)
Subjects: LCSH: African American children—Education. | Discrimination in education—United States. | Educational change—Social aspects—United States. | School-to-prison pipeline—United States.
Classification: LCC LC2771 .L68 2023 | DDC 371.829/96073—dc23/eng/20230512
LC record available at https://lccn.loc.gov/2023019663

First Edition: 2023

10 9 8 7 6 5 4 3 2 1

There is no bad luck in the world but white folks.
—Toni Morrison, *Beloved*

CONTENTS

PUNISHED
for
DREAMING

INTRODUCTION

I grew up in the 1980s and 1990s in Rochester, in Upstate New York, where I attended a vocational high school. That's where I met Zakia*, my friend and teammate. Everyone calls her Zook. In many ways, Zook is the impetus for this book. I have always been curious about Zook's life and the lives of other Black kids, who grew up like me during the eighties and nineties, labeled *disposable* because of our zip code, test scores, and Black skin.

The first time I interviewed Zook, I felt her words in the pit of my stomach. "I was No Child Left Behind *before* No Child Left Behind," she told me. In one simple phrase, she encapsulated the enormity of the era in which we came of age. Born in 1976, she is three years older than I am. Like me, she keenly recalls what it was like to be a Black public school kid in the Reagan, George H. W. Bush, and Clinton years. She told me that through thirteen years of schooling, she could not recall a single teacher who ever took an interest in her or positively impacted her life. A gifted athlete, in high school she became a basketball star, and she can still rattle off the names of numerous coaches who supported her. She cannot name one supportive teacher. No educator ever

---

* Some of the names of people who were interviewed for the book have been changed to protect their identity.

told Zook that she was smart, clever, or capable of excelling at school. In fact, she received no academic encouragement ever. She told me her motto in school was "Cs and Ds get degrees."

When she was eleven, Zook had been body-slammed and put in a choke hold by her elementary school teacher. This is still one of the most intense memories of her childhood and why she believes the only safety she ever felt at school was on the basketball court. Throughout middle and high school, she was routinely suspended for fighting and skipping school. She tells me that the anger she felt then came from her mother abandoning her at birth for a life of drugs and her community being taken over by drugs. No teacher or school counselor asked Zook why she was guarded around teachers, helped her understand that her emotions of loss and anger were required to heal, or just saw her as a grieving child. In school, Zook's trauma was grounds for punishment.[1] She estimates that she was suspended two to four weeks out of every year. In twelfth grade, she had a grade point average of only 0.62.

During Zook's senior year, with only a few weeks left in the basketball season, local media reported about a group of male athletes and included Zook as the only girl. The story painted them as rarely going to class and having GPAs that should have made them ineligible to play. In response, the school district changed our team's record from 22–2 to 2–22—every winning game that Zook had participated in was nullified, and she was kicked off the basketball team. Then, without Zook, we lost our first game in the playoffs and were eliminated. After being suspended from school and dogged by rumors of cheating, Zook attended her school disciplinary hearing feeling betrayed by every teacher and administrator in our school.

Alone in a room full of adults, Zook was accused by a teacher of skipping class and failing to complete assignments. She remembers bristling, "I felt used. They used me to win games, but they punished me for dreaming that basketball was my ticket out of the hood." Feeling vulnerable and unprotected, Zook threw a punch at this teacher. Then she remembers running into the hallway as teachers shouted and security blared, "Zook Vanhoose on the loose. Vanhoose on the loose," over the school intercom. She was formally expelled soon after.

Before this, Zook was my idol. I wanted to be her. She could handle the ball like it was strung to her hands, she always had all the latest sneakers, she was popular, and she was funny. I would learn later that laughter was her defense mechanism. After Zook was expelled from our high school, I led the basketball team with Bri, another rising basketball star. I was averaging over thirty-one points a game, and, by my junior year, colleges were calling me almost every night.

Now Zook was my cautionary tale. I didn't yet have the analysis to see that overlapping forms of systemic violence had effectively pushed Zook out of school and off the court, or the language to speak about it. I also didn't understand that my classmates and I were living under those same systems. I just knew that I wanted a shot at a different outcome from the one Zook got. I decided that playing college ball was my way out. I stopped skipping classes and focused on doing enough work to remain eligible to play basketball. But I wasn't prepared for what came next. Since I was in a vocational high school, I was enrolled in shop class for ninety minutes a day, making T-shirts and business cards. I never took Advanced Placement or high-level math courses. When it was time to take the SAT, I was lost.

Mrs. Van, a Black woman who taught math at my high school, also tutored students at the local library. I thought she would be the perfect teacher to help me improve my SAT scores. When I asked for help, however, she made it plain how she felt about me. "You are not college material," she told me. Her words stung. I was sixteen years old, and I needed help, but to Mrs. Van, I was

Zook all over again. Mrs. Van believed that athletes like me were undeserving of help because getting into college on a basketball scholarship was skipping the line. Luckily, I found another math teacher to help me. Ms. Nix attended many of the after-school events and coached girls' volleyball. And I got connected with a woman who offered SAT tutoring to athletes for five dollars a class. I never did well on standardized tests, and the SAT was no different. After four tries and countless hours of tutoring, I scored a 720, the exact number I needed to be eligible to play college basketball.

After being expelled, Zook was sent to an alternative high school, where she was just another star athlete from Upstate New York who blew it. But she refused to go down easily and worked diligently toward her GED. And in 1997, despite our three-year age difference, we both started college. After three years of hating herself for the mistakes she made, Zook got a second chance to play college basketball, this time at a historically Black college. There, she excelled athletically *and* academically.

Zook's and my story might sound like an after-school special with heartbreaks and setbacks—and ultimately happy endings. Education reformers would label our stories as perfect examples of grit and resilience. In doing so, they would disregard how the educational system punished Zook, assaulted her, and then threw her away. And how it never invested in her at all. Sadly, Zook's story of feeling betrayed, unsafe, and punished and mine of being academically undervalued are all too familiar for millions of Black students in this country. It has taken Zook many years of therapy to talk about her past and heal from the wounds of her public school education. As it has me.

And my story didn't end there. After I went to college, the perils of being on a non-academic track in a racist public school system continued to impact me. Once I started college, I was punished for dreaming that I could become more than an athlete. After graduating high school, I left Upstate New York for Old Dominion University in Norfolk, Virginia. At the time, ODU was a women's basketball powerhouse. My dreams were beginning to take shape. I was in a top-ranked women's basketball program, and the WNBA had just started the year before I graduated high school in 1996. But I didn't play right away. I was skinny, and in practice, I got pushed around like a pinball. I could score on almost anybody, but I didn't comprehend the fundamentals of the game. Frustrated, I spent my freshman year on the bench. I returned as a sophomore, still skinny, but more determined than ever to play. But it still didn't happen. I decided to get serious about my education. It was all I had left. For the first time in my life, I realized I needed a plan beyond basketball.

That's when I had a sobering realization: none of my teammates were in my classes. For two years, I had taken classes that were barely classes, let alone college-level courses. As one of the only Black girls from the inner city on my team, I was registered for first aid, outdoor recreation, and indoor recreation courses. And the students in these classes with me were mostly Black male basketball players who came from the same kinds of predominantly Black inner-city high schools that I did. We had all been labeled "dumb Black jocks" on arrival.

I started asking my White and more middle-class Black teammates what they were studying. They were taking classes in biology, physics, chemistry, and journalism. They were majoring in subjects such as premed and communications. I had simply been placed in classes for the recreation and leisure major. I didn't know what I wanted to major in, but it was definitely not recreation and leisure.

I went to see my athletic academic advisor, Mr. Robert. He was short, White, and had a strong Southern accent. I told him that I wanted to change my major to education. As I thought about what I wanted to do and who I wanted to be, memories of my earliest teachers came back to me. And I realized that my dream was to become one of the amazing Black teachers I had in elementary school.

When I asked Mr. Robert if I could change my major to education, he answered bluntly and without hesitation, "You are from the inner city and went to an inner-city school. You are here to play basketball." I didn't know how to respond to him. And I began to wonder if it was too late for me to take school seriously. I questioned whether I was college material. I questioned my intellectual right to be there since my SAT scores were low and I hadn't done any advanced coursework in high school. I left his office deflated. Instead of being encouraged, I felt punished for believing I could be more than an athlete. And then I called my high school athletic director, Mrs. Judy Knight.

When I told her what my athletic academic advisor had said, she said, "I am on my way." She flew from Upstate New York to Virginia for the next home game. After meeting with my coach, she said, "Bettina, you have to leave this place." I knew she was right. At the end of my sophomore year, I withdrew from ODU and returned to Rochester.

At the time, my best friend was being recruited by the University of Pittsburgh. Determined to get me back into college, Mrs. Knight made some calls and got me an interview with the head women's basketball coach there, where she knew I'd have at least one person whom I knew and trusted. She drove me from Rochester to Pittsburgh—a five-hour car ride. When I met the coach, Traci Waites, she told me something I had needed to hear for a very long time: "You are a student first and an athlete second." I remember slowly trying to process her words to make sure she got the order right. Then she let me know that each player on her team was required to attend study hall for at least eight hours a week. If a player fell short, we all had to run a mile for each minute missed.

With these new rules, expectations, and mandatory time to study, I began to excel. I wanted to read every book I got my hands on, especially when I took my first African American studies course. Reading *The Autobiography of Malcolm X,* I saw how much books helped transform his life. "I could spend the rest of my life reading, just satisfying my curiosity," Malcolm wrote, and I felt the same way. With Coach Waites's guidance, I didn't just get my BA, I also pursued my master's degree, all while playing basketball. I left the University of Pittsburgh with two degrees and became an elementary school teacher.

And the whole time I studied education, I thought about Zook and my high school experiences. Why was our education made up of a series of barriers that we, as children, were expected to jump over? Why, instead of learning, were we punished with low expectations, physical violence, surveillance, standardized testing, and frequent suspensions? For us and Black kids like us, school, instead of being a place of learning, was a place of harm. I now know that each barrier was intentional and put there to punish Black folx for fighting for racial equality in public education.

I was born a scant four years before the release of *A Nation at Risk: The Imperative for Educational Reform,* the Reagan administration report on the state of American education. The report was crafted under the leadership of education secretary Terrel Bell, and its alarmist language about the systemic failure of American schools to provide adequate education, coupled with its emphasis on reform as a solution, cast a long and dark shadow over young Black people of my generation.

A Nation at Risk, together with Reagan's war on drugs, set in motion the merging of prisons and schools under the guise of "getting tough" on education. "Getting tough" was a euphemism for "punishment," sold to the public as high-stakes testing, school choice, vouchers, charter schools, and school safety. At the same time, police officers were placed in schools along with metal detectors, police dogs, and surveillance equipment to control the students they now openly called *thugs* and *criminals.*

In *Punished for Dreaming,* I argue that Reagan's presidency ushered in a new type of American Black bondage: the War on Black Children, in which his war on drugs worked in concert with school reform to pathologize and penalize Black children under school safety policies. As the country watched and cheered for the militarization of police departments to fight crack in America's inner cities, the Reagan administration told the world that America's schools were failing and in need of discipline. All these reform measures were informed by what prison abolitionists call *carceral logic,* or "a punishment mindset."[2] Punishment became our primary solution. We were tough on crime and tough on public education. Under the slogans of "school accountability" and "school safety," schools morphed into spaces of surveillance, confinement, and state-sanctioned violence to Black bodies; schools became part of the police state resembling prisons. The government told Black parents that no child would be left behind, but they did not specify who would be taking their children—the testing industry, the prisons, or the punitive charter schools, which all too often only concerned themselves with teaching Black children the basic skills for America's low-skill labor demands. For-profit charter school companies cashed in on their contracts with nonprofit charter schools, including leasing properties, supplying curriculum, food services, personnel, cocurricular programming, technology, and, of course, management fees.[3]

The aim of this book is to understand how a thirty-six-page

educational report manufactured an educational crisis of cata-strophic proportions that destroyed generations of Black families. Eighties babies witnessed and, more important, experienced the joining of these industries—prisons and education—that ex-panded the prison industrial complex and created an educational system where Black children attended schools that structurally placed punishment, violence, police, standardized testing, and profits before learning. I call this the *educational survival com-plex*. I define this phenomenon as the exploitation of compulsory education by the ever-expanding carceral state, private corpora-tions, wealth managers, philanthropy, education reformers, local and state politicians, celebrities, real estate, the testing industry, and each U.S. president to fill school buildings with Black chil-dren who are educated to make profits for the über-rich and to undo America's democracy. Black children are put at the nexus of this education auction block.

My generation—part of the post-civil rights generation and the hip-hop generation—is like no other because we came of age when mass incarceration and educational policies put un-mistakable, identical targets on our backs. Crime reform and education reform merged to call us *crack babies, super pred-ators,* and *thugs* and told the world that we put this nation at risk. They referred to our educational experience as *the achievement gap,* which was another way to say we would never be as smart as White children. They only knew us as either fatherless teen moth-ers, criminals, or dropouts—or a combination of all three—who, to many, did not even deserve three strikes. When they looked at us, the theme song of *Cops* played in their heads. We were bad boys (and girls), and our bodies belonged to the state.

The conjoining of schools and prisons is not a conspiracy the-ory or something found on the dark web. It is a well-executed plan that for the last forty years has taken the lives of Black chil-dren with surgical precision. There is no big conspiracy in this book. When White supremacy is entrenched in every institution in this country and intoxicated by capitalism and anti-Blackness, Black people will suffer. White supremacy and capitalism work in unison, even in education. It is beyond a pipeline of corruption; it is a deliberate, massive, intentional, and profitable mechanism for the educational death of Black children.

My life and the lives of my peers were forever shaped by coming of age in a generation whose own government declared war on them, not only in the streets but also in the schools, at the intersection of economic gain and racist ideology. Long-standing public institutions (education, housing, health care, public assistance, and labor) were abandoned; the impact of this intentional "organized abandonment" criminalized our everyday lives inside and outside of schools, making carcerality inevitable.[4] The stories people told themselves about kids who came from zip codes like mine, which they heard only on the nightly news, didn't end in high school. That story traveled with me to college along with the shame of being stamped *inferior*.

Punished for Dreaming is the story of the past forty years of education reform, which deliberately crafted policies to punish Black people for believing in and fighting for their right to quality *public* education. The cruelest part of the so-called reform efforts that have shaped education in the past four decades is that they have relied on and taken advantage of Black people's aspirations— their hopes for education, self-determination, economic mobility, and, ultimately, freedom. When Black people have dreamed big, organized effectively, and fought hard enough that justice and grand-scale change seem not only possible but imminent—the insidious pushback to this comes in the form of reform. Reform, as it has been deployed in education, becomes punishment by implementing and creating punitive laws, regulations, and school policies that disproportionately label Black children as unruly, violent, and *academically inferior.* Reformers are comfortable with these labels because anti-Blackness remains the uninterrogated heart of reform. Anti-Blackness, the steadfast refusal to see Black people as fully human, manifests in the belief that Black people need fixing due to inherent negative qualities, such as criminality, laziness, and poor life choices. These beliefs allow reformers to step in as saviors with federally and privately funded "quick fixes," such as vouchers, charter schools, and character education. Fixes that harm Black children in their anti-Blackness while ultimately proving lucrative for the reformers. "School choice," for instance, is code for Black children's choices after White America has divvied up the resources needed for their children's education and Black parents in the inner city and poorer suburbs are left with educational scraps. This reform/savior mentality rests on the idea that White people are best able to determine the types of choices Black people have in housing, employment, safety, medical care, and education.

Throughout this book, I share stories, like Zook's and my own, of Black adults who grew up as targets of our own government's domestic wars, not only in our neighborhoods but also in our schools. These interviews are more than data points or individual grievances about a bad school experience; they represent generations of pain, trauma, and loss inflicted on Black children by America's public school system. The voices of Black people in this book tell the story of how a pillar of democracy—public education—put Black children on the educational auction block. In these pages, readers will meet over two dozen Black adults whose stories contextualize the concept that, if we are to move toward educational justice, then we must understand what education was before *Brown v. Board of Education,* after *Brown,* and the attack that was unleashed on my generation in 1983 because of White resistance to *Brown.*

In 2019, I wrote the book *We Want to Do More Than Survive: Abolitionist Teaching and the Pursuit of Education Freedom*. My goal was to center abolitionist approaches in the field of education. Since then, *abolition* has become a buzzword in education without an actual understanding of abolition or the courage to move beyond reform. With *Punished for Dreaming*, therefore, I seek to have us embrace educational reparations and start the path toward repairing, with the goal of ultimately transforming, our education system. Educational reparations are more than compensation for harm; it's the processes of accountability, truth-telling, cessation, collective healing, and transformation. If we embrace the process of educational reparations, I believe we can work toward something resembling true democracy.

In its twelve chapters, *Punished for Dreaming* tells the story of how my own family was impacted by *Brown* and how the court decision sparked the creation of a public school system that differed from the era of de jure segregation but was just as racist. This new system was drawn up by White liberals, White Southerners nostalgic for the Old South, the ultrarich, leading economists, and politicians. The book details how education reform was solidified with the release of the 1983 report *A Nation at Risk*, which was filled with lies that ultimately undermined public education, heightened America's disdain for Black people, opened schools to the free market, and left Black children with the educational scraps of White resentment. I also expose the big business of education entrepreneurs and philanthropists and how they profit and flourish from ensuring the failure of Black schools. And I cover the appointment of Betsy DeVos and the "Stop W.O.K.E Act" hysteria to continue White America's distrust in public education for privatization, as well as the promises and failures of the Biden administration.

Punished for Dreaming shows, too, how benevolent school policies and programs make carcerality an inevitability for Black students. It relates how the founders of the largest charter school network in the country, Knowledge Is Power Program, got their ideas from a Black woman, Harriett Ball—while she died trying to open her own school. It sheds light on how the work of reform is painstakingly ornamental and oftentimes protects Whiteness. If White people are going to fight for justice, I argue, they first need to save themselves and detach from White disposability and stop being duped by the lies of Whiteness. I also contend that when one sees Black people for who we are, one understands that we have shown this country—physically, mentally, materially, and spirituality—how to work toward justice with grace, love, dignity, and collective accountability and healing. Finally, *Punished for Dreaming* offers a road map for healing and transformation through the arduous and intensely emotional work of reparations. The book offers not only a critique of reform but a way forward. A way to a more just world for all children—and a nation finally ready to commit to ending harm and starting the long process of educational justice.

1

SETTING THE STAGE:
EDUCATIONAL WHITE RAGE

White rage doesn't have to wear sheets, burn crosses, or take to the streets. Working the halls of power, it can achieve its ends far more effectively, far more destructively.

—Carol Anderson, *White Rage:*
The Unspoken Truth of Our Racial Divide[1]

Lightning Rod

Mrs. Victoria Ali grew up in Virginia during the Jim Crow era. She remembers having to use separate water fountains, separate bathrooms, and a separate door—out back—to get a hot dog from her favorite childhood eatery. Growing up in the South in the 1950s and 1960s, Mrs. Ali accepted segregation as her reality.

Mrs. Ali attended all-Black schools throughout her youth— and she has fond memories of them. She talks about her twelfth-grade English teacher, Ruby B. Archie, who went on to become mayor of her small town. "She demanded so much of us in that class . . . but we enjoyed the atmosphere of learning." Mrs. Archie's classroom was filled with laughter and snacks, so long as there was enough to go around for everybody. She patiently worked with her students, meeting them where they were and ensuring they understood the concepts she introduced. "She was compassionate with those students who may not have had as much experience or exposure as others," Mrs. Ali told me, referencing the economic class divides among her peers. Years later, when Mrs. Ali became a teacher and learned how to differentiate instruction, she realized that Mrs. Archie had been an expert at adjusting lessons to meet each student's needs and gave them various entry points to success. "She didn't expect you to sit there and say, 'I can't,'" Mrs. Ali told me. "That wasn't a part of her philosophy."

Growing up, Mrs. Ali attended schools led by Black educators who addressed students' needs and cared for them. She recounted stories of teachers who went above and beyond the call of duty, getting to know students and their families. "It was a community," she told me. But while the Jim Crow South had plenty of classrooms led by warm, highly educated, and demanding teachers like Mrs. Archie, it was not an idyllic place for all Black students to be educated. Before *Brown v. Board of Education*, which overturned *Plessy v. Ferguson*, the infamous 1896 Supreme Court decision that upheld the policy of racial segregation known as "separate but equal," many Black children attended schools that were no more than shacks—they had no indoor plumbing or electricity, let alone respectable libraries. In Atlanta's Black schools in the mid-1930s, there were eighty-two students for every teacher.[2] Schools were so overcrowded in the city that "85 percent of all black elementary school students attended class for only half the day during the 1947–48 school year."[3] In Virginia's Prince Edward County, there was no high school for Black students until 1939, even though the state required "public schools and compulsory attendance."[4] And where there were public schools, funding disparities were wide. During the 1943/44 school year, the state of Louisiana spent $76.34 per White elementary school student; their Black counterparts got only $23.99.[5] The disparity was even worse when looking at the state's elementary and high school students combined: $95.98 for White students and $27.30 for Black students.

Brown seemed to signal a shift in the legacy of White scraps for Black children. But the reality is that this Supreme Court victory set into motion unprecedented White rage that unleashed decades of anti-Black educational policy. In *White Rage,* Carol Anderson makes clear that White rage is not just angry White parents shoving and spitting on Black children attempting to enter an all-White school. White rage is what has built America's institutions, working to cunningly craft laws, policies, covenants, and approaches that undercut democracy, halt Black advancement, and cage Black bodies while leaving White supremacy intact and often even stronger.

The resistance to *Brown* was immediate and intense. Special commissions and committees were formed to circumvent the threat of school desegregation.[6] Little Rock, Arkansas, closed public high schools for a year—for both Black and White students. Instead of integrating schools, Virginia's Prince Edward County shut down its entire public school system for five years. Many White people across the country were incensed by the idea that government could undo their segregationist lives. Enraged by *Brown,* White America took its tax dollars, resources, home values, economic mobility, and all-White schools and ran to the suburbs, accelerating a pattern of White flight. To keep their neighborhoods White, they continued using racially restrictive covenants prohibiting Black folx from buying homes in White enclaves, even though the Supreme Court had deemed the practice unenforceable in 1948. In the South, they opened private schools known as "segregation academies," which were granted tax exemptions by the federal government.[7]

"There is only one solution in the event segregation is banned by the Supreme Court," Georgia senator Herman Talmadge had warned in 1952.[8] "And that is abolition of the public school system."[9] Talmadge also said that after *Brown*, "blood will run in the streets of Atlanta."[10] In the lead-up to the high court's decision, President Eisenhower tried to placate Southern segregationists, particularly South Carolina governor James Byrnes, who lobbied him relentlessly. Eisenhower hosted a dinner party at the White House to enlighten Chief Justice Earl Warren on the ins and outs of Southern hospitality. The president told the Los Angeles–born justice that Southerners "are not bad people. All they are concerned about is to see that their sweet little girls are not required to sit in school alongside some big overgrown Negroes."[11] The tactic failed to sway Warren.

Senator Talmadge's followers made good on his promise. Anticipating the integration of Atlanta public schools, six years after the initial *Brown* decision, an all-Black school on the west side of Atlanta was bombed.[12] *Brown* infuriated White supremacists. Their rage became the momentum for a far-right movement to counter what they considered the "liberal establishment" after the *Brown* decision. The notion that the government could enforce school integration was an overreach to many White Americans, one that threatened states' rights. When conservatives argue for states' rights, they are arguing to expand the "collective freedoms" of White people at the expense of civil rights, women's rights, and LGBTQIA rights. States' rights is dog-whistle politics for preventing or erasing Black freedom and civil rights in general.

A year later, the Supreme Court decision in *Brown II* put the country on notice that the desegregation of public schools must happen "with all deliberate speed." But even a second court directive to integrate schools could not undo the resistance to *Brown*. In Louisiana, the governor went so far as to "empower state police to arrest any federal judge or U.S. marshal who tried to implement *Brown*."[13] Arkansas argued that the governor—not the Supreme Court—had the power to determine the state's law. And Mississippi declared *Brown* "unconstitutional." To Southern politicians, "Massive Resistance to *Brown* was not some base, primeval white supremacy," Anderson writes, "but rather a principled, patriotic stand to defend the Constitution."[14] White supremacists viewed *Brown* as a "declaration of war."[15]

After the ruling, Roy Wilkins, then executive secretary of the NAACP, admitted, "My sense of euphoria was a bit naïve. Swept away, elevated, exalted, I failed to anticipate the ferocity of the resistance that quickly grew up in the Deep South."[16] The resistance to *Brown*, he added, was a "cold, clinical cruelty of a response."[17] It was a response that destroyed Black education—an education that had nurtured so many students, including Mrs. Ali.

No Longer Seen

Mrs. Ali told me things changed after the *Brown* ruling. As someone who researches and studies the history of Black education, I had only read about how education for Black children changed for the worse after *Brown*. Hearing Mrs. Ali's words helped me understand just how devastating the aftermath of *Brown* was and how its devastation persists today. "They leave us to flounder in public education, knowing these schools will not serve our needs," she said. "Working as fast as we can, scratching our heads the entire time, making a way for our children. . . . Schools were not designed for our children," said Mrs. Ali. "They were created for White children."

Mrs. Ali wanted to teach in her hometown. Beginning in 1972, she taught there in an elementary school, then a middle school. She eventually became an elementary school vice principal and ultimately a principal, retiring in 2004. She was immersed in the education profession before high-stakes testing, No Child Left Behind, charter schools, and police in schools. When I asked how she determined if her children were achieving without standardized tests, she said, "I knew my students. I knew their families. I built a relationship with my students, so I knew what they needed. . . . It was hard work, but my students learned and enjoyed school." Reflecting on how schools had changed from when she was a student, she said, "Teachers don't have any tolerance for children of color, and they do not know the difference between discipline and punishment. . . . As a teacher, I would wonder why all the Black kids were in the office. When I became a principal, I understood why. I now had a thirty-thousand-foot view as an administrator." She saw White students routinely treated with kid gloves and given the benefit of the doubt, while Black children's behavior was held to a higher and more rigid standard. Much of this had to do with teachers' assumptions about how students' home cultures differed. "A lot of teachers, even Black teachers, felt that these White students were so overly prepared or so exposed that whatever they did was okay," Mrs. Ali told me. "When they messed up, it's like, 'This is probably what they're used to doing at home, so I'll just let that go,'" she said. Because of the tight-knit nature of her own school community while growing up and her professional commitment to understanding students as whole people, she knew these teachers were failing to create the bonds that are fundamental to positive school environments.

By the end of her career, tests were getting in the way of building teacher-student relationships, she said. Two years before she retired, No Child Left Behind, the most punitive educational legislation to date, was signed into law, mandating standardized testing. NCLB hampered educators' ability to build meaningful relationships with students and let young people know they were seen and valued. "Schools became so restrictive," she told me. "Taking kids to the park or socializing with children was forbidden [because] so much time was spent on testing."

Erasing Black Teachers and Black Culture

As underfunded as Black schools were under Jim Crow, teaching by Black educators was often exceptional. In her book *Their Highest Potential: An African American School Community in the Segregated South,* eminent educational historian Vanessa Siddle Walker writes, "Although black schools were indeed commonly lacking in facilities and funding, some evidence suggests that the environment of the segregated school had affective traits, institutional policies and community support that helped black children learn in spite of the neglect their schools received from white school boards."[18]

Describing her upbringing in Kentucky, feminist icon bell hooks wrote that her "almost all" Black female teachers "were committed to nurturing intellect so that we could become scholars, thinkers, and cultural workers—Black folks who used our 'minds.'"[19] She added, "To fulfill that mission, my teachers made sure they 'knew' us."[20] Her words echo Mrs. Ali's. hooks's education was rooted in Black liberation because a "devotion to learning, to a life of the mind, was a counter-hegemonic act, a fundamental way to resist every strategy of white racist colonization."[21]

Many Black parents resisted school desegregation, anticipating the racism and anti-Blackness their children would endure, the firing of Black teachers, and the unequal outcomes of Black students, even in shiny new buildings. And they were right. After *Brown,* more than thirty-eight thousand Black teachers were pushed out of their jobs.[22] Black principals fared the worst, with 90 percent losing their jobs.[23] White educators largely erased Black students' culture and community. Black students were put in classrooms with White teachers who had low expectations of their intellectual capacity. The late legal scholar Derrick

Bell maintained that Black folx would have been better served if the Supreme Court had enforced the "equal" part of "separate but equal."[24] In making his assertion, Bell echoed W. E. B. Du Bois, who in 1935 noted that, "Negro children need neither segregated schools nor mixed schools. What they need is education."[25] Du Bois and Bell are right, but Black children also need Black teachers.

The push out of Black teachers after *Brown* was swift. Before 1954, there was an abundance of highly credentialed, skilled Black teachers; some were Ph.D.s. According to historical records, in 1940, 56.9 percent of college-educated Black women and 35.9 percent of college-educated Black men were teachers.[26] These remarkable teachers had fewer resources but were committed to Black excellence. They were given the pink slip after *Brown*.[27] According to education scholar Leslie Fenwick's data, in the seventeen states with nonsegregated school systems before *Brown*, 35–50 percent of the teaching force was Black.[28] After *Brown*, barriers were established to keep Black teachers out of the profession. Expensive and irrelevant teacher licensure exams were now required.[29] These tests are incapable of predicting what kind of teacher one will be, but states used them to deny Black teachers the opportunity to teach or renew existing teacher contracts.

According to educational scholar Linda Tillman, "Between 1984 and 1989, about 21,500 black teachers were displaced because of new requirements for teacher education programs and certification."[30] Enterprising students matriculating at colleges and universities saw the writing on the wall and steered clear of the profession altogether. From 1975 to 1985, the number of Black students majoring in education declined by 66 percent.[31] Black teachers have never made up more than 10 percent of the teaching U.S. population in the last forty years.

Not only was there a large applicant pool of highly educated, skilled Black people entering the teaching profession before

Brown, but Southern Black teacher associations challenged institutional racism, aligned their educational goals with the civil rights movement, and advocated for equal salaries to their White peers, more resources for Black schools, and the right to work during desegregation.[32] However, the ultimate goal of Southern Black teacher associations was power. On April 12, 1930, in Montgomery, Alabama, Dr. John Hope, civil rights leader and president of Morehouse College, told a room of all Black educators, "The need of the Negro is pressing . . . If they are going to work out of it at all it will have to be done through their teachers. . . . We as teachers must realize that we have the power."[33] The White rage over desegregation destroyed Southern Black teacher associations and the power they sought for their profession and Black children. Subsequently, *Brown* created another Great Migration: the Southern Black teacher migration—as Black teachers were displaced from their jobs after *Brown,* many headed North to teach. My mother's first Black teacher was a displaced teacher from the South.

"Oh My God, Were They Strict"

My mother's father and mother, my grandparents, migrated from South Carolina in 1950 to Rochester, New York, which was first the land of the Iroquois Nation. Philip Washington, my grandfather, was nineteen, and Rosetta Washington, my grandmother, was fifteen when they married and left Hemingway, South Carolina. My grandfather's older brother had been the first in the family to leave Hemingway, known for cotton and tobacco, for Rochester in search of better jobs. At the time, this small town in western Upstate New York was home to major companies such as Eastman Kodak, Bausch + Lomb, and Xerox. In 1945, roughly five thousand Black people were living in Rochester; by 1964, almost thirty-two thousand more had settled in the city.

My grandmother grew up poor and never learned to read or write. My grandfather was literate. According to my mother, Patricia—but everyone, myself included, calls her *Patty*—once her parents got to Rochester, my grandfather found work right away. Patty was born three years after they arrived, in 1953; she was their third child. Although my grandmother was illiterate, she stressed education to the ten children she would eventually have. My grandmother stayed at home, while my grandfather opened up his own floor-cleaning company.

My mother loved school and was top of her class. When she started kindergarten in 1958, there were rarely any Black teachers in the city. Justin Murphy's book, *Your Children Are Very Greatly in Danger: School Segregation in Rochester, New York,* documents the years my mother was in school there and accurately reflects her experience. Murphy writes, "In 1963 there were just 96 Black teachers among a districtwide corps of 2,220, and many schools had none at all."[34] By the late 1960s, local organizations like FIGHT (Freedom, Independence, God, Honor, and Today) and Rochester's branch of the National Association for the Advancement of Colored People (NAACP) pushed for recruiting and hiring more Black teachers. These organizations actively recruited teachers from the South to Rochester, knowing that many of the South's well-educated and effective Black teaching force had just been laid off due to *Brown*. Even before organized recruitment efforts by the city, Black teachers were moving north to teach. Patty got her first Black teacher in third grade: Mrs. Nancy Jenkins, a Southern transplant, whom Patty remembers as being from Alabama or Georgia. As I interviewed my mother for this book, I was in awe of her memory. At sixty-nine years old, she remembers her elementary teachers' names. Her voice is raspy from years of smoking, but her memory is clear. "For some reason, I don't know, Rochester brought in all these Black teachers from the South because the White teachers weren't teaching the Black children, they weren't learning. So what they did, they brought these teachers from the South and—oh my God, were they strict!" Patty told me. Sitting outside on her porch in her yellow-and-brown nightgown, Patty burst into laughter just thinking about Mrs. Jenkins's high expectations.

The words Patty used to describe her Black teachers from the South match everything I have read about Black educators from that era and echo Mrs. Ali's experience in Virginia. When I asked Patty how her Black teachers taught, she said, "I mean, those teachers taught you rather than just make you sit there and listen to them. The White teachers would just walk around saying, 'Yes, Johnny,' and 'Yes, Patty.' They would give you an A or a B. They didn't care. If they liked you, you passed . . . Our Black teachers were intelligent." Patty could still name the three Black teachers she had in elementary school: Mrs. Jenkins, Mrs. Castleberry, and Mr. Williams—all three from the South.

Rochester's recruitment and hiring of Black teachers from the South was possible because of the city's rich history of activism, grassroots organizing, and cooperative economic strategies. In the 1960s, Black folx in the city had street dance parties on the weekend. During the summer months, festivals representing the African diaspora filled the summer breeze with good food, music, and a sense of community. However, outside the loving community, racial tensions in the city were always high. Housing discrimination was one of the "most visible instruments of segregation," along with severe state-sanctioned police violence toward Black people.[35] Racial covenants were created, trapping Black folx in the poorest and most under-resourced parts of the city. Their schools followed suit. These covenants were also state-sponsored "with elected officials openly, intentionally, and legally forcing neighborhoods to become 'Whites Only.'"[36] Black folx who came from the South to Rochester to teach and for better job opportunities still faced racism, anti-Blackness, and overcrowded Black schools, things they thought they'd left behind in the South. The city's redlining housing policies and Rochester City School District's (RCSD) racist educational policies ensured that Black students learned separately from their White peers in substandard conditions. In the 1950s and 1960s, RCSD put portable trailers outside Black schools instead of sending Black children to White schools.[37] In 1964, James Baldwin wrote an essay warning White people that their children, not only Black children, were endangered by the consequences of school segregation and the dehumanizing effect of racism on all people, including White people and children.

> I know you didn't do it, and I didn't do it either, but I am responsible for it because I am a man and a citizen of this country and you are responsible for it, too, for the very same reason: as long as my children face the future they face, and come to the ruin that they come to, your children are very greatly in danger, too.[38]

Baldwin warned us all, but White rage rarely listens, and it never comprehends.

Patty was in sixth grade and attended a nearly all-Black school on the city's west side when Baldwin published these words of warning. Like many other cities in the 1960s and beyond, Rochester faced hostile White opposition to desegregation as White people fled to the suburbs. Things came to a head in 1964 when police physically assaulted a well-known Black store owner, Rufus Fairwell. To protest police violence, Black folx took to the streets for three days; 4 people died and another 350 were injured. Patty was just eleven years old during the uprising. She told me, "I remember the state troopers and the National Guard walking our neighborhood streets with guns and kids throwing rocks at them. It was happening right on my street corner. Mama made us stay on the porch. It was terrible."

The racial violence didn't stop after 1964; it spilled over from the streets into the schools. After my grandparents watched the violence in their community and became frustrated with the lack of resources of all-Black schools, they decided to enroll my mother in an all-White school on the other side of town for seventh grade. Although my grandmother couldn't read or write, she always knew her daughter deserved more. At the time, Rochester had a program that allowed a very small portion of Black students to enroll in all-White schools; roughly 450 students participated in the program.[39] My mother remembers my grandfather enrolling her in the program and paying for her daily bus ride to Charlotte High School, one of the all-White schools in town. She only remembers one other Black girl at the school: "I don't remember her name, but her family had money," she told me.

Patty didn't last a school year at Charlotte. The racism was horrific. With tears in her eyes, my mother told me how White students called her the n-word and threatened her. While describing the verbal violence she endured, she got up and walked away. It was "just too much," she said. I never knew this story about Patty's school experience before this interview. After seeing her cry, which my mother rarely does, I now understand why she never told me. It was just too painful to talk about, even six decades later. My grandparents from South Carolina were too familiar with how the story of racism and threats could end for their daughter. They promptly unenrolled Patty from Charlotte and put her back at Madison, the all-Black high school near their home.

Patty didn't graduate from high school. She stopped attending school in tenth grade to care for her younger siblings. Remembering my grandmother wanted her children to have the education she never had, Patty cries again. Of her nine brothers and sisters, Patty thinks fewer than half graduated high school.

In March of 1970 (six years after Patty left Charlotte), Rochester City School District closed for a day after teachers threatened to boycott over a plan to desegregate schools. A year later, a full seventeen years after the first *Brown* decision mandating school desegregation, RCSD initiated a plan for integration by busing Black students to White schools. The busing program only lasted two months. The White rage was massive and swift, and Rochester, fresh from one uprising, chose to avoid another. Black parents' hopes for integration also waned. Black children returned home from school bloodied by rocks thrown at them by White classmates and having read racial slurs spray-painted on school walls.

Decades later, Rochester is now second in the nation for child poverty; nearly half of Rochester's children live in poverty, with Black and Brown[†] children overrepresented within that population.[40] Rochester's per-capita homicide rate in 2021 was fifth among major U.S. cities; Black people are overrepresented among

---

[†] In this book, I use the term "Brown," not referring to the legal case, when discussing student populations that have been systemically designated as "Hispanic" and "Latinx" within education-related data. I want to be clear that when I use the word "Brown," my intention is not to add to the erasure or the simplification of the various Indigenous identities that make up the student populations historically and currently categorized as Hispanic or Latinx. The Oxford Dictionary defines the term "Hispanic" as "relating to Spain or to Spanish-speaking countries, especially those of Central and South America" and "relating to Spanish-speaking people or their culture, especially in the U.S." I understand that "Hispanic" as a label is not only colonial in essence [centering Spanish colonization], but it also does not account for the many diasporic and Indigenous identities, languages, and cultures that exist within such a colonial categorization. To be clear, in this book, whenever I use the term "Hispanic," I do so only because I am utilizing the actual terms used in the data that I analyzed which classified its participants as Hispanic; otherwise, I will use the term "Brown" to refer to the many identities that make up this inaccurate and oversimplified category.

homicide victims.[41] ZIP codes where Rochester's violence is concentrated are also those with the lowest median income per household and the highest concentration of Black and Brown residents.[42] And in 2017, Rochester's schools were ranked last in the nation for academic growth.[43] A mixed bag of Black excellence and educational White rage after *Brown* created the school system in my hometown. I was fortunate enough to experience some Black excellence, but my path was all too similar to Patty's.

Johnson & Clayton

Like my grandparents, Patty and my father, Gene Love, thought sending me to a high-performing, well-resourced private school would be the best option. Although neither of my parents graduated high school, Patty got her GED, and they both had working-class jobs that put food on the table and a roof over their children's heads, and left enough over to send their last child of three to private school. For kindergarten through third grade, I attended St. Monica's, a private Catholic school a few minutes' walk from my house. Black children, a scattering of White children among them, filled the school. The school administrators were also Black, but the teachers were overwhelmingly White. I don't recall many Black teachers in the school, and I stayed in trouble. The school called my parents a lot because I was fighting and joking around. To be honest, the White teachers were scared of me and Patty, and I knew it, so I played the stereotyped role they expected of me—an unruly and academically low-performing Black child. They never suspended me; I suspect they didn't want to deal with Patty. "They called, but I always handled that. You were going to school the next day, and that was that . . . I would put you to the side and tell you, 'Don't let nobody make you small, don't let anyone put their hands on you and send you back to school." Patty was telling me what her mother told her when she entered that all-White school.

I remember Patty's pep talks because she was fearless in her tone, body language, and stance. Most days, before I left for school, she would urge me to "give them hell." To her, "them" were racist White folx or anybody who saw me as inferior. My mother taught me to resist and fight, like her mother taught her. And every life lesson she imparted started with an idiom: "Loose lips sink ships," "Don't rob Peter to pay Paul," and "A hard head makes a soft behind." One Christmas, I asked my mother if Santa Claus was real. "Do we have a chimney?" she asked. And before I could reply, she told me, "Ain't no White man getting credit for all my hard work." I would tell my own children the same thing about Santa Claus decades later.

I went to school every day giving them hell. My mother tried to protect me from enduring harm similar to what White students and teachers had inflicted on her, but by the time I entered third grade, my parents had enough. My mother's survival tactics of being ruthless, calculated, and scared of no one could only protect me against Whiteness for so long. I was labeled a disruptive kid, and although I was passing all my classes, my teacher wanted to hold me back. My mother intervened. My parents decided that for fourth grade, I would be going to the public school in my neighborhood.

When I entered School #19, I had Mrs. Helen Johnson, my first black teacher. She was tall and skinny and wore braces, yet I had never seen a woman, any woman of any race, have such a commanding, powerful, and stern presence. A native of the South—New Orleans, to be exact—Mrs. Johnson didn't just love us students, she believed we mattered. She made us believe that caring for herself also meant wrapping our lives up in hers. Testimony to her power is that even Patty feared her. I remember walking into Mrs. Johnson's class and knowing deep down that my days as class clown were over. And, frankly, I was relieved.

I was ready to be more than what White people thought I was or could become. Mrs. Johnson embodied the best of us; smart, thoughtful, and funny, I wanted to be her.

Mrs. Johnson wore bright clothes every day and had the most beautiful penmanship I'd ever seen. She also demanded excellence from each one of us. She knew that we needed a survival plan and that school was key to our achieving one. For that to happen, she had to teach us that school mattered beyond our grades, and so she taught as if the fate of her family and the fate of our families were connected. She made herself vulnerable in front of us and shared stories of her childhood in New Orleans. When she would call our parents, she would talk about us as people worthy of respect, not just students who were her job. Her sense of responsibility for us made us all feel like we were a family. Disappointing Mrs. Johnson meant disappointing our class, our family, and our community. Her classroom created a collective spirit of love, accountability, and purpose. Each one of our voices mattered, she listened to each one of us. We felt and knew that we genuinely were her priority.

The following year, we had Mr. Clayton as our fifth grade teacher. He wore a tie every day and he was my first and only Black male teacher until college. Like Mrs. Johnson, he never dressed down. Every day he showed up embodying the respect he wanted to instill in us. And he called us by our last names. I can still hear him call to me, "Miss Love, would you like to answer the question?"

It was around this time that I started showing up to school dirty after playing basketball with the boys in the morning. My parents left for work early, so it was my responsibility to get to school on time. I would play basketball in rain, wind, or snow. I didn't care; I just wanted to be on the court. One morning, I came to Mr. Clayton's looking particularly a mess. "Miss Love," he said, calling me over. "Miss Love, you are pretty good at basketball," he said. Those words coming from him felt like deep validation. Then he continued, "But you can't keep coming to class filthy." I wasn't ashamed because I could feel his words coming from a place of love and deep concern. He told me that I could play ball in the morning as long as I also brought a fresh change of clothes to school. He wanted me to know that I could play hard with the boys while also fulfilling my obligations to his classroom. It was a powerful lesson on how to negotiate competing identities and one that I never forgot.

Mr. Clayton and Mrs. Johnson were more than teachers; they were also parental figures. The respect they brought to their classrooms and the respect they demanded from us, for each other, and for ourselves were linchpins of my early development. I needed their presence because my stable and supportive Black family was starting to unravel. My older siblings were out of the house living their lives, and my parents became hooked on drugs. Patty was no longer around to tell me to "give them hell," but now I needed her words to survive the community that raised me. Drugs and crime overtook my community. When I entered kindergarten in 1985, there were 26 murders and 1,072 robberies in the city of Rochester. By the time I was a high school sophomore (in 1995), murders had increased more than 200 percent while robberies were up nearly 150 percent. In a single decade, the decade in which I attended elementary and middle school, the decade in which I began to prepare for my adult life, my city became mired in violence, a trend that sadly continues today.

Crime, drugs, and educational White rage were conjoined, and my generation stood at the crossroads as America put targets on Black children's backs. The educational White rage experienced by generations of my family did not happen by accident. What Patty experienced was not by accident. Patty's experiences, along with Zook's and my own, were orchestrated by powerful individuals who used White resentment toward civil rights achievements to set up an education system that punished Black children, Black communities, and Black dreams.

The *Brown* ruling, a monumental civil rights achievement, was supposed to give Black children greater access to educational opportunities, but my family and my friends got the backlash. *Brown* incited a loosely coordinated but tightly aligned attack on public education by the right, the far right, White liberals in the North, poor White folx, and the ultrarich. Ironically, *Brown* marks the formal beginning of an anti-Black educational agenda that would become the norm by the 1980s and 1990s. By the 1980s, the racism Patty had experienced at an all-White school in the 1960s would become subtler but remain dangerous. There was no longer any need to yell racial slurs at Black children because the system was created to treat us as such.

The effort to destroy *Brown* and the public school system in general was possible because powerful individuals who held some of the most critical positions in government, policy, and economics worked in unison to destroy the good-hearted and morally driven intentions of desegregation. These individuals worked strategically to codify educational White rage. Their approach was cruel, direct, and predatory. The goal was singular: undermine public education at every turn and then profit from its demise. Some of these powerful actors are now well known, and others intentionally remain publicly obscure, but all were ideologically and politically aligned in the gutting of public education to the detriment of Black folx like myself and my friends. I believe that to undo a system and move it toward repair, you must understand who did the harm and hold them responsible.

Let's Name Names

Historian Nancy MacLean argues that influential economists were part of a network of wealthy elites who used their power to "restructure state and federal policy to protect their rights (and their privileged positions) from being diminished by the majority

of Americans."[44] According to MacLean, James Buchanan, a Nobel Prize–winning economist from Virginia, was the catalyst for
"alter[ing] every branch of government to disempower the majority."[45] In her book *Democracy in Chains*, MacLean shows that Buchanan viewed the *Brown* ruling as perpetuating the "problems of
equalitarianism," "income redistribution," and "the welfare state."[46]
He brazenly advocated for school segregation and recommended
that Virginia schools privatize public education in the aftermath
of *Brown*. Buchanan opposed civil disobedience and characterized peaceful protest and sit-ins as anarchy. In response to student
protest in the 1960s, he wrote:

> Unrestrained and with little or no sense of mutual respect
> and tolerance, [students flout] ordinary rules of conduct;
> they disrupt others in the pursuit of their affairs; they have
> almost destroyed the basic order that once prevailed on
> campuses everywhere. All of this would be disturbing
> enough if the students' excesses were confined within the
> ivy walls . . . But having learned none of the simple virtues
> in either family, church, or school, why should we expect
> the child-men to behave differently in the great society
> beyond the groves? The animals are in the streets, liter-
> ally, and if college buildings burn so do banks, as we are
> finding this year.[47]

Buchanan worked behind the scenes for decades, undermining democracy and writing the playbook for the far right.

This desire to blow up the system rather than grant access to
Black children was not confined to Southerners. For decades,
Milton Friedman was a juggernaut among the economics faculty at the University of Chicago. His theories became known
as the "Chicago School of Economics" and influenced governments worldwide. Affectionately known to his followers as Uncle

Miltie, Friedman and his free-market philosophy promoted and sustained structural racism, authoritarianism abroad, small government, and corporate profits with no social responsibilities. A year after the *Brown* ruling, in an essay titled "The Role of Government in Education," Friedman called for applying free-market principles in the field of education and provided a race-free analysis of school choice. Many refer to Friedman as "the father of the modern school choice movement."[48] He was a master at helping White people feel good about their racism, anti-Blackness, and greed. Scholar Jon Hale explains:

> In a belief that is widely shared among school choice advocates, Friedman claimed that race did not and would not matter in an ideal application of choice. He predicted marked improvement through school choice plans for "the ablest and most ambitious Negro youth." . . . He placed the onus to desegregate on those who supported integration. It was up to them, not the government, to persuade individuals to support desegregation.[49]

When it came to Black folx, Friedman relied on the meritocracy myth. The idea of school choice in an anti-Black educational system puts the burden on Black families and ultimately Black children to overcome racism as magical Negroes—young people who can demonstrate a type of Black exceptionalism that makes White America feel good and lets White people take credit for Black children's success.

Friedman understood racism to be a matter of what he called "taste," writing, "When the owner of the store hires white clerks in preference to Negroes in the absence of the law, he may not be expressing any preference or prejudice or taste of his own. He may simply be transmitting the taste of the community."[50] Friedman was adamant that the government's sole purpose is "to protect our freedom both from the enemies outside our gates and from our fellow-citizens: to preserve law and order, to enforce private contracts, to foster competitive markets."[51] His laissez-faire economic policy would eventually become part of America's cultural norms, completely disregarding the impact of race, class, and inequality on a person's chances of achieving economic prosperity.

Friedman's beliefs, summarized by his words that if "government got out of the way, the economy would grow and everyone would benefit,"[52] would have an outsize influence in politics and government. As the story goes, when the former actor Ronald Reagan was running for governor of California in 1966, one of his aides noticed that he was carrying a copy of Milton Friedman's book *Capitalism and Freedom*.[53] Reagan's education agenda directly reflected Friedman's philosophies. Friedman believed that government could not justify the expense of subsidized loans and grants that support students' college tuition.[54] Reagan put this theorizing into practice.

While campaigning for California's governorship, Reagan called for the end of free tuition and a 20 percent cut in higher education funding. He insisted that "a small minority of hippies, radicals, and filthy speech advocates" were causing disruption on campuses and should be removed permanently.[55] He told Californians that the young people protesting the Vietnam War and fighting for civil rights and women's rights were "spoiled" and "didn't deserve the education they were getting." He added that the state "should not subsidize intellectual curiosity." Reagan won in a landslide. He then called in the National Guard to remove liberal activists from college campuses. He cut $11 million from the University of California's operating budget. He eliminated $116 million from university and state college budgets statewide. And so began the rapid acceleration of skyrocketing college debt in California and, soon, elsewhere.

As Reagan's popularity grew, so did Friedman's—"the Economist of the Century" won a Nobel Prize for Economic Sciences in 1976. His ideas about school choice, small government, and corporate greed spread rapidly. In 1980, his book *Free to Choose*, written with his wife, Rose, was adapted into a popular ten-part PBS series. The series espoused Friedman's beliefs that public housing contributed to racial inequality, that public assistance (welfare) should be eliminated, that the declining academic achievement of students was due to government control, and that school vouchers would cure what ailed public education. The series was updated and rebroadcast in 1990. Friedman's ideas inspired everyday Americans, but they amounted to marching orders for policy makers and presidents who would draft laws and policies based on his economic model, giving tax cuts to the rich, destabilizing unions, deregulating industries, and calling for fewer government interventions to address poverty, inequality, low wages, environmental destruction, housing segregation, and racist banking practices. Black people experienced the unforgiving realities of Friedman's ideas of capitalism while being locked out of its potential or perceived benefits and put in a "state of perpetual depression" by their own government.[56]

As influential as Friedman was in crafting the modern playbook of neoliberalism, he was not alone. Other economists played key roles in defending the interests of White elites—namely, Friedrich Hayek, Ludwig von Mises, and Murray Rothbard. In 1947, Hayek, along with Mises, Friedman, and others, founded the Mont Pelerin Society to spread the doctrine of neoliberalism. Proponents of neoliberalism believe that "the market ensures that everyone gets what they deserve."[57] In 1977, Rothbard helped found the Cato Institute, the libertarian think tank funded by Charles Koch.

The Koch brothers, Charles and the late David (who died in 2019), are extreme libertarians who have weaponized their wealth to suppress the Black vote, deregulate corporations, undermine the power of unions, shift the burden of taxes onto the middle and working classes, and work to privatize and thus abolish public education.[58] They were not the first Koch family members to use their wealth to weaken civil rights gains and destabilize democracy. Their father, Fred Koch, a very wealthy businessman, was one of the founding members of the John Birch Society, the notorious archconservative, conspiracy-spinning group. Incensed by the *Brown* ruling, Birchers bought billboards across the country calling for the impeachment of Supreme Court chief justice Earl Warren. These rich White men believed that "communism" was infiltrating American politics, regardless of political party, and that Black people securing civil rights threatened the status quo.[59]

The Koch brothers have spent hundreds of millions of dollars of their personal wealth and funds raised from their donor networks to found and bankroll radical organizations like Americans for Prosperity, FreedomWorks, and the American Legislative Exchange Council. Americans for Prosperity is the nation's most prominent conservative political organization, advocating for reducing or ending taxes, cutting government spending, eliminating environmental restrictions, and promoting school choice—which is code for ending public education. FreedomWorks is a powerful conservative advocacy group that mobilizes its base to oppose expanding health care, raising taxes on the rich, or supporting climate change policies. The American Legislative Exchange Council (ALEC) writes legislation for conservative lawmakers and lobbyists. More than six hundred pieces of ALEC's "model legislation" have become law. Among them is Florida's "Stand Your Ground" law, which moved "home-defense principles into the streets."[60] Ultimately, the law played a role in the acquittal of George Zimmerman's White-rage killing of teenager Trayvon Martin in 2012.

As I write this, the Koch brothers, along with the Manhattan Institute, the Bradley Foundation, and America First Legal are financing the attack on racial and queer justice in education by lying to the American public that critical race theory (CRT) is being taught in our nation's schools and drag queens are grooming children. The Koch brothers don't simply aim their wealth at model legislation and shifting public perceptions. They also attempt to directly influence electoral results by financing right-wing candidates and movements like the Tea Party.

And their support of candidates matters. Three years before Murray Rothbard—another of those key economists—died, the libertarian economist called for a president who embodied the following qualities:

> And so the proper strategy for the right wing must be what we can call "right-wing populism": exciting, dynamic, tough, and confrontational, rousing and inspiring. . . . We need a leadership that can reach the masses and cut through the crippling and distorting hermeneutical fog spread by the media elites.[61]

Rothbard was expressing his excitement for David Duke, the former grand wizard of the KKK who ran for president in 1992, but he accurately describes the man who would be elected president in 2016.

Who Are the Real Super Predators?

By the 1980s, what began as resistance to school integration had grown over three decades and was now a conglomeration of well-funded think tanks, foundations, nonprofits, academic institutions, and political movements from both parties. The forty years beginning in the 1980s are different and worth studying because this conglomeration is both big business and also anti-Black, all the while wrapped in the language of justice. To-gether, these rich White men, allied with White women, teamed up to create a radical right wing that would defund and try to eliminate public education. I prefer to call these men—and the women who worked with them—by a different name: super predators. A term popularized in the mid-1990s ostensibly to describe the rise and imminent explosion of teen criminals in general but immediately understood to be referring to Black boys, the idea of the "super predator" was used to justify mass incarceration. But the real super predators need Black people to remain civically, institutionally, economically, and educationally vulnerable to maintain the status quo, which is rooted in anti-Blackness, inequality, and White privilege.

Some super predators are ruthless autocrats (e.g., Ronald Reagan, Milton Friedman, George H. W. Bush, William Ben-nett, Donald Trump, Ron Desantis, Betsy DeVos, and the Koch Brothers), determined to create a plutocracy. Though they might profess a love of democracy, their actions directly contradict its basic principles. Other super predators view themselves as com-passionate conservatives (e.g., George W. Bush and Jeb Bush); their sympathy toward Black people is rooted in anti-Blackness and paternalism as they use education to make millions for their fellow billionaires. There are liberal super predators like Bill and Melinda Gates, Mike Bloomberg, and Barack Obama, who use the platform of progressive politics to perpetrate harmful edu-cational practices. And lastly, there are the super predators be-loved by neoliberal philanthropy (e.g., Wendy Kopp, Michelle Rhee, Priscilla Chan, Mark Zuckerberg, David Levin, and Mike Feinberg), who gain fame by peddling anti-Black approaches to Black communities in the name of justice. They believe they can fix Black people with accountability standards, data, merit pay, charter schools, and an emphasis on grit—as if we lack it. Regard-less of their approach or "good" intentions, these "reformers" are all predators. They raid and pillage urban education for their gain while sacrificing Black children and Black communities.

Some might balk at my use of the term "super predator," but I use it to elucidate a larger point. We need incisive language to wake us up to the effects of actions that are presented as helpful but in fact continue to cause harm. If we give centrists and Democrats a pass and focus only on conservatives, we don't strike at the root of the problem. The resistance to *Brown* anchored itself in a bureaucratic opposition that drew from across the political spectrum, gutted the aspirations of integration, and galvanized a new form of White rage by 1983: educational reform.

2

BLACK CHILDREN AT RISK

Slavery persists as an issue in the political life of black America . . . because black lives are still imperiled and devalued by a racial calculus and a political arithmetic that were entrenched centuries ago. This is the afterlife of slavery—skewed life chances, limited access to health and education, premature death, incarceration, and impoverishment.

—Saidiya V. Hartman[1]

"There Is an Assumption That Black Kids Won't Have an Advocate"

Mr. Roc moved with his family from Macon, Georgia, to New York City when he was two. His mother raised him and his six siblings on her own and had an outsize influence on his life. Mr. Roc was in his midtwenties when she died, and he decided then that he wanted a career that would allow him to help single mothers, those who—as his own mother had—were trying their best to move their children toward healthy, successful adulthood. He chose the field of education.

He became an elementary school teacher in the mid-1980s,

but soured on the relentless emphasis on testing, preparation for which dominated the reading curriculum every year from November until April. "Everything relied on the results," he told me. "I noticed that my children in sixth grade, before they got to me, were trained to cheat or ask for assistance on the test. They would be reading the test and call me over. The student would point to the question. What I came to find out was that the teacher who had them in the fifth grade would point to the answer." Frustrated, Mr. Roc left the lower grades to teach high school, where he quickly learned that the school environment was largely shaped by forces beyond the schoolhouse doors. By that time, New Yorkers had more than two decades of experience living under policies that terrorized Black communities and treated Black life as disposable.

In March of 1964, New York State passed two anti-crime laws that gave police the ability to "stop-and-frisk" and perform what became known as "no knock" warrant searches. Critics of the anti-crime laws told *Time* that these police measures were "ominously dangerous enactments threatening a reign of unrestrained terror in our state."[2] Decades of punishment would prove those critics right. Police disproportionately enforced these laws in predominantly Black communities, creating a direct pipeline for Black youth into what abolitionist and transformation justice educator Mariame Kaba calls the "criminal punishment system,"[3] a phrase that describes the interlocking policies and procedures without suggesting justice can be found therein.

As illegal drugs flooded the streets, Black people who were pushed by a failing and racist economy to sell drugs on the corners were caged, intended never to be seen again. Black drug users, besieged by an addiction, were labeled criminals. Americans were told they needed to get tough on crime to keep themselves safe. In 1973, New York State established minimum sentencing laws known as the *Rockefeller drug laws*. The laws

mandated a fifteen-year minimum sentence for selling or pos-
sessing cocaine, heroin, or other controlled substances. Other
states throughout the country followed New York's lead in creating egregious and harsh minimum sentencing laws targeting
Black communities.

Mr. Roc's reality as a newly minted educator was informed
by the merging of education and law enforcement that was becoming common as he entered the profession. Still, he continued climbing the ranks in education and eventually became vice
principal of a high school. In that role, he saw how the larger system of criminal punishment had begun to shape discipline inside
schools. He recalls a Black student who, when asked by a dean to
remove his hat, refused to do so. The administrator didn't take
kindly to being ignored. "The student didn't move fast enough,
and the next thing you know, the student was on the ground,"
Mr. Roc remembers. "That was the norm." Mr. Roc summarized
the pattern of how adults in power treated the Black teenagers
in their care: "It was gangsta." White kids at the school were not
disciplined the same way. "No, no. There is an assumption that
Black kids won't have an advocate," Mr. Roc said, explaining the
disparate treatment.

By the late 1990s, Mr. Roc had become a principal in what he
calls a "traumatized" New York City high school. "On any given
day, there would be four hundred kids standing around outside
and another three hundred kids in the hallways." He told me that
teachers at the school would lock the doors to the classroom
when the bell rang, and the school administrators would hold
the students then caught in the hallways in the auditorium while
class was in session. While there, they received no academic instruction. Once class ended, administrators would release those
students to go on about their days as usual, but after the next
bell, the adults would again sweep any stragglers into the au-

ditorium. This cycle continued throughout the day. The school was filled with teachers who had low expectations for students, he said.

None of this sat well with Mr. Roc. He told his teachers they had to keep their doors open to allow tardy students into the classroom to learn. Further, he told teachers they could only hold students accountable for rules about which they were informed. It took time for the mentality of the teachers to change, but Mr. Roc slowly turned the school around using a loving, firm approach toward the teachers. The district recognized him for his efforts. But to this day, he wonders whether the school system truly cared about the opportunities he created for Black children, or if the district was simply responding to praise from White folx in the community who were happy to no longer see hundreds of Black kids milling about outside the school.

Mr. Roc described schools as "flooded with police" during his tenure as an educator and advocate for students under zero-tolerance policies. When a student brought what could be considered a weapon to school, the punishment was an automatic ninety-day suspension. In some instances, it was a full school-year suspension. As a principal, Mr. Roc would recommend that a student receive a shorter suspension and be reinstated. He felt his duty was to make sure students made it back to school as quickly as possible, before they gave up on even trying to return and were completely pushed out of school.

During another phase in his career, Mr. Roc supervised the educations of New York City students incarcerated at Rikers Island, the sprawling New York City jail that has been called "a symbol of brutality and inhumanity" due to its well-documented culture of abuse and violence.[4] At that time, sixteen- and seventeen-year-olds were held at Rikers Island alongside adult prisoners. He was there to teach teenagers, but he knew many of the older inmates, too. "The saddest part for me is when I would go out to Rikers and hear my name screamed out by former students." He kept going back and was eventually able to create policies that helped students return to school after being imprisoned.

Now retired and sixty-one years old, Mr. Roc has synthesized what he learned over the years in classrooms and through conversations with students, families, and other educators. "The system, the school, is really like a plantation," he said of the racism he encountered. "As a principal, I was not the master but the overseer. I am not proud of that, but I tried to stay under the radar to fight for what's right for kids. It's a hard place to be in if you are really thinking about liberation or freedom. As I went up the ladder, it got Whiter, Whiter, and Whiter, and they want to exert more control. Eventually, I realized I could not serve two masters. I could not serve the children and the system. The system was not about helping children; it was about helping the system. If you are a part of the system, by default, you are helping to maintain the system."

Mr. Roc entered the teaching profession as a motivated twenty-something driven by love, dedication, and the memory of what his own mother had given him and his siblings. He had wanted to do what was best for Black families. Instead, he spent his career fighting a post-*Brown* public school reality that left him feeling as though he could never truly impact the system in the interest of Black children. As a teacher and administrator in the 1980s, he found himself no less emotionally impacted by the merger of the carceral state and reform politics in education than his students did. In this way, we see the scope of the harm these school policies enacted on Black life. Even Black teachers and administrators were helpless to transform the violent racism that undergirded their time in public schools. Multiple generations, each one helpless to protect Black children.

The Undoing of Brown

Richard Nixon, the only U.S. president to resign from office, will go down in history as having covered up the crimes of Watergate. What's less known is how he laid the groundwork for the gutting of *Brown* and criminalizing the pursuit of civil rights. Before Nixon took office in 1969, a 1968 Harris Poll revealed 81 percent of respondents believed that "law and order has broken down in this country," and 59 percent of those blamed "Negroes who start riots."[5] Angry White voters put Nixon in the White House, and he was the first to declare a so-called war on drugs.[6] This "war," though, was little more than a front to criminalize and incarcerate the president's biggest critics: Black people and Vietnam War protesters. John Ehrlichman, Nixon's domestic policy chief, revealed that the administration's goal was to "arrest their leaders, raid their homes, break up their meetings, and vilify them night after night on the evening news."[7] Specifically, the Nixon administration sought to disparage Black people for demanding civil rights.

He also disarmed civil rights coalition demands for wealth redistribution by co-opting the rhetoric of Black capitalism.[8] He neutralized the Black Power movement and satisfied his White base by touting a self-help strategy for Black people that required no structural or policy changes to provide economic relief. Nixon successfully played both sides, diminishing the rights of Black people while also calling for "more black ownership, black pride . . . and yes, black power."[9] He wasn't alone. His head of urban affairs, Democrat Daniel Patrick Moynihan, proposed that "the time may have come when the issue of race could benefit from a period of benign neglect."[10]

Keeping his campaign promise to supporters, Nixon crusaded against school busing. While in office, Nixon appointed four conservative Supreme Court justices. In 1974, the U.S. Supreme

Court—with Justice Thurgood Marshall on the bench—crushed *Brown* with its decision in *Milliken v. Bradley*. The lawsuit had initially been filed in a lower court in Detroit. At issue was whether school districts could be held responsible for desegregation if no one could prove that district lines were drawn with racist intent. The 5–4 Supreme Court ruling sided with the district, accepting its claims of innocence. All four Nixon appointees sided with the majority opinion.

In his dissenting opinion, Marshall wrote: "Under such a plan, white and Negro students will not go to school together. Instead, Negro children will continue to attend all-Negro schools. The very evil that *Brown* was aimed at will not be cured but will be perpetuated."[11] Sure enough, in the years following *Milliken*, Detroit Public Schools became even more segregated.[12] The student body was 35 percent White in 1974, but by 2020, it was 82 percent Black, 14 percent Hispanic, 3 percent White, and 1 percent Asian. Many inner-city school districts around the country mirrored Detroit schools' racial imbalance.

Not only did *Milliken* stop the enforcement of *Brown*, it also perpetuated racial inequality in school funding. Desegregating schools is not just about attempting to force racial harmony. It is also about non-White students gaining access to the same resources and opportunities White students have. *Milliken* allowed White families to maintain school lines that paralleled their racial housing covenants, end racial quotas and busing, and keep a greater, inequitable share of public school funding.

Having access to equitable resources makes a significant difference in students' experiences and outcomes. Research shows that between 1970 and 1990, the educational attainment for Black and Brown students attending integrated schools improved. They learned more, got better grades in college, graduated at higher rates, and secured jobs.[13] Rucker C. Johnson, coauthor of *Children of the Dream: Why School Integration Works*, writes:

> Desegregation and related policies are commonly misperceived as failed social engineering that shuffled children around for many years, with no real benefit. The truth is that significant efforts to integrate schools occurred only for about 15 years, and peaked in 1988. In this period, we witnessed the greatest racial convergence of achievement gaps, educational attainment, earnings and health status.[14]

Johnson adds that this growth did not come at the expense of White students. However, data on the positive effects of school integration were disregarded to create an educational crisis.

The Manufactured Crises of the 1980s

Before the 1960s, the federal government played a small role in K–12 education. The *Brown* ruling engaged federal courts in desegregation efforts, but that wasn't the only way new powers were centralized at the national level. In 1965, Congress passed the Elementary and Secondary Education Act, or ESEA, which provided federal funds, known as Title I, to economically disadvantaged students. School districts could access Title I funds by providing evidence of effectiveness.[15] U.S. senator Robert F. Kennedy was adamant that there be an evaluation provision in Title I to "whip" or "spur" changes in schools he deemed ineffective.[16] The goal was for ESEA to strengthen the efforts of Head Start, a program for early childhood development. Policy makers naively believed Head Start and Title I could "eliminate poverty and provide equal opportunity for all children."[17] These unrealistic goals were not achieved, and policy makers grew frustrated. As the scholar Jean Anyon astutely observed, "As a nation, we have been counting on education to solve the problems of unemployment, joblessness, and poverty for many years. But education did not cause these problems, and education cannot solve them."[18]

Reagan's first attempt at the presidency in 1976 hadn't been successful. But he'd been intent on carrying economist Milton Friedman's worldview into the White House even then. During his first campaign for national office, Reagan told Washington lawmakers "to heed Friedman's views on policy."[19] By 1980, when Reagan ran again, the influence of neoliberalism guided at least two of the platforms Americans had to choose from: Reagan for the Republicans and David Koch, the ultra-wealthy businessman, running for vice president on the Libertarian ticket. Koch and his running mate, Ed Clark, supported vouchers and wanted to abolish public education.

When Reagan took office in 1981, he had four education goals: abolish the Department of Education, put prayer in schools, drastically cut the federal education budget, and introduce school vouchers to allow public dollars to be spent at private schools.[20] These policy initiatives would set the stage for his undermining of public education. On October 14, 1982, Reagan declared illicit drugs a threat to U.S. national security and greatly expanded Nixon's war on drugs. The president announced plans for twelve new drug task forces and the hiring of about 1,200 additional agents and prosecutors. His plan increased law enforcement to target Black communities and ensured that the government had enough prosecutors to convict. Reagan also supported death sentences for individuals convicted of certain drug crimes. As for the people who were addicted to drugs, he called them "parasites" and "vermin." On the campaign trail, Reagan told Americans that his policies would "make America great again"—a catchphrase that Donald Trump used to galvanize the same base almost four decades later.

Reagan enlisted his wife, Nancy, to tell kids to "Just Say No" to drugs. In Black communities, the message reinforced the cruel stereotype that Black people are lazy and lack self-control. Award-winning filmmaker Stanley Nelson's documentary *Crack: Cocaine, Corruption, and Conspiracy* tells the story of how U.S. officials turned a blind eye to drug traffickers who were funneling cocaine from Central and South America to inner-city Black neighborhoods in the United States. As the government allowed illegal drugs to be smuggled into Black communities, Black Americans in the 1980s faced staggering rates of unemployment, reduced wages, mass incarceration, the loss of manufacturing jobs due to globalization, and anti-Black education reform policies.[21] Let's be clear: the Reagan administration pushed law enforcement and the Justice Department to target Black communities for using and selling the drugs that they themselves played a role in putting in inner cities.

In 1973, the National Advisory Commission on Criminal Justice Standards and Goals recommended that "no new institutions for adults should be built and existing institutions for juveniles should be closed . . . There is overwhelming evidence that these institutions create crime rather than prevent it."[22] When Reagan took office, the U.S. prison population totaled about 329,000 people.[23] By the end of Reagan's term, the prison population had almost doubled to 627,000.[24] At the same time Reagan was filling prisons with Black bodies, he was eliminating federal funds earmarked to advance desegregation.[25] Reagan's war on drugs and education provided the groundwork for what Naomi Klein calls "disaster capitalism" in her analysis of Friedman's economic philosophy. Friedman professed that when a crisis arises, the economy should take advantage of that crisis: "Only a crisis—actual or perceived—produces real change. When the crisis occurs, the actions that are taken depend on the ideas lying around."

To advance the war on Black people further, both Democrats and Republicans embraced a theory made popular by two other academics. In 1982, *The Atlantic* published a piece by political scientist James Q. Wilson and criminologist George L. Kelling titled "Broken Windows." Wilson and Kelling argued that allowing even one disorder in a neighborhood could escalate and get out of control. The authors considered a broken window a visible sign of disorder and urban decay; other signs included panhandlers, graffiti, prostitution, and drug use. They proposed that police focus their resources on maintaining order instead of major crimes. This logic spread to police departments across the country and transformed public policy, increasing surveillance and aggressive policing tactics in response to minor infractions.

It also transformed education. Black children were already seen as criminals, and the broken windows theory further promoted a focus on order in the classroom and a school culture of strict student discipline, the forerunner of zero tolerance in schools. Mayor Rudolph Giuliani of New York was the most famous public official to profess that he could reduce crime by implementing the broken windows theory. Later, Mayor Michael Bloomberg used Giuliani's broken windows approach in twenty-two New York City public middle and high schools. Under the Impact Schools Initiative, Bloomberg used a $6.25 million grant from the U.S. Department of Justice to add 50 police officers to a force of 150 stationed in schools.

The broken windows theory was also the precursor to charter schools' "no excuses" discipline approach. The national call to see urban schools as broken windows was tailor-made for Reagan's war on drugs and his 1983 manufactured education crisis, for which he started gathering "evidence" before he took office in 1981. Shortly before the former California governor won the presidency in 1980, he created an education policy advisory committee (EPAC). The committee was chaired by W. Glenn Campbell, a conservative economist and former director of the Hoover Institution. An ardent anti-Communist, Campbell was a longtime confidant of Reagan and argued that the free market was the answer to the country's problems.[26] Campbell had no expertise in K–12 education, but on October 22, 1980, his committee submitted a "tentative draft" of its report.

In their book, *The Manufactured Crisis: Myths, Fraud, and the Attack on America's Public Schools,* David Berliner and Bruce Biddle assert that this draft "offers good insight into how the far-right viewed education during the crucial period."[27] The draft was packed with skewed data. For example, it claimed that educational achievement was declining sharply. However, the National Assessment of Educational Progress (NAEP), a nonpartisan government entity that provides group-level data on U.S. student assessment, reported at the time that there was "very little change over the past two decades." The report also asserted that SAT scores were declining—without adequate data to support that conclusion. There had been a narrow decline in SAT scores between 1963 and 1975, ranging from sixty to ninety points depending on the year; however, as Berliner and Biddle write, "such small shifts in SAT scores are not meaningful, and by themselves aggregate SAT scores provide no information about the performance of American schools."[28] In reality, the SAT scores tell us more about a student's family income than their academic abilities.[29] After decades of lies, misleading data, and instigating public panic linking education and crime, the groundwork for the big lie was set.

The Betrayal

The United States' attack on Black life escalated on April 26, 1983, when Reagan's White House released an education report titled *A Nation at Risk.* Under Reagan, the position of education secretary served as the bully pulpit for the Republican education agenda.[30] The first person to fill the role was Terrel H. Bell, who commissioned the report. *A Nation at Risk* begins with "An Open Letter to the American People," warning of an imperiled nation hobbled by its education system:

> Our Nation is at risk. Our once unchallenged preeminence in commerce, industry, science, and technological innovation is being overtaken by competitors throughout the world. This report is concerned with only one of the many causes and dimensions of the problem, but it is the one that undergirds American prosperity, security, and civility. We report to the American people that while we can take justifiable pride in what our schools and colleges have historically accomplished and contributed to the United States and the well-being of its people, the educational foundations of our society are presently being eroded by a rising tide of mediocrity that threatens our very future as a Nation and a people. What was unimaginable a generation ago has begun to occur—others are matching and surpassing our educational attainments.[31]

Like the education report released by Reagan's camp the month before he was elected, *A Nation at Risk* was comprised of cherry-picked data to villainize America's schools. Reagan wanted the report to "make American public schools look as bad as possible."[32] The report continued: "If an unfriendly foreign power had attempted to impose on America the mediocre educational performance that exists today, we might well have viewed it as an act of war. As it stands, we have allowed this to happen to ourselves. We have even squandered the gains in student achievement made in the wake of the Sputnik challenge."[33] News of *A Nation at Risk* appeared on front pages across the country.[34] The report barely mentioned race. It did not have to. The framing of an educational crisis played on White Americans' fears about desegregation. In short, it created the perception that Black children were putting this country at risk of war simply by being Black and fighting for equally funded education.

Just weeks after *A Nation at Risk* was released, *Heritage Today*, a publication of the right-wing Heritage Foundation, covered the report.

> The most damaging blows to science and mathematics education have come from Washington. For the past 20 years, federal mandates have favored "disadvantaged" pupils at the expense of those who have the highest potential to contribute positively to society . . . By catering to the demands of special-interest groups—racial minorities, the handicapped, women, and non-English speaking students—America's public schools have successfully competed for government funds, but have done so at the expense of education as a whole.[35]

A Nation at Risk created a faux national crisis and ushered in the far right's education agenda. It was nothing short of propaganda—thirty-six pages of lies and attacks on public education to advance anti-Blackness and diminish Americans' trust in public education. Berliner and Biddle wrote, "*A Nation at Risk* merely gave public voice to changes about education that right-wing ideologies had already been telling one another."[36] It was all a "politically inspired hoax."[37] The NAEP reported that from the 1970s to the early 1980s, the performance of elementary and secondary pupils dropped slightly on some examinations. During that same period, though, scores increased moderately on other examinations.[38] The report intentionally omitted such positive educational data. It was a wink and a nod to those who believed Black people imperiled public education. It also reinforced support for defunding and abolishing public schools.

A Nation at Risk was embraced with great fanfare by both political parties because it aligned with their views on education and linked education to the labor market and the economy. Education was now solely focused on productivity, preparation for the workforce, and global competition for technological innovations. After 1983, education no longer had time for critical-thinking skills, civics education for a better world, teacher-student relationships, or divergent thinking. With this shift, corporate America became the savior of public education. The report was released during a recession, which some considered the severest recession since World War II. Reagan and the coauthors of the report played host to a series of public hearings at which they urged Americans to testify about how badly schools were failing. Failing schools—not economic policies that favored the rich—were responsible for the economy. Both parties not only endorsed the hoax but tried to outdo each other over who could punish Black children the most and profit the most from their suffering. *Education Week* reported in 1987 that *A Nation at Risk* accomplished what "would have taken 30 years to enact through regular education channels: the wave of reforms many states have adopted in the past three years."[39]

After the release of the education report, Reagan began to explicitly make the link between the nation's failing schools and the crime-ridden neighborhoods on which he'd declared war. Both needed new forms of surveillance and control. More specifically, American schools, he said, lacked "good old-fashioned discipline." Speaking at a National Forum on Excellence in Education in 1983, months after the release of *A Nation at Risk,* the president told over two thousand educators that to improve education, he would direct the Department of Education and the Department of Justice "to find ways we can help teachers and administrators enforce discipline" in schools.[40] "American schools don't need vast new sums of money as much as they need a few fundamental reforms," he said.[41] Over the course of Reagan's years in office, this message would be amplified by nightly news reports that endlessly depicted Black people as criminals, drug users, welfare "queens," teenage mothers, and high school dropouts draining the American economy.

In 1984, the Reagan administration released another scathing report, *Disorder in Our Public Schools*. The twenty-three-page document cited crime and discipline problems such as assault and robbery in urban schools. Many officials, even within the administration, admitted that the report was outdated (it was based on data from 1976). And teachers who were critical of the report told *The Washington Post* that the most common discipline issues they dealt with were "age-old and hardly severe: tardiness, cutting class, and back-talking."[42] School discipline issues were actually declining.

Reagan's presidency was thus the launching point for an educational reform agenda that ushered in a new sort of Black bondage, a system in which Black Americans would be educationally neglected, economically starved, denied assistance, and incarcerated for selling drugs that the government itself allowed to be put out on the street. Every president since Reagan has made a moral and financial commitment to the American people to throw as many Black drug dealers and Black drug users in prison as possible by turning police officers into soldiers, with America's Black neighborhoods and schools as its battlefields.

One Term of Historic Damage

George H. W. Bush got elected by stoking White fears of Blackness. Bush was trailing Democratic opponent Michael Dukakis, and his campaign aired the now-infamous "Willie Horton ad" that painted the Massachusetts governor as soft on crime and fueled a fear of rampant Black criminality. Willie Horton raped and murdered a White woman and stabbed her partner while on a weekend pass from a Massachusetts prison. The ad was created by Bush's campaign strategist and legendary Republican political operative, Lee Atwater. Atwater was one of the masterminds behind the GOP's "Southern Strategy." The goal was to use White resentment toward civil rights and *Brown* to marry conservative policies resisting busing, integration, and government assistance programs to cutting taxes for the rich and privatizing the government. In 1981, seven years before the Willie Horton ad, Atwater told a reporter for *Southern Politics*:

> Y'all don't quote me on this. You start out in 1954 by saying, "Nigger, nigger, nigger." By 1968 you can't say "nigger"—that hurts you. Backfires. So you say stuff like forced busing, states' rights and all that stuff. You're getting so abstract now [that] you're talking about cutting taxes, and all these things you're talking about are totally economic things and a byproduct of them is [that] blacks get hurt worse than whites.[43]

Atwater understood how to use racism, anti-Blackness, and White resentment for votes and for the disposal of Black life. The Willie Horton ad showed Horton's mug shot as the off-screen narrator informs the viewer of Horton's horrendous crimes while noting that "Dukakis not only opposes the death penalty, he allowed first-degree murderers to have weekend passes from prison." The ad essentially tanked Dukakis's presidential run but also led the many Democrats to mirror the Republican's racially driven tough-on-crime agenda and rhetoric for decades to come.

After making Willie Horton a household name, in his first Oval Office address as president in 1989, Bush held up a small plastic bag of drugs. "It's as innocent-looking as candy, but it's turning our cities into battle zones," he intoned. "This is crack cocaine, seized a few days ago by drug enforcement agents in a park just across the street from the White House." In truth, agents from the Drug Enforcement Administration (DEA) had lured eighteen-year-old Keith Jackson to Lafayette Square, across the street from the White House, to get a prop for Bush's speech on the war on drugs. Jackson was then convicted of three counts of distributing drugs, including selling crack within one thousand feet of a school, a crime that carried an automatic ten-year sentence.[44] Jackson was sentenced under a mandatory minimum law established by a 1988 update to the Anti-Drug Abuse Act. Enacted under Reagan, the 1986 Anti-Drug Abuse Act appropriated $1.7 billion to fund the war on drugs and shifted federal drug rehabilitative efforts to punitive measures that punished drug users, imposing longer sentences for crack than for cocaine. Before the Anti-Drug Abuse Act, "the average federal drug sentence for African Americans was 11 percent higher than for whites. Four years later, the average federal drug sentence for African Americans was 49 percent higher."[45]

George H. W. Bush wanted to be tough on crime. He also wanted to be known as "the education president." Bush and his enablers painted inner cities as spaces filled with criminals and dangerous schools. Educational policy and myths of Black criminality went hand in hand. Although Bush was a one-term president and never passed any education bills, he was the architect of the modern-day school reform movement that married entrepreneurism and government.[46] In 1991, Bush debuted the America 2000 strategy, a set of goals and policy initiatives that largely focused on school choice and standardized testing. Republicans in Congress responded by introducing the America 2000 Excellence in Education Act, which was endorsed by many Democrats nationwide, including then Arkansas governor Bill Clinton. The legislation never passed, but it galvanized a faction in Washington calling for national standards and national testing. America 2000 would be ramped up with vengence by Bush's sons George and Jeb, ultimately leading to the former's No Child Left Behind policy. While America 2000 fizzled out due to a lack of support from Democrats, many of its policy initiatives were taken up without congressional approval.[47]

In 1991, under the auspices of America 2000, George H. W. Bush subsidized the creation of the New American Schools Development Corporation, also called New American Schools (NAS). A private sector venture, the organization was made up of prominent corporate CEOs who by the 1990s realized that public education was a "potential $600 billion investment opportunity."[48] Bush promoted the idea, through NAS, that America's public education systems could be "reinvented" through experimental schools. Of course, it was easier to sell such a concept when the American people were told that public schools were a national security risk, lacked high standards and accountability, and were overrun by lawless Black children.

In 1991, the same year NAS was created, Minnesota became the first state to authorize charter schools, despite critics warning the public that these schools "would turn kids into guinea pigs."[49] By 1993, Jeanne Allen, an education policy advisor for the Heritage Foundation, created the Center for Education Reform, which was funded by the Koch brothers to further invest in the expansion of charter schools. Less than a decade after the first charter school was opened, more than 2,500 of them were enrolling upwards of half a million kids across the country. Today, those numbers have risen to more than 7,000 charter schools enrolling more than three million students.

As scholar Marc Lamont Hill writes, the corporate takeover of public education relies on "market-driven logic that privileges economic efficiency and individual success over collective justice."[50] However, the takeover of public education in the last forty years is not simply a set of educational policies. It is part of an attack on Black people from both political parties. As the late historian Manning Marable wrote, reforms "exist not to develop, but to underdevelop Black people," transforming the role and function of government in the process.[51]

Following Reagan's lead, Bush exploited America's racism to advance his agenda and support those seeking to profit from reform, auctioning off Black children's education in the process. Every president since has used the same approach. I started this chapter with Saidiya Hartman's notion of the afterlife of slavery. Following the Supreme Court's landmark *Brown* decision, the White supremacists did not simply resist school integration— they built a profitable educational enterprise rooted in the exploitation of Black people's pursuit of education that has led to "skewed life chances, limited access to health and education, premature death, incarceration, and impoverishment." This is the afterlife of *Brown* putting Black children at risk.

3

SCRAPS

Raising black children—female or male—in the mouth of a racist, sexist, suicidal dragon is perilous and chancy. If they cannot love and resist at the same time, they will probably not survive.

—Audre Lorde[1]

The Ultimate Sacrifice

To understand why Black children only get the scraps of school choice, we need to interrogate what the phrase *school choice* has meant in the years between the *Brown* ruling and today. Initially, Black families sought more choice in their children's education. More precisely, they wanted access to schools that were better resourced than those established for Black children—a decision my grandparents and parents both made. My family, like many others, bought into the American myth that education would be the great equalizer—that obtaining a "good" education would keep their children safe and afford them their piece of the American dream.

School choice promised to allow parents, irrespective of race, to choose outside of their zoned public school in the interest of their children's education, while in reality, that choice was fraught at best and damaging at worst. Money that would have gone to making local public schools more equal and more viable for Black children was made available for transfer to already more privileged White schools. Black parents who could afford it could choose to send their children to private schools or suburban schools removed from their community, and in doing so, expose their children to racial violence. The hope education fostered in the hearts of generations of Black parents was paid for by having to watch their children endure violence, racial isolation, and psychological trauma in predominantly White schools and under-resourced, understaffed, less credentialed, and policed predominantly Black public schools.

The sacrifice of leaving local public schools was made most evident in the lives of Ruby Bridges and Linda Brown. Ruby Bridges was just six years old in 1960 when she walked to school in New Orleans escorted by four U.S. marshals. On her first day, Ruby was accosted by two White women, one who threatened to poison her, the other who held a display of a Black baby doll in a coffin. For her safety, Ruby was not permitted to eat food prepared at school. She spent the entire school year alone. No White parent would allow their child to be in the same classroom with her. Linda Brown was thrust into the national spotlight by her family's commitment to ending racial segregation in public schools. The Brown name entered the annals of history by chance. Thirteen families were involved in the civil rights lawsuit, but the Brown case was chosen because it was alphabetically first: *Brown v. Board of Education.* These two Black girls still embody both the hope and the terror that Black parents are faced with generation after generation as they choose an educational path for their children.

Thirty years later, access to White schools continued to offer Black children nothing more than a mixed bag: a chance at more advanced academics but at a negative and often damaging social cost. Aja, who is forty and Black, grew up in my hometown of Rochester, New York. She works for a local nonprofit in the city. Educators raised her—her grandmother and mother are teachers—and she loved to read as a child. She remembers being a first grader who often finished schoolwork before her classmates. When she did, she would put her pencil down, hand the work to her teacher, then walk over to the reading nook to quietly lose herself in a book, careful not to disrupt her classmates. Rather than give Aja more challenging work or encourage her independent reading time, her White teacher labeled Aja's trips to the reading nook disruptive and called Aja's mother to complain. "I was a precocious little kid," Aja told me. "My thirst for knowledge was a problem for this teacher."

Aja's mother searched for a better school for her daughter, one that would nurture her love of learning. Private school was too expensive, so Aja's mother filled out an application for her nine-year-old daughter to attend Urban-Suburban, the "first and oldest voluntary desegregation program in the United States." Established in 1965 through an agreement between the Rochester City School District and a neighboring school district, the program transfers inner-city students to suburban schools and vice versa. Urban-Suburban's goal is "to decrease racial isolation, deconcentrate poverty and enhance opportunities for students."[2]

The ruse of school choice left Aja's mother with few options for her daughter. White people who had fled to the segregated suburbs left underfunded urban public schools in their wake, and programs like Urban-Suburban were designed to fill the gap. However, to seize the opportunity offered by Urban-Suburban, Aja would have to leave her city behind. "It was overwhelming. It was terrifying. It was traumatizing," Aja said about attending a nearly all-White school. The suburb her school was in was 87 percent White. "It was also the realization that, damn, we're poor," Aja continued.

Aja had to leave her house by 5:30 a.m. to arrive at school on time. She took a bus to downtown Rochester, then transferred to another that would take her to a suburb called Penfield. The bus was full of Black faces hoping their proximity to the privileges afforded Whiteness would save them. Aja played basketball, so during basketball season, she remembers leaving home at 5:30 a.m. and not returning until 7:00 or 8:00 p.m. "I never got the chance to hang out with kids from my neighborhood." I can attest to this because even though Aja and I only lived streets away from each other, we didn't meet until we were selected for the same summer basketball team at seventeen. I played at almost every gym on my side of town, and I never ran into Aja because she was either at school twenty miles away or didn't have any friends from the neighborhood to go to the gym with.

Listening to Aja describe her experience hit me hard. I had applied to that same program for high school, but I had been rejected. I thought Aja was lucky—until I interviewed her for this book. When Aja and I met as teenagers, we instantly became best friends. We both noticed right away that I needed Aja's help. We were in the same grade and the same age, but I was years behind her educationally. She was well read, and I had never finished a book. She began to tutor me. I needed her guidance in every subject. We joked and laughed about how far behind I was, but Aja would reassure me that she had my back. And I, in turn, gave Aja the Black female friendship and camaraderie that she had missed out on at a segregated school like Penfield.

But Aja's access to rigorous academics came at a price. She recalls sitting in classrooms in those moments before or after the bell rang, the moments when students had time to mill about and talk. That's when she'd find herself surrounded by White peers who shot rapid-fire questions at her "tommy-gun-style," she told me. They wanted to know what it was like to live in Rochester, but first they had to make their assumptions known.

"Are you in a gang? Do you have a gun?" Others asked about her hair and talked about Black people in only stereotypical ways. Aja said she felt like "an exhibit in a zoo." All she could do was look at them incredulously, hopeful that the look on her face showed her disgust at their ignorance. "I knew I was dealing with White people's perceptions," she told me. "But I didn't have the framework to understand what was happening." Aja made do, building community with other Black students who, like her, were bused in from the city. She got used to White classmates trying to correct her English and stopped expecting anyone in leadership at the school to bridge the gap between the culture she came from and the one she'd been "imported" into.

While I was skipping classes and playing basketball at my inner-city school, I made lifelong friends. Mrs. Knight, my high school athletic director, unofficially adopted me into her family, and when I was seventeen and my father died, my basketball coach, Coach Mike Nally, stepped up to fill the role. Aja had the resources and instruction to excel, but I had the love of my community, the love of my friends, and a sense of identity. Aja told me she would give anything to have had my high school experiences of belonging and care.

Looking back at her teen years, Aja is not sure that the education she received at White schools was worth the emotional harm. "It's a conundrum," she said. "There are no good solutions for us." Aja recalled coming home to her neighborhood and feeling alienated. Neighborhood kids accused her of speaking like a White girl. She was not accepted at school or in her community. In both worlds, she felt like a pariah.

What's infuriating is that neither one of us should have had to sacrifice one experience for the other. I should have had educational opportunities and support, and Aja should never have had to leave her community to access a well-resourced education.

Black children are often exposed to soul-crushing social challenges and psychic damage when they attend majority-White schools. Even today, Black families take huge risks to send their children to districts they perceive as offering more educational opportunities. Sometimes they are even criminalized for this pursuit. In 2011, Kelley Williams-Bolar, a Black mother, served nine days in jail and was sentenced to eighty hours of community service for using her father's address to enroll her two daughters in a school with more resources and opportunities.[3] Tanya McDowell was charged with first-degree larceny for using her son's babysitter's address to enroll him in a school. McDowell and her son were homeless, and the babysitter's address was the only address she had at the time. McDowell told the judge at her sentencing, "I have no regrets seeking a better education for him."[4]

A common thread exists between the civil rights era, the period when Aja and I were in school, and today. The burdens of choice, travel, and risk fall on non-White families. Then as now, school choice relies on Black resiliency, Black ambition, and Black people's relentless pursuit of education to create the façade that our children have choices in life to mitigate racism and anti-Blackness. In reality, we have educational scraps. Black parents' sacrifices are expected, and the awareness that many of us will do whatever it takes to help our children is systematically exploited. Our sacrifices are celebrated as America's watershed moments for the appearance of civil rights, but once the cameras leave, we are met with resistance in the courts—and legislation often quietly unravels the gains of our sacrifices. We are expected to be America's moral conscience, and we are unceremoniously punished for it.

For Black parents, the White rage of the educational system is ever present because we were once children who were traumatized by the same system to which we now send our children. In 1979, Linda Brown again sued the Kansas Board of Education, reopening her famous civil rights case. This time, the case was brought on behalf of her children. Brown filed a lawsuit arguing along with eight other parents that her children's school was segregated. Brown's attorney at the time stated: "Twenty-five years later, the only thing that has changed for black people here is that the quality of their children's education has declined . . . The Supreme Court's decision hasn't changed a thing."[5]

Aja is overwhelmed by the stress of sending her son to school in our hometown of Rochester. Today, it is one of the poorest cities in the country.[6] Its graduation rate in 2020 was only 68 percent, compared to 85 percent statewide.[7] A mere 10 percent of the city's school population is White.[8] In the fall of 2020, the district was contending with a potential budget deficit of $117 million. One reason for the shortfall, writes local reporter Justin Murphy, is that the city has "far more children in poverty and with disabilities than any other district in the region . . . while not receiving proportionate state funding."[9] Some neighboring suburbs have median household incomes of more than $70,000, while that figure is less than $31,000 for Rochester residents.[10]

This divide was heightened in the spring of 2022 when six Rochester teachers were put on administrative leave after a student discovered a text message thread where these six teachers used vulgar slurs to describe their students. One text message read: "Dave said I have to take my clothes off in the garage and put them in a bag and put them in the dryer on hot, and then get a job in Penfield."[11] A neighboring suburb of Rochester, Penfield, where Aja was bused to school, is currently 90 percent White. Another text referred to calling parents, stating: "I'm calling to remind you that you are a [expletive] parent, and your kid is a [expletive] like you. Thanks." All the students referred to in these text messages were Black. What makes this even more disturbing is that according to a study published in 2022, White teachers "bonded with each other more quickly and effectively" when communication centered on racially stereotyping their students.[12]

I fear for the kids being educated in my hometown by teachers who bond over disparaging and anti-Black ideas about them and the city I love. The parents I interviewed all expressed significant concern not just for their children's physical safety as Black children but also for the psychological damage of educational White rage that is just as present today as it was after *Brown*.

"Oh, Your Dad Lives with You"

Leo and Tia, who are in their midforties, were high school sweethearts and have been married for over twenty years—when asked, they laugh and can't agree on exactly how long. One thing they know for sure is that they love being parents. They have four children, ages nineteen, sixteen, thirteen, and six. Tia is a social worker, and Leo works at a hospital as the sterile processing supervisor. They live in one of the largest suburbs outside metro Atlanta, Cobb County. Demographically, the county is 55.8 percent White, 28.7 percent Black, 13.4 percent Hispanic, 6.1 percent Asian, 5.6 percent "other," and 3.4 percent two or more races.[13]

Cobb County Schools is a district consistently in the news for racist incidents. In 2017, a Black mother challenged her son's social studies curriculum when her son was called a slave by his White classmate on Civil War Dress-Up Day.[14] Also in 2017, a student at a high school in the district threatened on social media to kill Black students.[15] In 2021, the district passed a resolution banning the factual teaching of U.S. history. The resolution read in part: Cobb County "will not implement Critical Race Theory, also called CRT, in our schools—not under that name nor by any other name, nor will we be using *The 1619 Project* in our schools—

not under that name nor by any other name."[16] In 2022, professor and activist Jillian Ford, together with the Southern Poverty Law Center and the ACLU, sued Cobb County Schools for intentionally drawing school maps that placed Black and Brown students in overcrowded schools.[17]

Leo and Tia told me that none of their four children have ever had a Black teacher. They moved to Cobb because they wanted their children to "experience diversity, different cultures, different people . . . What we didn't realize is that although we wanted diversity in children, there wasn't going to be diversity in educators. I think we didn't think about that point." Tia recounts many challenges educating her Black children in a district where the teaching population is overwhelmingly White. Many times, she noted her children's teachers were not teaching Black history. So she and Leo supplement their education.

I spoke with their oldest child, Isa, a second-year college student. She is a nineteen-year-old junior because she took college credit classes in high school. Isa shared about her parents' extra assignments, "I was fortunate enough because my mom would take teaching Black history into her own hands. But a lot of my classmates didn't know much about Black culture or even, like, slavery, systematic racism, or that the government sets us up to fail." It was insightful to hear Leo and Tia's teachings in Isa's responses, especially because I interviewed them at separate times. Isa was in her dorm room, miles away from home.

Isa also told me how the absence of Black teachers influenced her thinking; growing up, the only Black people she saw working in her schools were the cleaning staff. She said,

> It's not saying I didn't think Black people were capable of certain things; I learned that at home. But when you see every position being the same color . . . I see my principals are only White and teachers. Not saying Black people can't

be teachers. But you know, it wasn't until maybe college that I actually saw a Black person teach in a classroom. Wow. Or actually, scratch that—I have a Black president at my college [Georgia State]. So I think that's the first time I've actually seen, like, oh, wow, like we're capable. You know, that's the thing.

Isa's comments speak to her parents' work ensuring she sees Black representation.

In middle school, Isa was inspired by NFL star Colin Kaepernick's silent protest of refusing to stand during the national anthem in response to the killings of Black folx by police. After learning about Black Lives Matter and how Black people were being gunned down in the streets by police, she felt that the flag did not "represent" her, so she decided to sit down during the Pledge of Allegiance. Her principal saw her sitting during the pledge and was "furious," according to Isa. She told me,

> The principal was like, "What are you doing? You need to stand up." I was like, "I don't need to stand up." She was like, "You know how disrespectful that is?" going on and on and on and on. In a hallway full of people, people are looking at me. And then she told me, "You need to come to my office." She then goes on about how disrespectful it is that I don't stand for the flag and tells me about all this country's done for us. And implied something like, I don't know history. How disrespectful is she? My great-granddad was in World War II. My granddad fought in wars, too.

Tia wrote a long email explaining that according to the Cobb County Schools rule book, students don't have to stand for the Pledge of Allegiance. Isa was well within her rights as a student to sit, her mother argued on her behalf. Tia also made it clear that berating her child in front of her peers was unacceptable and would not be tolerated again. With confidence and boldness, Tia told me that the principal understood her very clearly after that incident about her child's rights and how Isa would be treated moving forward. Only after Isa's mom got involved did the principal apologize to Isa.

But what frustrated Isa the most throughout K–12 schooling was teachers assuming she didn't have a dad present in her life. Leo told me that teachers often assumed his kids came from a fatherless home, even though he regularly attended school events. He told me, "Isa would notice when teachers only want to reach out to her mom. Isa would tell them, 'You can reach out to my dad. Go talk to my dad. Why can't you reach out to my dad?' Yeah, she would say it regularly." When I asked Isa about her teacher assuming she didn't have a dad, she told me about the time her dad attended and took her home after her chorus concert. She told me,

> She was like, "Oh, your dad came?" I was like, "Yeah." But why do people say that? But I learned the connotation. Oh, you're Black, so you don't have a dad in your life. But even in elementary school: "Oh, you have a dad?" "Oh, your dad lives with you in your house with your mom?" I'm like, "Yeah . . . even, like, my little siblings." "Oh, y'all have the same dad?" Yeah, we have the same dad, you know, this type of stuff.

The racist myth believed by Isa's teachers is that Black men are not a part of their children's lives; however, research shows that Black fathers are more active fathers compared to White fathers.[18] Not to mention, welfare reform systematically removed Black men from two-parent homes. Starting in the 1940s, Black women entering the U.S. labor market, faced with low pay, discrimination, and job instability, also faced a racist, sexist, and anti-Black welfare system that determined eligibility based on White Christian morals.[19] Aid to families was denied due to the "man-in-the-house" rule. Unmarried Black mothers couldn't receive funding assistance if there was found to be any adult male presence in the house. Caseworkers would make unannounced visits to catch Black men (whether fathers or not) in the home.[20] Welfare reform tore Black families apart as Black mothers had to choose between their children's father and federal assistance in a precarious labor market. In 1968, the Supreme Court struck down the "man-in-the-house" rule, but the racist myth that Black fathers are not in the home is alive and well today, as Isa's teachers demonstrated.

Isa was not the only of the couple's four children to face struggles in schools that have only White adults in leadership positions. Their now-sixteen-year-old daughter Kim had a traumatic experience with a White teacher when she was in preschool. "I was the only Black girl in the class," Kim remembers. "I just felt the teacher treated me differently, and I told my mom about it. I ended up switching schools, but I don't know, it just wasn't like a great start to school."

That interaction at four years old has affected Kim's trust in White teachers even today. She hears White teachers making "slick remarks about Black students," which puts her right back in her pre-K classroom, the only Black girl and so mired in feelings of being isolated and singled out. When I heard Kim refer to slick comments directed at Black students, I thought immediately of those texts found on teachers' phones in Rochester. Listening to the hoops Black parents have to jump through, not only to educate their children but to teach them to stand up to Whiteness, was heartbreaking. At the same time, it is the reality I know as the parent of two Black children myself. I tell my children what Patty told me: "Give them hell."

Leo and Tia echo that lesson for their children. It's important that their children know how to speak up for themselves, stand up to authority, and communicate their feelings because they never want them to feel unheard or small next to their White peers. They make sure they have countless conversations with their children about racism in America and teach them to "never shrink yourself" because of the racism and anti-Blackness their children will face in schools and this world.

This is the additional labor of being a Black parent. We have all the worries any parent would have, such as "Are my kids reading on grade level?" "Are they writing complete sentences?" and "Are they learning the times table?" We also have a whole additional set of questions surrounding race, racism, harm, trauma, self-esteem, safety, and pain when we send our Black children to school. Sadly, asking ourselves these questions is followed by uncontrollable emotions, knowing that we must send our children daily to a place that will demand they endure its pain. For parents, this is a hard reality to quiet in the mind. To know this pain as a student and then become a parent yourself? Sometimes it's too much to bear.

Predatory School Choice

Students who are my contemporaries, like my friend Aja, were bused to majority White districts following *Brown*. Some Black students in recent decades have the experience of growing up in districts in which White students are a slight majority but the educators are overwhelmingly White, as is the case with Leo and Tia's children. However, charter schools move Black students into environments where they are more likely to have Black peers and Black teachers.

Ace and Val, who are in their midforties, met during college in Philadelphia. After graduation, they moved to Atlanta, which is where Val was born. I interviewed them early one morning via Zoom. They had just returned from dropping their thirteen-year-old daughter and six-year-old son off at school. They say their experiences as Black parents have "run the gamut." Their daughter attended a private school for grades K–3. She then attended a public charter school, then a different charter school, and is now back at the private school at which she'd started. Her younger brother also attends that private school.

"Where you live has a huge impact on the kind of education you can give your kids," Val told me. "Because it's so separate, educational excellence appears to be very segregated." Val is right. In 2021, the Brookings Institution determined that Atlanta was one of the most racially segregated cities in the U.S.[21] The same study found that in 2019, homes in White-majority neighborhoods had a median home value of almost $500,000; in Black-majority neighborhoods, the median home value was roughly $150,000.[22] Val, who owns a social media marketing agency, and Ace, a real estate agent, know how much money it takes to buy a home in an area of the city with schools they feel offer a "more rigorous education."

Val and Ace moved their child from the private school where she attended K–3 to a charter school because they wanted her to have exposure to extracurricular activities and technology that was not available at the private school. They looked for a school with "all the bells and whistles." They found what they thought was the perfect school for their daughter, a charter school specializing in technology. Val told me,

> Because of where it was located, it had a lot of partnerships that allowed them to have extracurriculars like coding, gifted class. They had gifted class in the [nearby] aquarium's classroom. They had marine biology . . . They had the Atlanta Falcons [players and the cheerleaders] on their first day of school, all that kind of stuff going on.

Ace interjects, "But the teacher was never there." According to the couple, all the extracurricular activities were great, but "inside of the classroom, it was dismal." Val said,

> Her teacher was just never there. She would be there only three days out of the week. And then, the other days of the week, they had random substitutes. The teacher would randomly be gone for a whole week or two weeks. And as parents, we complain to the principal, but, you know, we're assuming that there was a family situation, because how do you maintain a job? . . . But as a result, our child did not see any growth in math.

After a disappointing academic year filled with inconsistencies, Val and Ace pulled their daughter from the "shiny" charter school. They then enrolled her in a different charter school that was more academically focused. Ace shared that the school lacked any structure. He said, "Structure, discipline, and consistency—that's big for me." They both agreed that their daughter was settling into mediocrity because the school lacked rules and structure. Ace also felt that, like Leo, he experienced being ignored by teachers as a Black father. "I do think in the educational system, we're [Black fathers are] overlooked a lot."

I asked Val about moving her daughter from charter to charter after being promised world-class extracurricular activities by school leaders who failed to educate her daughter in the core subjects. Val vividly explained the predatory nature of school choice for Black parents:

> I think in Black neighborhoods and schools that are being designed and led by people who are not of color to serve children who are of color, [leadership] will often use the

shiny balls to distract Black families into thinking that this
is the best option for their child. When they actually get in
there, they're not giving them what they originally came
for . . . It's like all the shiny keywords and buzzwords, and,
you know, all the cool swag. The brand attracts people. But
at the end of the day, are you able to deliver the education
for these Black kids that they came to get? And they can't
do that.

In the decades following George H. W. Bush's administration,
the proliferation of charter schools, virtual schools, and vouchers were just three of the many ways the super predators began
siphoning public money and selling Black children's education.
The super predators essentially set the schoolhouse on fire, set
the water hose to a drizzle, and then charged for the water. Diane Ravitch served as George H. W. Bush's assistant secretary
of education and strongly advocated for school choice, charter
schools, and merit pay. A Democrat, she has since apologized
for her role as an educational reformer in the 1980s and 1990s
and now writes and speaks against many of the reforms she once
championed. In her book *Reign of Error: The Hoax of the Privatization Movement and the Danger to America's Public Schools,*
she writes:

> The "reform" movement is really a "corporate reform"
> movement, funded to a large degree by the major foun-
> dations, Wall Street hedge managers, entrepreneurs, and
> the U.S. Department of Education. The movement is de-
> termined to cut costs and maximize competition among
> schools and among teachers. It seeks to eliminate the geo-
> graphically based system of public education as we have
> known it for the past 150 years and replace it with a com-
> petitive market-based system of school choice.[23]

Black children, especially those in poor communities, are offered devalued school choices based on the "racial calculus" of reform, effectively creating what scholar Noliwe Rooks calls "segrenomics," which is both a "business strategy" and an "educational ideology" that work in tandem to make school segregation profitable. Racial and economic segregation allow White parents to provide their children with an education that functions to maintain their privilege. Black parents, meanwhile, are left to navigate unproven educational reform models. We are instructed to abandon our neighborhood schools, which are intentionally neglected and underfunded, for school choices that White parents might hear about only on NPR. We are told to leave our schools full of Black faces, like our own children's faces, because those children are lawless, low-achieving, "behind," and lacking "college readiness skills."

To make matters worse, Black parents are pitted against one another and other folx of color for coveted spots at charter and virtual schools or for the limited allocation of vouchers that are touted by reformers as the best choices for Black children. Enrollment at charter school networks depends on traditional public schools failing, closing, and being viewed as unsafe. Black parents often win a lottery to attend one of these networks.

These schools are predatory because they bank on our desire for a system that leads our children to social and economic mobility while creating educational enterprises that profit from their repeated failed experiments. Our resiliency is thus taken for granted and exploited for profit. It's a vicious and seemingly inescapable cycle, as many of these same people have made divestments that ensure that we cannot learn in our own zoned schools.

Shockingly, the enterprise of educational exploitation is entirely legal. Derestricting charter school capacity to grow allows corporate school reformers to essentially sell Black children's futures. Investors such as Mark Zuckerberg are motivated to get involved in corporate education reform.[24] In 2010, Zuckerberg launched a foundation called Startup:Education (now the Chan Zuckerberg Initiative) and announced he would donate $100 million to Newark, New Jersey, schools to transform that city's failing system. The tycoon made the announcement on Oprah Winfrey's show, joined by Newark mayor Cory Booker and New Jersey governor Chris Christie. Another $100 million was then raised by foundations and private donors. As journalist Dale Russakoff documented in her book, *The Prize,* the $200 million was spent building political careers, paying consultants, disregarding public schools in favor of charters, and ignoring parents and students in the decision-making process. Once again, Black families and their struggles to overcome divestment in public education were used as props to advance those in power.

Tellingly, many of the nation's richest hedge fund operators have investments in charter schools and other efforts to privatize public education. David Tepper (whose net worth was $15.8 billion in 2021) founded Appaloosa Management, a hedge fund firm, and Better Education for Kids, a New Jersey political action committee that has campaigned for vouchers and other reforms. Steven A. Cohen of SAC Capital Advisors ($16 billion) has donated hundreds of millions of dollars to charter schools.[25] Celebrities looking for tax breaks and investments also open charter schools that produce questionable results, if not educational malfeasance. Retired tennis great Andre Agassi founded the Andre Agassi College Preparatory Academy in his hometown of Las Vegas in 2001. A few years after the school opened, Agassi started a hedge fund to build schools and rent the buildings to charter school networks.[26]

In 2012, former football star Deion Sanders opened Prime Prep Academy in Texas. Prime Prep's two locations closed a few years after opening amid accusations that Sanders was violent and intimidating toward former academy staff members.[27] "The high school was chaos," former Prime Prep executive director Kimberly Carlisle told *The New York Times*. "Academics didn't even play second fiddle. It was all about getting those athletes scholarships and contracts."[28] The Texas Education Agency revoked Prime Prep Academy's charter after allegations of mismanagement of funds. The school could not even be ranked academically because of missing data.

In Harlem, meanwhile, rapper and businessman Sean Combs teamed up with the charter school network Capital Preparatory to open a school focused on social justice. However, an investigation found that the network's central location in Hartford, Connecticut, permitted athletes to bypass the state's normal lottery process for enrollment—for the school to have dominant sports teams.[29] Another investment strategy corporate school reformers use is the New Market Tax Credit, which provides a 39 percent tax credit to investors who fund projects, including the construction of new charter schools, in low-income communities. Finally, investors lobby against caps on charter schools to allow for the unregulated proliferation of charter schools, which incidentally maximizes investors' profits.

In 2019, a pair of reports by the Network for Public Education found that the U.S. government had wasted up to $1 billion on charter schools.[30] Between 2009 and 2016, one in four schools awarded grants either never opened or were shut down due to mismanagement of funds, poor performance, lack of enrollment, or fraud.[31] In Michigan alone, seventy-two charter schools that never opened received a combined $7.7 million from the Department of Education's Charter Schools Program.[32] From 1995 to 2005, the department did not require states to report how they spent federal dollars from this program.[33] Since 1995, the Elementary and Secondary Education Act has given out $4 billion to charter schools.[34] The Network for Public Education reported that many applications for charter school grants were given "without scrutiny."[35]

The organization also uncovered how some nonprofit charters operated as shell companies for for-profit corporations. For example, the Ohio-based for-profit company White Hat Management functioned as a for-profit charter management organization overseeing the operations of sixteen Life Skills charter schools in five states. Some of the charter schools within the network of White Hat Management paid 97 percent of their funding to White Hat. The corporation also functioned as a real estate company that leased buildings to schools.[36] White Hat Management was founded in 2000 by David Brennan, an industrialist known for wearing a white hat. Brennan championed school choice in Ohio and used his wealth and influence to campaign for the expansion of the state's charter schools.[37] He also was among the largest Republican donors in Ohio.[38] White Hat Management charter schools had low test scores and "soaring high school dropout rates," and some of its own schools eventually sued the company. The schools argued that White Hat violated its financial duty to the schools because textbooks, computers, and furniture purchased with public funds belonged to White Hat, not the schools. Ohio's supreme court disagreed, ruling in favor of White Hat in 2015.[39]

Ron Packard, a former executive at Goldman Sachs who "specialized in mergers and acquisitions," acquired White Hat schools in 2014 and 2019 through Accel Schools, a charter school network based in Virginia.[40] In 2021, the network had more than 54 schools, more than 3,000 educators, and more than 23,500 students in seven states.[41] Before creating Accel Schools, Packard was the CEO and cofounder of K12, an online charter chain.[42] William Bennett, the former secretary of education under the Reagan administration and drug czar, is its other founder—the same William Bennett who in 2005 said, "If you wanted to reduce crime, you could, if that were your sole purpose, you could abort every black baby in this country, and your crime rate would go down."[43] Bennett and Packard secured seed money from Michael Milken (who was pardoned in 2020 by Donald Trump for violating U.S. securities laws), Larry Ellison of Oracle Corporation, and Andrew Tisch of the Loews Corporation.[44] As CEO of K12, Packard made $5 million a year.[45] Bennett stepped down from the company in 2005 after his offensive comments about aborting Black babies caused controversy.[46] The company is publicly traded and worth an estimated $1.5 billion.[47]

One reason virtual public charter schools are so widespread—despite the lack of evidence showing their effectiveness—is that beginning in 2005, the American Legislative Exchange Council (ALEC), backed by the Koch brothers, provided the template for lawmakers to introduce virtual charter schools.[48] The Virtual Public Schools Act, written by ALEC and backed by K12's lobbyists, states that its goal is to provide "additional educational resources to improve academic achievement" and that virtual charter schools "must be recognized as public schools and provided equitable treatment and resources as any other public school in the state."[49]

Reformers use the language of inclusion, diversity, and equity misleadingly so that it appears, on the surface, as if their investment in public education is for the greater good. K12 operates more than seventy online schools in thirty states, accounting for 30 percent of all virtual charter schools in the U.S.[50] In 2017 and 2018, two virtual charter school chains alone—K12 and Connections Academy—made up a whopping 50 percent of online enrollments in the U.S.[51] And yet the average four-year graduation rates for virtual schools linger around 50 percent, compared to 84 percent in public schools.[52]

In 2011, Agora Cyber Charter, the second-largest virtual

school in Pennsylvania—and one managed by K12—was on track to receive $72 million in taxpayer money, even while the state's education budget was dramatically cut.[53] That same year, however, *The New York Times* reported that Agora, which served more than eight thousand students at the time, was failing by almost every educational measure.[54] According to *The Times*, 50 percent of the students were behind in reading, 60 percent were behind in math, and a "third do not graduate on time."[55] The story also revealed that "hundreds of children, from kindergartners to seniors, withdraw within months after they enroll."[56] K12 has paid more than $175 million to settle false student-performance claims and false advertising.[57]

That same year, 2011, Tennessee passed the Virtual Public Schools Act. Introduced by Representative Harry Brooks, who served on ALEC's Education Task Force, the law "allowed school districts to open and operate online public schools and receive the same per-pupil funding as traditional public schools, despite not incurring the expenses that go along with brick-and-mortar facilities."[58] The Tennessee Virtual Academy, run by K12, received over $5,000 per student enrolled, yet it ranked as one of the lowest-performing schools in the state.[59]

Like charters, virtual schools are more than simply alternatives to brick-and-mortar public schools—they are a school choice option that facilitates the closing of public schools and funneling taxpayer dollars into private for-profit companies. Rooks documented how Pennsylvania governor Tom Corbett, a Republican, cut statewide funding for K–12 education by $900 million. The cuts disproportionately targeted the Philadelphia School District, which lost $198 million. As a result, thousands of teachers were laid off, class sizes were increased, extracurricular activities were cut by 40 percent, and dozens of schools were closed. "School buildings," Rooks said, "became so unpleasant that virtual education almost seemed like a respite."[60] Because of public school closures, parents were pushed into virtual education, with corporate online networks like K12 reaping the profits.

Like charter schools, virtual schools enlist celebrities to attract students. Bridgescape schools, run by EdisonLearning—a for-profit company that in the 1990s became the largest publicly traded educational organization, signed a marketing deal in 2012 with basketball legend Magic Johnson.[61] Johnson's star appeal was part of the lure to working-class parents.

The push to open so many charter schools—when studies have consistently shown that, overall, they do not academically outperform public schools—has everything to do with profit.[62] As the charter school bubble erupts, Black communities are left with what renowned educational researcher Gloria Ladson-Billings calls "education debt."[63] Researchers have equated the "rapid, unfettered expansion of charter schools" with predatory subprime mortgages because both have little federal oversight, target Black communities that have been historically denied access, and create a "bubble"[64] that, when it bursts, leaves Black people in debt, whether educational or financial. Additionally, charter schools facing closure find independent charter authorizers who will reauthorize their charter instead of addressing their harmful practices.[65] And some charter schools have engaged in practices reminiscent of predatory lending, such as offering gift cards and cash rewards to parents who refer other parents to the school.[66]

Black parents need more than what White schools offer. We need more because of the burden of racism and anti-Blackness. We need schools that understand, affirm, and love Black people for more than just the month of February. Schools that honor their child's language. Schools that teach Black children the beauty of what it means to be a Black person. Schools that treat their child like a child and not a criminal. Schools that confront the legacy and continued existence of racism in schooling head-on.

Schools that nurture their child's potential. Schools that are welcoming not only to children but to their families as well. Schools that center Black people's contributions, not just their oppression. Schools where Black children feel valued for their language, heritage, and community. Schools where Black Lives Matter. This is the type of education that reform can't provide.

4

NO ENTREPRENEUR LEFT BEHIND

> No one experiments on other children the way our children are guinea pigged. I want for our children what the best get.
>
> —Marva Collins, legendary Black educator[1]

"A Band-Aid to a Gunshot Wound"

Shani Robinson never intended to be a teacher. It was the family profession. Her mother and grandmother were teachers, but Shani's dream was to be broadcast into people's homes nightly, especially Black people's homes, informing them about what was happening in their communities. She wanted to be a news anchor and tell "positive Black stories," she told me. Shani grew up in Atlanta, Georgia, then moved to Nashville, Tennessee, to attend Tennessee State University, a Historically Black College and University (HBCU). In 2006, Shani graduated with a double major in psychology and African studies. Her passion remained journalism. After college, Shani got an internship at the local news station in Nashville; then, she was hired as an entry-level associate producer. At first, the work felt like a dream come true. Shani's face lit up, telling me about the first time she reported the news on air. But the longer she stayed in the job, the more she realized she'd been naive about the world of journalism and how nightly news worked. She learned that working the "Black beat" in the newsroom meant covering crime. The revelation devastated Shani.

While at the station, Shani had occasionally worked as a substitute teacher to make money on the side. So when a friend told Shani about Teach for America (TFA), Shani thought this might be the right way to change career paths. TFA is a nonprofit that places college graduates in urban and some rural classrooms across America without the requirement that they've majored in education or obtained teaching licensure. Shani applied and became a corps member in 2007. She didn't want to leave Nashville, but at the time, TFA didn't place corps members in Nashville. They did have placements in Atlanta, so Shani decided to move back home as a TFA corps member. There, Shani was thrown into a five-week summer teaching boot camp to prepare her to be a full-time teacher. "We worked with the kids who failed the state test and constructed lesson plans," she said of the boot camp. "We all were in one class teaching ten kids . . . It wasn't realistic." At first, Shani thought the training had prepared her well for the classroom. But once the school year began, she realized much more about the demands of the profession. "When you get in and you realize, okay, you have a whole classroom to yourself. You have a lot to prepare," she remembered. "No, five weeks is not enough to give them [students] everything that they need, you know, a holistic approach to teaching and learning. You are trying to put a Band-Aid to a gunshot wound."

Shani at first felt her lack of training would not cause too much harm because her position as a teacher would be temporary. She told me, "The way it was explained to me was that we would be filling in for teacher shortages. It made sense to me, like, they don't have enough teachers. It just seemed okay." If students were faced with either having an unprepared temporary teacher or no teacher, Shani felt she was serving the students. "It wasn't until later when I learned actually, they are replacing some teachers," she said. "We had no idea they were replacing traditional teachers." Reflecting on the bait and switch, Shani emphasized, "It's been more of them trying to put a Band-Aid on deeper, deeply rooted issues."

These deep issues, Shani told me, were poverty, students coming to school hungry, and parents who were also pushed out of school and now struggled to help educate their children. In other words, those deep-seated issues are the result of educational White rage, still reverberating generations later. After fulfilling her two-year commitment with TFA, Shani returned for a third year of teaching. After three years, Shani resigned. By then, the former psychology major had a new passion: counseling. She wanted to put her degree to use working with youth in her hometown. Shani thought she was done with education—until she became part of the biggest standardized testing cheating scandal in recent U.S. history.

Teach America's Black Children

The education crisis manufactured by Ronald Reagan and George H. W. Bush created an entire job sector for education entrepreneurs who hijacked public education using government funds. TFA is a prime example of an entrepreneurial venture that used the unproven idea of taking uncertified teachers like Shani and putting them in classrooms with students that need the most skilled teachers, ultimately sacrificing Black children's lives and education along the way.

In the late 1980s, there was a growing debate about whether teachers needed credentials, experience, or even the most basic qualifications (a debate that is alive and well in 2023). As someone whose job is to prepare teachers, I am confident that teacher preparedness positively impacts student learning.[2] The far-right think tank Mackinac Center for Public Policy is among those who argue that teacher certification is unnecessary, using private school teachers and homeschooling parents as evidence.[3] Others say that all you need to teach is "the potential" to be a great teacher.[4] Inspired by the debate—and with no real job prospects— Princeton University senior Wendy Kopp stepped into the burgeoning field of education entrepreneurship by creating Teach for America. She secured $26,000 in funding from the philanthropic wing of the oil company Mobil (now ExxonMobil); from the start, she was bankrolled by corporate America and philanthropists. Kopp proposed enlisting college graduates from elite universities to teach for two years in urban schools—precisely the schools that White America had abandoned a few decades earlier. America's so-called brightest students, with zero teaching experience, would spend two years in an inner-city school, experimenting on Black children. These young and eager graduates were tasked with working in struggling schools that were designed to fail. That is to say, schools that were underfunded, had high teacher burnout, and administered tests that punished students. TFA recruits were given only two years—if they could make it that long—to "make a difference."[5] Shani exceeded her two-year commitment, becoming one of the 60 percent of TFA corps members to do so.[6] Kopp's model, which launched in 1989, was perfectly timed, given the move toward privatization that had occurred under the first President Bush.

In the 1990s and 2000s, the reformers rebranded themselves as education entrepreneurs, inspired by the notion of "entrepreneurial government"—a term coined by Ted Gaebler, city manager of Rancho Cordova, California, and journalist David Osborne in their book, *Reinventing Government: How the Entrepreneurial Spirit Is Transforming the Public Sector*. They argued that instilling entrepreneurship into government would reduce bureaucracy and promote effectiveness. "There are ways to use choice and competition to increase the equity in our school system," the authors wrote.[7] Both political parties embraced the "opportunity to reinvent government" through entrepreneurship. Republicans saw a chance to "diminish the power of teacher unions."[8] Both parties were united in their belief that public schools were obsolete or at least in need of major reforms.

Nearing the end of the century, reformers needed to reinvent themselves as compassionate and caring to appeal to a broader base of White liberals and Black voters. Even as they rebranded, they remained tough on crime and promoted school choice to maintain the free market model of education reform. The reformers and politicians of the twentieth century were ideologues and entrepreneurs who truly believed they could "fix" Black people and repair the harm of their predecessors. At first glance, their paternalism was less damaging than that of the reformers and politicians of the past, but the results were the same.

Across the country, young do-gooders—convinced that public schools needed them—flew into inner cities to save the day, creating networks of charter schools and taking up teaching jobs through TFA placements. All you needed was a college degree, a deep-seated belief that public education was a failure, and the hubris that you could fix Black education with no experience. I don't think this is what Shani believed going into TFA, but they are the messages she received while being recruited and trained.

Education entrepreneurs are still just entrepreneurs, and failure is a key component of being a good entrepreneur. In their book, *Education Entrepreneurs Today*, Frederick M. Hess and Michael Q. McShane profess that failure is an essential component of problem solving. An education entrepreneur, they maintain, has to experiment. "Entrepreneurship does not guarantee success," they conclude. "If anything, it ensures that there will be failure."[9] As appealing as the strategy of failure as impetus to improve may sound, many overlook the fact that real lives—Black children's lives—are at stake.

Having raised funds based on ideas she put forth in her senior thesis, Kopp sent nearly five hundred uncertified teachers into the under-resourced classrooms of New York, Los Angeles, eastern North Carolina, southern Louisiana, and rural Georgia.[10] Critics of TFA emerged quickly: current corps members,[11] former corps members,[12] and teacher educators[13] among them. By 2002, TFA had nearly 2,500 members in its teaching corps; by 2009, that number jumped to almost 7,500.[14] Public education was put in double jeopardy: not only were the reformers taking over schools with charters, but TFA and other teacher alternative programs allowed them to infiltrate the teaching force as well. Meanwhile, the nation needed to create jobs for high school graduates in the absence of industrial work. Instead, it provided jobs for college graduates like Kopp.

To maintain the nation's distrust of public education, reformers vilified teachers' unions, calling out the protection of tenure and the expenses of health insurance and pension benefits packages. TFA provides teachers without districts having to provide tenure or pay for pension benefits packages. In fact, school districts pay TFA directly for each TFA member they employ—$4,000–$5,000 for each inexperienced teacher.

Being a part of TFA looks great on the résumés of recent college grads, but there's no conclusive evidence that TFA is effective at educating students. A 2002 study found that, unlike certified teachers, TFA teachers had a *negative* impact on their students' outcomes.[15] Renowned educational researcher and policy expert Linda Darling-Hammond studied 4,400 teachers and 132,000 students in Houston and found that certified teachers' students consistently outperformed those taught by uncertified

TFA teachers. Other studies have come to the same conclusion, finding that new instructors are less effective than veteran teachers, and new teachers are least successful in their first two years. A few studies have detailed TFA's effectiveness; however, none are as comprehensive as Darling-Hammond's, and many lack meaningful high-impact indicators of achievement.[16]

The expansion of TFA and charter schools have gone hand in hand. In 2018, TFA sent almost 40 percent of its teachers to charter schools.[17] In major cities, charter schools employ a significant number of TFA teachers. For example, 54 percent of the teaching force in Houston is TFA. In San Antonio, the number is 58 percent, and in Los Angeles, it is 70 percent.[18] As a former elementary school teacher, I know firsthand how powerful it is to teach in a building with veteran teachers who have a deep understanding of the community and the children entering the school building every day. When I took my first teaching position in a school in Florida, it was filled with veteran teachers whom I asked to mentor me in building a classroom community, lesson plans, pacing, and how to read between the lines of the paperwork and tasks that were needed and the ones that could wait because they were bureaucratic busywork that nobody really evaluated. Teachers in schools with a majority TFA population are not as fortunate as I was.

While studies of TFA's effectiveness may be inconclusive, their funding is not. TFA ranks among the one hundred largest nonprofits in the nation, with an endowment of $208 million, over $245 million in awarded philanthropic grants, and $40 million received annually from the federal government as of 2016.[19] TFA is backed by some of the wealthiest people in this country, including the Walton family, who own Walmart, and retired Silicon Valley entrepreneur Arthur Rock.[20]

Kopp may have started with a grant from the petroleum industry, but she and other entrepreneurs have been able to keep their ventures funded by a network of philanthropists who are squarely focused on education reform. In 1998, entrepreneur Kim Smith and venture capitalists John Doerr and Brook Byers founded NewSchools Venture Fund. One of the first large-scale organizations to distribute philanthropic grants to education entrepreneurs, the fund has invested over $345 million in the past twenty years. One of its education entrepreneur pipelines is TFA, whose alums often become drivers of new entrepreneurial ventures themselves.

Among TFA's critics are people who have worked for the organization. Alex Caputo-Pearl, a former TFA corps member, said that TFA is a "main contributor to the characterization" of public schools as failing or in need of reform and their "privatization . . . rather than helping to address the teacher shortage in public district schools."[21] Many other TFA members have expressed dismay. Like Shani, many felt they were not prepared to teach students who were neglected by school systems entrenched in anti-Blackness. High teacher turnover has a significant negative impact on student learning.[22] While TFA requires a 2-year commitment, TFA's own data show that between 2012 and 2014 in some of their sites, as few as 78 percent of their first-year TFA corps members returned for their second year while in other sites, as few as 74 percent completed their second year.[23] While 60 percent of TFA corps members stayed for a third year, only 27.8 percent were still teaching after five years.[24] Perhaps this is not surprising, though, when you consider that Wendy Kopp herself states, "I think the way to understand Teach for America is as a leadership development program. We need political leaders, policy makers, doctors, lawyers, and probably more business leaders than we are producing right now who actually understand what it means to successfully teach in this context."[25] TFA is better understood as a business reform strategy that happens to involve education.

TFA's overwhelming presence in urban schools fits a reform model that ensures Black students get a second-rate education. It's no secret that TFA teachers are rarely in suburban schools. We do not send uncredentialed teachers into White schools, or at least not middle- or upper-class ones. Also, those schools would never allow uncredentialed, inexperienced instructors to teach a largely White—and more well-off—student body.

TFA opened the door to large-scale teacher for-profit alternative certification companies. Teachers of Tomorrow is the largest alterative certification provider in the nation; the program is entirely online and asynchronous. According to their website, the company has put more than 75,000 teachers in the classroom. In 2021, the Texas State Board for Educator Certification placed the company on probation for misleading marketing materials, failure to place teaching candidates with mentors, and the use of online curriculum that wasn't research-based.[26] The company also had an excessive number of complaints from teacher candidates.[27] That same year, in Texas, one in five new teachers hired entered the classroom without state certification; 40 percent of those teachers were placed in charter schools.[28] Nationally, less than 20 percent of teachers enter the profession through alternative certification programs, many working in urban schools.[29] Alternative teacher programs may seem to get one thing right: as an industry, they recruit a larger number of teacher candidates of color than traditional teacher certification programs;[30] however, Black and Brown prospective educators deserve high-quality teacher preparation, and so do their students. School reformers would never send their children to the schools where uncertified and alternatively certified teachers predominantly teach, and yet they promote and fund these programs to their profit.[31] Reformers need Black children to be underserved and failing, which supports their feel-good, quick-fix, gimmicky narrative. And who were among the biggest proponents of school choice around the same time TFA rose to prominence? Bill and Hillary Clinton.

The Clintons

In March of 1993, just a few months after Bill Clinton's inauguration, one of his administration's first objectives was to create the National Partnership for Reinventing Government. The initiative aimed to "adapt private sector management techniques to the public sector."[32] As Clinton famously proclaimed, "The era of big government is over."[33] Eliminating federal jobs was just one aspect of the program. The objective was also to create annual performance reviews and plans with target goals. For the first time in U.S. history, government agencies were creating strategic plans for Congress to review.[34] A year later, Clinton would sign the Improving America's Schools Act of 1994, an updated and nationalized version of South Carolina's Education Improvement Act of 1984. Clinton's secretary of education, Richard Riley, was viewed as a leader in educational reform in his home state of South Carolina, where he had served as governor. Riley's nomination received widespread praise from the education world.[35]

In the early 1980s, South Carolina was ranked forty-ninth in education in the nation. In 1983, as governor, Riley installed the Business Education Partnership. Its purpose was "to monitor [the state's] public school system to improve teacher quality, student testing and school funding."[36] A year later, Riley passed the Education Improvement Act, which called for more standards, increased spending, and holding schools accountable for test scores. While teacher salaries and per-pupil spending were significantly improved (reaching thirty-eighth and fortieth in the nation, respectively), a decade later, "South Carolina still ranks low compared with the nation as a whole, and test scores have not improved in the last two years."[37]

The Improving America's Schools Act, or IASA, was part of Clinton's education initiative Goals 2000, which itself was an offshoot of America 2000, Bush's reform strategy. Under IASA, a school district that sought to receive Title I funds (for low-income children) had to develop school improvement plans, performance standards, and show "adequate yearly progress"—a new standard that would foreshadow George W. Bush's No Child Left Behind Act. IASA also established that states could reward high-achieving school districts. Those districts that did not meet the "adequate yearly progress," or AYP, could be abolished. IASA also set aside $15 million to assist districts in creating charter schools.

While Clinton was increasing funding for charter operators and education entrepreneurs looking to collect their share of public dollars, he was also, like Reagan, telling the nation that schools lacked discipline and posed a "threat to the strength and vitality of America."[38] Clinton went so far as to call a summit to remind Americans that public schools were sites of crime; speaking at the 1998 American Federation of Teachers' annual convention, Clinton proposed the need for school uniforms, curfews, and anti-gun policies. "Teachers can't teach if they have to fight for respect or fear for their safety," he said. Laughably hailed as the nation's first "Black president," Clinton publicly stated that urban schools were unsafe for teachers. Whether he realized it or not, his language was racist and coded—urban connotes Blackness. Since over 80 percent of teachers in the country are White, Clinton effectively told America that White teachers were not safe with Black children. At the AFT convention, Clinton announced his White House summit on school violence that would bring students, school administrators, teachers, and law enforcement officials together in October of that year. He said the summit signaled "a new approach to restore discipline in our schools and order in our children's lives."[39]

At the conference, which explored young people's "violent behavior," First Lady Hillary Rodham Clinton was front and center. Four years earlier, she had promoted Clinton's Violent Crime Control and Law Enforcement Act of 1994, the largest crime bill in U.S. history, which "created longer mandatory sentences, reclassified less serious crimes as felonies and put tens of thousands more police officers on the streets."[40] In 1996, she had made the now-infamous comment that Black teenagers were "super predators" with "no conscience" and "no empathy." America's First Lady promoted crime bills and incited racial rhetoric that authorized the disposal of Black children. Calling Black teens "super predators" implicitly marks their schools as spaces of violence. And it makes school reform inevitable, branding it into something digestible and essential. Reformers know that when inner-city crime, school safety, and school discipline are made into national issues, dollars earmarked for public education are up for grabs.

Both George H. W. Bush and Clinton advanced the super predators' agenda of "privatization, deregulation, and competition between schools."[41] However, it is hardly a competition when public schools are fighting for funding, while many charter schools are awash in corporate sponsors, philanthropic dollars, and the expectation that failure is an important part of the entrepreneurial process. The Clinton administration thus paved the way for George H. W. Bush's sons.

The Bush Brothers

Many consider the Koch brothers and their father, Fred Koch, as the architects of weakening public education (and, in the process, democratic principles). But they were not alone among the very wealthy in selling public education to corporate America. The Bushes, too, were key players. In the 1990s and early 2000s, self-branded "compassionate conservatives" following the path to politics laid by their father, the Bush brothers Jeb and George W. used standardized testing and charter schools to plunder public education for crony capitalism.

While most states prohibit for-profit corporations from operating charter schools, the reality is that nonprofit schools often contract with for-profit corporations for key services. "Between September 2020 and February 2021, The Network for Public Education identified more than 1,100 charter schools that have contracts with one of 138 for-profit organizations to control the schools' critical or complete operations, including management, personnel, and/or curriculum."[42] Contractual elements called "sweeps" specify that the for-profit company has "the authority to run all school services in exchange for all or nearly all of the school's revenue."[43] Nonprofit schools qualify for federal grants, which are then "swept" to their contracted for-profit company. Public schools must engage in competitive bidding; charter schools are often exempt from these same financial regulations, allowing for-profit companies to charge obscenely inflated costs.[44] These practices encourage for-profit companies to cut costs to boost their profits, even when that cost-cutting directly impacts the educational experiences of the students for whose education they are receiving public dollars.[45]

George W. Bush rode into the White House from Texas on an educational reform lie he called the "Texas Miracle." In 1995, as governor of Texas, Bush revamped education in the state with Senate Bill 1. Running for governor, he promised more charter schools, more accountability, and more money for school vouchers. The goal of Bush's model was for school districts to abandon state regulations and create competition among schools that demonstrated high standardized test scores. Charter schools would be the incubator of this competition. Senate Bill 1 also replaced the traditional school governance model with a corporate structure that stripped most managerial and regulatory power away from the state board of education.[46]

Schools became "test-preparation academies" as test scores rose in the state.[47] The idea was that if all schools administered the same test, school leaders could measure and compare the academic achievement of Black and Brown students. Standardized tests became the sole indicator of school success, and the tenth-grade exams held particular importance. Schools pushed some students out before their tenth-grade test; they repeatedly retained others in the ninth grade and then promoted them directly to the eleventh grade.[48] Only 50 percent of non-White students who started ninth grade successfully graduated from high school.[49] Researchers found that the Texas tests developed by Pearson only measured students' test-taking skills, not their knowledge,[50] and the gains reflected in the Texas tests did not appear when those same students took tests not created and controlled by Texas.[51]

Governor Jeb Bush was also transforming his state's public education system in Florida. In the late 1990s, Bush worked with the Heritage Foundation to bring charter schools to the Sunshine State. To hold schools accountable, he proposed a public grading system that would rate schools from A to F. The legislature was ready to agree to that plan, but Bush revised it "to give its accountability measures a harder edge."[52] Having created one of the highest-stakes testing procedures in the country, Bush also created the first statewide voucher program and unleashed open season for charter schools.[53] In 1997, Jonathan Hage, a staffer at the Heritage Foundation who helped Bush open the state's first charter school, created Charter Schools USA, which he called a "classic business opportunity."[54] Bush also signed a provision that allowed charter schools to appeal denials by the local school board. By 2002, for-profit companies ran three-quarters of the state's charter schools.[55] And by 2015, Charter Schools USA managed seventy schools in Florida and six other states, with revenues exceeding $300 million.[56]

The Bush brothers and their father sold public education to the super predators while professing to care about Black and Brown students. Jeb, who is married to Mexican American philanthropist Columba Bush, is a father of three. At an event hosted by the National Reading Panel, he told attendees, "As the father of Hispanic kids, you become far more sensitive to disparities—kids who look like your kids not getting the skills they need or getting into the right colleges."[57] It was a nice sentiment, as long as one overlooked that Bush's children were attending private schools at the time.[58] In 1995, Jeb Bush declared that corporal punishment would deter school shootings because students need to experience shame, and public school students seemed to feel no shame in receiving poor grades. He therefore publicly shamed students and the communities they lived in by ranking schools by letter grades based on test scores and mandating that those grades be published yearly in local newspapers.

As a parent, I cannot imagine the frustration, anger, and hopelessness of waking your child up every morning to attend a school the state labeled failing. But what about the students? What does it mean to walk into a building every day thinking the school is failing not because of teachers, administrators, or the reforms that intentionally destabilize, terrorize, and divest from your education but because of you? I worked at an F school in Florida, so I know what it feels like from an educator's perspective. There were days as a teacher I was depressed at seeing a big F in the newspaper directed at the school I taught every day. I, along with my students and their families, was an F, and some days, it felt as though we all were trapped by that letter grade.

Bush's approach was also a road map for educational entrepreneurs to prey on those communities with the empty promises of charter schools. Bush wrote:

> In many of Florida's largest school districts, there is little that the teacher can do to make students feel some sense of shame. In some school districts, such as Walton County, one of the oldest forms of shame, corporal punishment, is alive and well, and despite protests by some parents and Florida's PTAs, the students have actually found that this doling out of shame is very effective. The students of these schools will tell you, as will anybody who experienced corporal punishment in school, that it is not the brief spanking that hurts, but the accompanying shame.[59]

The man who considered himself a self-made man (but who comes from one of the most powerful and richest families in the country) wanted to shame children with physical punishment, a practice that disproportionately impacts Black and Brown children and is associated with "a range of unintended negative outcomes . . . including higher rates of mental health problems . . . and lower cognitive ability and academic achievement."[60] This is the same governor who advocated building prisons for youth to stress "punishment over therapy."[61] As governor, Bush opposed a ballot measure allowing drug offenders treatment instead of prison, supported the growth of private prisons, blocked efforts to decriminalize cannabis, increased minimum sentences for juveniles, and executed twenty-one people.[62] The Bush brothers were racing to follow in their father's shoes and used the tools of disastrous education reform, crony capitalism, and privatization as they paved the path for at least one of them to occupy the White House.

Education was a piece of Jeb Bush's overall plan to end state-run services and weaken unions, including teacher unions.[63]

In 2003, he eliminated Florida's cap on the number of charter schools. Republican lawmakers then increased the allotment of taxpayer dollars to build charter schools and allowed "developers [to] build schools using the subdivision homeowner fees that they used for pools and other amenities."[64] When Bush left office in 2006, Florida had over three hundred charter schools.[65]

Then in 2008, Jeb Bush launched the Foundation for Excellence in Education. Patricia Levesque, his former deputy chief of staff, serves as chief executive officer; Levesque is also a lobbyist for education-technology companies. According to investigative reporter Lee Fang, Levesque openly lobbies lawmakers to diminish unions, move taxpayer dollars to religious schools, and legislate for more charter schools.[66] Among the approaches she takes to forward her agenda is introducing egregious reform bills she knows are illegal in order to keep teachers' unions "busy" and thus allowing the bills she supports to "fly under the radar."[67] While she "is a leader of a coalition of government officials, academics and virtual school sector companies pushing new education laws that could benefit them," she also coaches "notable charities like the Bill and Melinda Gates Foundation and the Michael and Susan Dell Foundation."[68]

In 2015, in preparation for his presidential run, Jeb Bush resigned as chairman of the Foundation for Excellence, as it faced accusations of working "as a backdoor vehicle for major corporations to urge state officials to adopt policies that would enrich the companies."[69] According to Layton's reporting, "The foundation has, for instance, pushed states to embrace digital learning in public schools, a costly transition that often requires new software and hardware. Many of those digital products are made by donors to Bush's foundation, including Microsoft, Intel, News Corp., Pearson PLC and K12 Inc."[70]

The Bush brothers and their father undermined and weakened public education as much as the Koch brothers and their father. But the Bushes' impact was direct and swift, given that they held such prominent public offices for decades. When George W. Bush surpassed his younger brother, becoming president in 2001, he said he would reform education by closing the achievement gap and saving Black children—leaving no child behind. How would he do this? With punitive testing measures and school closures.

The Gap

In July 2000, courting Black votes as the Republican candidate for president and keeping up his façade as the "compassionate conservative," George W. Bush addressed the NAACP at its convention in Baltimore. He told the crowd:

> My friend Phyllis Hunter of Houston, Texas, calls reading the new civil right. Equality in our country will remain a distant dream until every child, of every background, learns so that he or she may strive and rise in this world. No child in America should be segregated by low expectations, imprisoned by illiteracy, abandoned to frustration and the darkness of self-doubt. There's reason for optimism in this land. A great movement of education reform has begun in this country built on clear principles: to raise the bar of standards, expect every child can learn; to give schools the flexibility to meet those standards; to measure progress and insist upon results; to blow the whistle on failure; to provide parents with options to increase their option, like charters and choice; and also remember the role of education is to leave no child behind.[71]

Bush's words made him sound like a president ready to confront the nation's racism. But his approach to education actually meant doubling down on reforms grounded in anti-Blackness. Bush sought to tackle segregated schools and provide Black parents with options using a trusted move out of the preceding super predators' playbook: school choice.

And like his predecessors, regardless of party, Bush campaigned by stressing the need for morals in schools. Bush was a proponent of something called *character education.* As I have previously documented, character education mushroomed during the 1980s and 1990s when private, large-scale programs such as the Heartwood Program and Character Counts! infiltrated public education.[72] At the time, proponents of character education, such as Thomas Lickona, argued factors such as "the decline of the family" and "troubling trends in youth character" necessitated character education.[73] Lickona did not explicitly name race in his arguments; however, his argument is undergirded by coded language about "children of single mothers," the aggressive behavior of "especially boys, who are living in single-parent families," "poor parenting," and "the wrong kind of adult role models."[74] By 1996, 45 percent of school districts surveyed offered some form of character education, and 38 percent of the remaining districts had plans to do so in the near future.[75] President George W. Bush tripled funding for character education during his administration.

Bush also pushed funding for abstinence-only sex education, which, after years and millions of dollars, was found to be harmful to young people's sexual behavior, including increased rates of teen pregnancy and STDs.[76] In 2022, *The New York Times* reported that multiple studies conducted since 2017 found that most parents want their children to learn about contraception, sex education, puberty, healthy relationships, and abstinence in school.[77] While the majority of parents are not in favor of abstinence-only sex education, the federal government currently spends $100 million a year on the failed initiative, which is up from $50 million a decade ago.[78]

The president would put the achievement gap front and center of education reform and, fittingly, stole the slogan of a civil rights icon to make his pitch to the nation. Marian Wright Edelman founded the Children's Defense Fund in 1973. The organization's goal is to center the rights of children and families. An acclaimed author and winner of a MacArthur "Genius Grant," Edelman provided counsel for Martin Luther King Jr.'s Poor People's Campaign. The fund's mission is to "ensure every child a *Healthy Start*, a *Head Start*, a *Fair Start*, a *Safe Start* and a *Moral Start* in life and successful passage to adulthood with the help of caring families and communities." Its motto is "Leave No Child Behind." Bush blatantly purloined Edelman's words, but he disgraced her mission.

No Child Left Behind was a combination of educational reform approaches that had begun with Reagan. Bush took his unproven gubernatorial education reform approach to the White House by convincing Democrats and Republicans that accountability, high-stakes testing, merit pay, deregulation, data-driven decisions, charter schools, and competition would close the achievement gap.[79] And thus, a conservative Republican president, almost fifty years after *Brown*, radically expanded the federal reach of a government agency that Republicans under Reagan had wanted to abolish.

No Child Left Behind was years in the making. The act drew on Reagan's fearmongering, the senior President Bush's marrying of entrepreneurism and government, and Clinton's Goals 2000. Its accountability plan stated that schools and school districts were required to reach the goal of 100 percent proficiency by 2013/2014. It was finally time to "get tough" on education by punishing Black children and schools precisely because their country had left them behind.

Tests and Punishment

No Child Left Behind had one official goal: improving Black and Brown test scores in math and reading. Reformers pushed states to focus on basic skills; the humanities and teacher-student relationships were perceived as unimportant. Any state or school district that refused to comply with the federal mandates risked losing millions of dollars for students that needed the resources the most. If a school failed to reach "adequate yearly progress," the staff and principal could be fired, and the school could be closed. Closing schools became the solution for what reformers considered low performance. Alarmed researchers warned that school closings were another step in the movement to privatize education. "Closing public schools not only has a negative impact on student performance but also creates hardships for communities already struggling with disinvestment," argued Darling-Hammond.[80]

In 2013 alone, Chicago Public Schools closed forty-nine elementary schools and a high school. Along with displacing Black children from their communities, school closings are expensive—not surprisingly, the moving, the busing, and the school maintenance fees cost money even after the building is closed.[81] Furthermore, the Department of Education punished traditional schools for failing test scores while telling educational entrepreneurs that failure was expected.

Another brutal aspect of No Child Left Behind: students were required to make adequate yearly progress, regardless of their starting point. However, adequate yearly progress was based on scoring at or above grade level on a given standardized test. This meant that if a child entered school three grades behind in reading and by the end of the school year was only one grade behind, under NCLB, the child would be considered not to have made "adequate progress." In addition, if a child was at or above grade level as evidenced by formative and summative classroom assessments but scored poorly on the mandated standardized test, that child would also be considered not to have made "adequate progress."

Of course, another outcome for so-called failing schools was conversion into charter schools. Underfunded schools were especially under pressure, as they had to comply with NCLB or lose Title I funding, which supported low-income students. Under NCLB, those funds were used to hold low-income students captive. The federal government only provides about 8 percent of funding for K–12 public schools; the overwhelming majority comes from local and state taxes. But for schools in low-income communities, Title I funding is imperative. Low-income schools couldn't opt out of NCLB.

Making matters worse, NCLB's accountability measures ended up leading to unintended consequences, particularly for Black and Brown students. NCLB mandated test scores be disaggregated into four subgroups: race/ethnicity, socioeconomic status, limited English proficiency, and students with disabilities. If even a single subgroup did not make adequate yearly progress, the entire school could be closed for underperformance. A provision in the law stated that a subgroup population within a school or district that was under the minimum group size would not be analyzed and, thus, would not count as an indicator of that school's or district's adequate yearly progress. Later policy revisions led to some flexibility to better represent the learning of students with disabilities. It was in the school's, school district's, or state's best interest to ensure that subgroups remained under the minimum group size and that lower-achieving students were placed into a special education category to prevent their scores from impacting the school's, district's, or state's accountability outcomes.

Researchers at Portland State University and New York University found that the same student could be labeled with a learning disability in one school and not qualify for that same label at another.[82] Further, in a school with a small population of Black and/or Hispanic learners, those learners were more likely to be designated with a disability.[83] In 2007, experts, including representatives from the U.S. Department of Education, National Council on Disability, National School Boards Association, NAACP, and Mexican American Legal Defense and Educational Fund (MALDEF), went before the United States Commission on Civil Rights to detail how racial biases and lower academic expectations were disproportionately misplacing Black and Brown students in special education. In 2019, researchers found that Black and Brown students were more likely to be identified with disabilities if they attended a school where the student population is majority White and less likely to be identified with disabilities if the student body is majority Black and Brown.[84] The same was true for English learners, for whom English is their second language. Over time, Black students seen as low-performing were pushed out of schools to improve testing scores.[85] Civil rights groups revealed the link between inadequate school financing and high discipline rates: poorly financed districts had higher suspension and lower graduation rates.

Schools stopped focusing on teaching and learning and started focusing on strategies to stay open. This meant teaching to the test, putting Black children who do not need it in special education, and suspending Black children. As Radley Balko, author of *Rise of the Warrior Cop*, writes: "Systemic racism means . . . that we have systems and institutions that produce racially disparate outcomes, regardless of the intentions of the people who work within them."[86] Teachers who had gone into the profession to bring joy and lifelong learning to children were buying into a system of punitive testing because they were fearful for their jobs. Some teachers and administrators even believed that racist and anti-Black reforms were necessary.

In the end, NCLB did not improve education, students did not meet proficiency by 2014, and the policy dramatically reduced local control of schools. NCLB was a massive overhaul of public education that gave more power and money to testing companies and charter school operators and turned Black and Brown students into objects for sale in the educational marketplace. To understand just how far the super predators went to pillage public education, we need look no further than New Orleans after Hurricane Katrina.

The Crescent City

Three months after the levees broke in New Orleans, Louisianans were still searching for the remains of loved ones. The disaster was recent, but that didn't stop a frail ninety-three-year-old Milton Friedman from writing an op-ed for *The Wall Street Journal* rallying the super predators to take over New Orleans schools. It was time to take advantage of a crisis and snatch public education away from the public. Pointing out that most New Orleans schools and houses were ruined, he wrote, "The children are now scattered all over the country. This is a tragedy. It is also an opportunity to radically reform the educational system."[87]

Corporate lobbyists and right-wing think tanks descended on Baton Rouge, the state's capital, as developers, investors, and prominent Republicans began using language like "fresh start" and "clean slate" to describe their disingenuous motives for helping the people of New Orleans.[88] The super predators' goal was to emerge from this disaster with "lower taxes, fewer regulations, cheaper workers and . . . plans to level the public housing projects."[89] Their biggest priority, though, was the massive takeover of the New Orleans public school system. Naomi Klein writes that the "auctioning off of New Orleans' school system took place with military speed and precision."[90] The Bush administration coughed up millions of dollars to convert New Orleans public schools to charter schools. In 2003, Louisiana established the Recovery School District, or RSD. This governing body could take over the operations of schools that did not meet the state's academic standards. The RSD made post-Katrina New Orleans an educational reformer's dream. The entire menu of school choice and free-market ideas of education reform was possible because the disaster provided them with what they perceived as a blank canvas. For New Orleanians, this is exactly what it meant to be dispossessed in this country: first trying to survive a natural disaster with no help from your government and then being deprived of any control over your education.

In the months following Katrina, using millions of dollars in public funds, the Orleans Parish School Board and the Louisiana Department of Education fired all 7,500 public school teachers—most of them Black—and destroyed the city's teacher unions. At the same time, the Recovery School District turned all but 17 of 127 public schools into charter schools. Teachers were forced to reapply for their jobs. Before the storm, New Orleans's teaching force was 71 percent Black and 78 percent women.[91] The work of teaching the Crescent City was done by Black women. The Black community was hit hard by the firings, as veteran teachers who were staples in the community were replaced with inexperienced White teachers from Teach for America. Following Katrina, TFA's presence "tripled in size in the region."[92] In the 2014–2015 school year, 93 percent of the RSD's students were Black.[93] At the same time, less than half of their teachers were Black.[94]

After Katrina, Louisiana lawmakers established private school choice programs that allowed families to deduct up to $5,000 in state income taxes for private school tuition and provided vouchers for low-income students to attend private schools. The per-pupil spending in New Orleans also increased by more than $1,300, but the funding did not go to veteran teachers. The funds went toward administrative costs and busing kids all over the city because school zones no longer existed, and schools had to compete for students. About 40 charter school organizations were running schools in New Orleans, and all competed for students. And, of course, the usual suspects were funding the city's education takeover as one large entrepreneurship experiment: KIPP opened schools; TFA supplied teachers; the Gates Foundation, the Walton family, and the NewSchools Venture Fund donated philanthropic dollars; and right-wing conservative think tanks applauded the efforts. The American Enterprise Institute gleefully noted that "Katrina accomplished in a day . . . what Louisiana school reformers couldn't do after years of trying."[95]

The free-market competition model in New Orleans has created a school system where teaching to the test is expected. It promotes a culture of an endless chase for a limited supply of philanthropic dollars. In her book *After the Education Wars*, business journalism professor Andrea Gabor describes New Orleans's Recovery School District as a system where, "for children, there is the Darwinian game of musical chairs—with the weakest kids left out when the music stops and failing schools close, or when they are counseled out of schools that can't, or won't, deal with their problems."[96] This is education's version of *The Hunger Games*, in which reformers have already selected the victors; the rest of us are playing a rigged game of educational oppression.

There is no conclusive data that the New Orleans charter school takeover was an academic success. Some studies show gains, but those gains are modest and inconsistent. From 2008 to 2014, third through eighth graders scoring at or above grade level on standardized tests rose from 28 percent to 57 percent, and graduation rates went up. But these were still some of the worst graduation rates in the state. According to a 2015 Kaiser Family Foundation / NPR poll, 42 percent of the city's residents with children under nineteen were "very" worried that their kids would not receive a good education, while 62 percent felt that charter schools were a "good thing." White parents overwhelmingly approved of charter schools compared to Black parents, who made up the majority of respondents expressing doubt.[97] When reading those statistics, it is important to remember that those students and their families had no input on the charter school conversion plan. Endesha Juakali, a New Orleans resident, said it best: "What we need is the power to make decisions . . . We need a plan that comes from our own communities . . . We don't need a 35-year-old New York educator to come in and tell us what we need to do. We need to tell them [entrepreneurs], what to do."[98]

A Race to More of the Same

President Barack Obama was elected on a message of hope and change. His vision of change did not extend to public education, though; he continued high-stakes standardized testing and the expansion of charter schools. His slogan "Race to the Top" proved to be as harmful as No Child Left Behind. The policy's wording implies that every child starts at the same place and that the race is fair and equal. Race to the Top does not address years of racism, anti-Blackness, discrimination, the divestment of education, and the hoarding of resources by White parents. Obama's secretary of education, Arne Duncan, came from Chicago, like Obama, where he had been the chief executive officer of Chicago Public Schools.

As CEO, Duncan closed public schools in Chicago and replaced them with charter schools. First, though, he eliminated positions across the board, including custodial and kitchen staff; tenured teachers were let go and given ten months to find other teaching jobs before they were "honorably terminated."[99] It is easy to understand why Duncan said that Hurricane Katrina was the "best thing that happened to the education system in New Orleans." He later apologized for the comment.

Race to the Top was a $4.3 billion fund designed to give competitive grants to states and local school districts to expand charter schools, explicitly link teacher and principal evaluations to test scores with performance-based assessments, and promote Common Core State Standards. To manage Race to the Top, Duncan appointed Joanne S. Weiss, CEO of the NewSchools Venture Fund. Weiss is a seasoned education entrepreneur who has helped corporations create educational business ventures for decades. Many major foundations that influenced education were on Team Obama, including the Gates Foundation, the Michael & Susan Dell Foundation, and the Eli and Edythe Broad Foundation. In 2008, the Broad and Gates Foundations united to launch a $60 million campaign to promote longer school days, national standards, and merit pay.[100] The Obama administration's educational reform plans were then crafted by these neoliberal super predators. When referring to the Obama administration's education agenda, *Washington Post* editorial page editor Fred Hiatt wrote: "You might call it the Obama-Duncan-Gates-Rhee philosophy of education reform."[101] During the Obama years, many of Duncan's appointments were former Gates officials or former Gates grantees.[102] People who followed Duncan's hires and policy agenda jokingly called the administration "the Gates Administration."[103]

Gates also funded Michelle Rhee, an inexperienced educational entrepreneur who would soon embody all the flaws of Gates-funded education reform. Rhee was young, brash, and had no real school leadership experience. She talked tough, however, and convinced the super predators that she could get results. She had never even been a school principal. Yet she came highly recommended for the position of chancellor of Washington, D.C., schools by Joel Klein, then chancellor of the New York City Department of Education, who himself lacked in-school experience.

Rhee had three years of experience as a Teach for America teacher in Baltimore. She claimed, though data were never produced, that the proportion of her students who read on grade level soared from 13 to 90 percent. "Those kids, where they lived didn't change," she told *Newsweek*. "Their parents didn't change. Their diets didn't change. The violence in the community didn't change. The only thing that changed for those 70 kids was the adults who were in front of them every single day teaching them."[104] Rhee put the education reform world on notice that she would clean up education. In 2007, after serving as CEO of the New Teacher Project, a nonprofit that helped recruit teachers, Rhee was appointed chancellor of Washington, D.C., schools by Mayor Adrian Fenty. The D.C. Board of Education had been stripped of decision-making power, so the new mayor didn't need board approval to hire Rhee as chancellor.

Within months of her appointment, Rhee implemented drastic reforms. She fired central office staff, closed under-enrolled schools without public hearings, and banished principals she felt did not meet her standards. She tried to abolish teacher tenure by offering to supersize teachers' salaries up to $130,000 a year in exchange for eliminating tenure; the proposed salary increase was funded by the Gates Foundation and the Broad Foundation. Rhee appeared on the cover of *Time* magazine holding a broom to indicate she was cleaning up education. But by 2010, Rhee was out. The Obama-Duncan-Gates-Rhee-Broad education philosophy was popular, but it was rooted in a hubris that communicates that educational philanthropy knows best. Although the Obama administration pushed for criminal justice reform and established civil rights guidelines to halt the unfair discipline of Black and Brown students who faced higher rates of suspension than their White counterparts, Race to the Top resulted in widespread test-cheating scandals, one of which landed teachers in prison.

Cheating Scandals

When Obama took office, the nation was in a recession, and Race to the Top offered billions of dollars to states that desperately needed cash. Georgia was one—its "plummeting tax revenue was compounded by years of [Governor Sonny] Perdue's austerity cuts."[105] The governor decided that Georgia would benefit from Race to the Top, and the state submitted its grant application. The application failed to mention that 20 percent of the schools in Georgia were suspected of cheating on the state's standardized tests. In February 2010, *The Atlanta Journal-Constitution* reported on an analysis of the state's 2009 test scores commissioned by the Governor's Office of Student Achievement, an independent agency. Data showed that one in five schools in Georgia were flagged for high numbers of wrong-to-right erasures; fifty-eight schools in Atlanta Public Schools were flagged, which amounted to 69 percent of elementary and middle schools in the district.[106]

The district was led by Beverly Hall, who had become superintendent of Atlanta Public Schools in 1999. Before arriving in Atlanta, she had a controversial record of improving education through private investment. Hall had been hired as superintendent of Newark Public Schools after the state of New Jersey took over the city's failing school system. While there, Hall fired five hundred employees in "one fell swoop," in what Newark residents called the "Beverly Hall massacre."[107] Hall had a reputation as an autocrat, and many of her reforms were met with protests by parents and district employees. But Hall did not waver in the face of opposition, ousting principals and linking test scores to pay raises.[108]

Atlanta was ready to recruit Hall: the state of Georgia had already been paying teachers rewards for high test scores and attendance.[109] Hall's annual salary in Atlanta was $165,000, with $49,500 in bonuses if she met performance goals. That meant raising test scores, improving attendance, and increasing the number of students in advanced classes.[110] A decade into Hall's tenure as head of Atlanta schools, evidence emerged that Atlanta teachers had cheated. Elected officials, hungry to mete out punishment, proposed a new law that never passed but would have made altering test results a "misdemeanor punishable by 30 days in jail and a $1,000 fine."[111]

In August 2010, Perdue launched a $2.2 million state investigation into the Atlanta Public Schools and one other school district where cheating was suspected. However, just days after the start of the investigation, Perdue called a press conference to announce the Peach State had won $400 million in Race to the Top funding. Not surprisingly, test scores submitted to the Department of Education for the grant were inflated. Perdue's investigation eventually implicated 178 Atlanta educators in cheating. Most received little, if any, financial reward for high test scores, but Hall took home $365,000 in bonus pay tied to test scores.[112]

Investigators released a lengthy report that said teachers aware of cheating felt they would "face retaliation from higher-ups" if they reported it. Hall reportedly created "a culture of fear and a conspiracy of silence," telling her staff that to meet academic goals, she wanted "no exceptions, no excuses."[113] In the end, Hall and thirty-four Atlanta educators were indicted. They were charged with racketeering, theft, influencing witnesses, conspiracy, and making false statements. Hall, at age sixty-seven, faced up to forty-five years in prison. Of the thirty-five indicted educators, all but twelve took plea deals. Hall would ultimately die of breast cancer before her trial. Teachers were granted immunity if they "admitted to cheating and accused their colleagues."[114] To avoid prosecution, another teacher gave investigators Shani Robinson's name.

Shani left her career in journalism and started teaching when she was twenty-four years old. As a first-grade teacher, she gave her students practice tests. She maintains that she did not do what she is accused of doing: erasing her students' incorrect answers and filling in the bubbles that correspond to correct responses. She received no bonus money. Four years later, her trial started, the longest and the most expensive in Georgia's history.[115] Shani was offered a deal of home confinement, probation, and other punishments instead of prison—if she admitted guilt. She refused.[116] She gave birth to her son ten days after being convicted of racketeering. Shani is now thirty-eight years old, and still, at any moment, she could be sent to prison. Only a bond agreement has kept her out of prison so far. Today, Shani has two sons, and her biggest fear is that someday she won't be able to raise her sons and be with her husband.

Why has Shani's adult life been consumed by the criminal punishment system? Another teacher, wanting to avoid prosecution, told officials that Shani had cheated. While Shani was on trial, she had long left education and worked for the Department of Juvenile Justice as an administrator of a group home for formerly incarcerated girls. Her work involved picking up young girls from jail and helping them reenroll in school and access the necessary resources to continue their education. Shani told me, "I would leave court and then go to the juvenile court down the street to advocate for someone. It was maddening to both work for the Department of Juvenile Justice, trying to help young people succeed in their education, and be prosecuted as an educator at the same time."

Shani worked with journalist Anna Simonton to write the book *None of the Above: The Untold Story of the Atlanta Public Schools Cheating Scandal, Corporate Greed, and the Criminalization of Educators*. In it, she condemns the system surrounding the cheating scandal. Harshly prosecuting educators, she writes, "drained public resources, deepened racial disparities and distracted from unjust policies."[117] Shani told me, "I don't see how the trajectory that we've been on is going to help solve problems in the Black community. All you have to do is look and see who is bankrolling these reforms, all these corporate execs and CEOs and all these rich and powerful people." All except one of the educators convicted in the Atlanta cheating scandal, including Beverly Hall, were Black. This was no accident; what happened in Georgia and elsewhere was the culmination of decades of education reform entangled in the "criminal punishment system."[118]

These policies and reforms created a system in which some educators responded rationally (although not ethically) to a system that punished what it considered failure. This same logic did not extend to the state itself, however. Under Governor Perdue, Georgia was awarded $400 million in federal grants. In exchange for the funds, the state promised bold and ambitious goals of reforming "standards, assessments, data systems, teacher effectiveness systems, certification, educator preparation programs, professional learning and low achieving schools."[119] A Georgia Partnership for Excellence in Education report documents that many of the ambitious goals outlined by Perdue's application for Race to the Top funds were never met. The report found that the scale of the project was too big and did not have statewide coordination, many teachers and school and district leaders had no real understanding of the measures themselves, and leadership changes delayed implementation. Georgia received millions of dollars by creating unrealistic, unachievable goals and suffered no consequences for its failure to meet them.

Shani has not told her children about her vulnerable position. "I don't want them stressed out about their mom possibly going to jail." She can try to shield her children from this stress, but she cannot protect herself from it. Fighting back tears, she shared, "I've been in and out of counseling for the past seven years for PTSD," she said. "We were indicted nine years ago. When is it going to be over? Anytime I look on the news, they are still discussing the trial. The lead prosecutor, Willis, still wants to see us go to prison." Shani went from first wanting to report the news to learning that the "Black Beat" meant reporting on crime to finally being the news she never wanted to cover.

The emotional toll of the scandal extends to students, as well. Dre was a senior in Atlanta Public Schools during the period when teachers allegedly cheated and in college when news of the scandal broke. Valedictorian of his senior class, Dre told me the cheating scandal made him question his academic abilities. "Did anyone change my answers?" He continues, "It definitely made me feel some level of shame because I was a proud graduate of Atlanta Public Schools . . . I had to check myself." This deep reflection on how the broader school context affects students impacted not only his perspective on his past but also his future. Dre taught for three years and is now a middle school principal.

I was floored when Dre told me that one of the teachers involved in the cheating scandal now works at his school. Working with her gave him the opportunity to address something that's been on his heart for years. "I just couldn't wrap my mind around how educators could go that far." Dre says that they have spoken about what happened and that she admitted to changing students' test answers. She explained that she was a young teacher and felt significant pressure to follow the orders from her superiors. Unlike Shani, this teacher was not convicted. The fact that she altered test answers over a decade ago is not evidence that she is unqualified to work with children. Indeed, Dre identifies her as one of the top teachers at the school.

Atlanta teachers were not alone in being under investigation. Cheating scandals were reported in more than one thousand school districts across the country. In his first term, George W. Bush chose Rod Paige to be secretary of education (and one of the architects of NCLB) because of Paige's reputation as a miracle worker when he was superintendent of Houston schools. These results were later found to be due to cheating. Some Houston teachers promised merit pay for increasing test scores went so far as to tell struggling students to stay home on test day.[120] In 1999, thirty-two New York City schools were embroiled in a cheating scandal. During Obama's first term, standardized test score manipulation was widespread at both public and charter schools. After years of merit pay scandals, Race to the Top was still filled with merit pay incentives, which the Gates Foundation supported.

The educational reform superstar Michelle Rhee was also flagged in the test score scandal. Talk of inflated test scores out of Washington, D.C., public schools started soon after Rhee arrived. Possible test cheating took place in at least seventy schools under Rhee's watch. One father told reporters he had become suspicious of his daughter's high math test scores because she had struggled with basic math functions.[121] Rhee's administration paid principals and teachers up to $12,000 in annual bonuses for raising test scores, which amounted to $1.5 million. Rhee also fired more than 600 teachers for low test scores. On one day alone, in 2010, she fired 214 teachers. She was alerted to test irregularities in 2009.[122] But Rhee claimed she never saw the memo and that there was "no widespread cheating" in her district. Only one educator lost his job over the scandal, and many of Rhee's critics thought the investigation did not go far enough.

When Washington, D.C., mayor Adrian Fenty lost his race for reelection, Rhee resigned. She was the focus of a 2010 doc-

umentary *Waiting for "Superman,"* along with Harlem education reformer Geoffrey Canada. Backed by the Walton Family
Foundation and the Doris & Donald Fisher Fund, the film was
propaganda for the charter school movement. After leaving her
controversial post as Washington's chancellor, Rhee founded a
political lobbying group called StudentsFirst. The organization
works to pass state laws that expand charter schools and weaken
teacher tenure.

The backlash for eight years of a Black man as president was
seismic in intensity. Donald Trump's campaign brought back big-
oted, inflammatory rhetoric that resembled the race-baiting of
Nixon, Reagan, and the first President Bush. But Trump's words
as he rallied support for his candidacy were much brasher and
carried more overt contempt for non-White people. The current
anti-Black education reform system *was* tailor-made for Trump.

5

ERASURE

The Handbook

Joe Biden took office during a global pandemic after a year of school closings and teachers forced to transition to online classrooms with little preparation or training. When schools reopened, the nation was not only divided on the issues of climate, racial justice, and the economy but also on how to keep our children safe in school. The overlap between parents opposed to critical race theory, or CRT, and mask and vaccine mandates was significant enough to consume national headlines and turn mundane school board meetings into spaces that might require riot gear.

The Biden administration, committed to appearing dedicated to both racial justice and reopening schools, released a COVID-19 handbook for reopening schools safely. The handbook, unbeknownst to me, included a link to a guide I helped create with cofounders and board members of the Abolitionist Teaching Network (ATN). We founded this nonprofit in 2020 to support teachers and parents fighting injustice in their schools and communities. The guide was an invitation for "abolitionist teachers [to] promote justice, healing, joy, and liberation for all Black, Brown, and Indigenous students, inclusive of all intersecting identities."[1] The guide also called for "a commitment to learning from students, families, and educators who disrupt Whiteness and other forms of oppression."[2]

After the Biden administration released their handbook with a link to ATN's guide, people in the organization, myself included, started receiving requests from the press to comment on the guide. Without asking our permission or giving us a heads-up, the Department of Education turned our small nonprofit into one of Fox News's biggest headlines, and I was their main target. Because ATN's guide denounced Whiteness and White supremacy, we were thrown into the far right's manufactured CRT controversy. A broad conceptual framework that documents how structural racism is foundational to our legal system, governmental policies, and institutions, critical race theory has been around since the 1980s. Still, it was new to the American lexicon and a perfect ideological bogeyman for the Republican Party.

ATN's staff began receiving violent racist emails and calls. People called the University of Georgia to demand that they fire me. These White supremacists went so far as to call in a bomb threat at a university I had spoken at years before. The emails were loaded with racial epithets and violence. ATN was not equipped to handle this level of attention or threats.

To make matters worse, when the Biden administration was asked by Fox News why they had included ATN in the handbook, they replied, "The Department does not endorse the recommendations of this group, nor do they reflect our policy positions. It was an error in a lengthy document to include this citation."[3] An error? Calling for justice cannot be labeled an error. I became paranoid and frightened by the constant threats of violence to my family and me. I was furious that the Department of Education had thrown me and other people of color who work with us and believe in the work of ATN under the bus to appease a base of voters who want nothing more than to uphold White supremacy. One cannot stand for justice only when it serves their political career.

After about three weeks, the conservative media moved on, the death threats stopped, and I attempted to move on, too, but the oppressive anxiety brought on by such threats never went away. Creating this lingering anxiety is precisely the point. People calling you the n-word, threatening to kill you, and calling for your job silences you and gives power to hate. They want to erase you, to make you feel powerless and alone. Silence can feel like your only protection. You begin to erase yourself. And erasure means that the people or the institution who harmed you never have to apologize for their wrongdoing. There is no need to apologize, compensate, or even acknowledge harm when it has been erased from society through textbooks, book bans, legislative bills, and ultimately America's memory.

I remember repeating to myself the words of the great Audre Lorde: "When we speak we are afraid / our words will not be heard / nor welcomed / but when we are silent / we are still afraid / so it is better to speak."[4] I knew all of this, but I still resorted to silence as I watched every unfamiliar car coming down my street. I feared for my family and the families of those who worked for ATN.

ATN and I were pulled into the nation's controversy around critical race theory during the Biden years. But to understand how this widespread misinformation campaign took hold of the public consciousness, we need to look at Biden's predecessor. The previous forty years of education reform had made it possible for Trump to make Black history, anti-racism, and LGBTQIA rights the new *A Nation at Risk*.

Fake News

The Trump administration's most shameful educational legacy will be its attack on teaching this country's racial history and preventing anti-racism work in education—in other words, manufacturing another education crisis. In 2020, Trump went on a crusade to restore "patriotic" education in our schools. In particular, he took aim at the 1619 Project, a *New York Times* initiative that examined U.S. history through the context of enslavement and the contributions of Black Americans. Nikole Hannah-Jones, an accomplished journalist, won a Pulitzer Prize for her work on the 1619 Project, and some schools across the country incorporated the project into their school curricula. In an attempt to discredit the 1619 Project, Trump created the 1776 Commission consisting of eighteen conservative members loyal to the presidency. The commission declared the 1619 project as "reckless re-education,"[5] fueling a national movement led by conservative media to rewrite history by erasing the contributions of Black people and the brutality of enslavement. Their intended erasure would also undermine the fragile racial progress made after the killings of George Floyd and Breonna Taylor. It was revenge; again, Black folx were being punished for fighting for justice. As protests erupted around the country, school districts scrambled to respond to the call of Black Lives Matter; their work was met with educational White rage.

The 1776 Commission report, similar to a *Nation at Risk*, inspired local and state politicians, along with far right grassroots organizations funded by some of the richest super predators, to spark a political and cultural war to undercut Black Lives Matter and attempts at racial progress in schools made under the umbrellas of diversity, equity, and inclusion (DEI) and anti-racism. The far right found what they considered the "perfect villain" to wage a broad and invasive cultural war: critical race theory.[6] Conservatives made buzzwords of *race* and *critical,* turning them into ideal weapons for baiting White parents into believing that CRT was infiltrating schools across America. The tactic had been tried in 2012 when Breitbart News, a far right syndicated news website, posted a video of President Obama as a law student at Harvard, introducing Harvard Law School professor Derrick Bell, one of the founders of CRT. That attempt did not gain traction, but Trump had a different approach: executive order. Almost ten years after the Bell/Obama/CRT connection fizzled out, the Trump White House issued an executive order prohibiting federal contractors from receiving diversity training focused on racism or sexism.[7] The day before Juneteenth, Trump declared the teaching of CRT "psychological abuse."[8] By the time Trump left office, the letters *CRT* became a catchphrase for what the far right most hates: racial progress, gender justice, and LGBTQIA rights.

According to Media Matters, in 2021 Fox News mentioned CRT 3,900 times.[9] Attacking Black people to destabilize public education is a tried-and-true trick out of the Nixon, Reagan, and Atwater playbooks. Advancing the hysteria, Republican-led states around the country began banning the teaching of CRT, which was not being taught in the first place. Republican governors and right-leaning school boards banned anything the far right deemed "divisive" or hostile toward White people, calling it "anti-American" and a "dangerous ideology."[10] School districts held town hall meetings to address angry White mobs of parents enraged that their children might learn about systemic racism. Jeff Porter, a school superintendent in Maine, said his district was "almost held hostage" by the national hysteria over CRT.[11]

Republican governors signed bills banning the teaching of CRT, going so far as to use *CRT* as an all-encompassing term to ban anti-racism and diversity efforts in public education. The New Hampshire chapter of the conservative mothers' group Moms for Liberty told supporters they would pay $500 to anyone who catches a teacher discussing racism or sexism, arguing that such a discussion would violate the state's ban on lessons that teach "one's race, sex or other characteristics are 'inherently superior' to others, or that people are inherently racist, sexist or oppressive on account of their race, sex or other characteristics."[12] The Miami-Dade chapter of Moms for Liberty called for gay and queer students to be put in separate classes from straight and cisgender students.[13] The group lobbied for Florida's Parental Rights in Education bill, known around the country as the "Don't Say Gay" bill, which was signed into law in the spring of 2022.[14] The "Don't Say Gay" bill bans teaching about sexual orientation or gender identity in grades K–3. A year later, the Florida Board of Education approved an expansion of the bill to grades K-12. Florida's governor, Ron DeSantis, doing his best Trump imitation, made attacking CRT, anti-racism, and LGBTQIA students and families one of the centerpieces of his administration. DeSantis took the pop culture word *woke,* which means to be mindful of injustice and to fight racism, and turned it into another ban. The "Stop W.O.K.E. Act" was signed into law in the spring of 2022.[15] The bill attempts to restrict any teaching about the U.S.'s history of racism. That includes banning conversations about racism in the workplace, essentially ending DEI work in schools and businesses in the Sunshine State. In the fall of 2022, a federal judge partially blocked the bill because it violated the First Amendment.[16] In January 2023, DeSantis took his White rage even further when Florida's Department of Education banned an Advanced Placement African American Studies course from being taught in public schools in Florida because it taught students about the importance of Black feminism, intersectionality, and reparations.

The erasure of Black history and America's racism galvanized Republican governors and lawmakers around the country. From January 2021 to February 2022, thirty-five states introduced 137 bills banning the teaching of historical accuracy, racism, and discussions about gender identity and queer families.[17] Florida may have received the lion's share of media attention for its bans, but book bans across the country were rewriting the educational landscape in ways that signaled who belonged in Trump's America. Curriculum deeply impacts sense of belonging, signaling to students who is worthy of visibility and who is not. Curriculum studies scholar Denise Taliaferro Baszile argues that "curriculum is the story and stories that we tell our children about who we want them to believe that we are and who we ultimately want them to be. So when those stories are untrue, or those stories are half told, or those stories don't acknowledge both the beauty and the complexity of our society, of our country, then they are not narrating belonging."[18] Bills banning the teaching of America's racial history, Black people's resistance to oppression, and queer people's existence tell children who belongs in school and in this country. Curriculum that erases people's struggles for justice, their contributions to this nation, and how they loved, found joy, and built community while facing the violence of anti-Blackness is White supremacy. Curriculum is one of the most powerful tools in education to teach all children that people like them and people from whom they are different are beautiful, powerful, and valuable, and so were their ancestors.

There have been incidents around the country of teachers and principals losing their jobs for supporting Black Lives Matter, calling out White privilege, or assigning a book that discusses racism. Conservative school boards banned books on anti-racism, diversity, civil rights, or Black people's fight to integrate schools. A group in Tennessee attempted to ban a book about Ruby Bridges. In Texas, a group of educators proposed that the state teach enslavement as "involuntary relocation."[19] According to the American Library Association, book ban challenges more than doubled from 2021 to 2022.[20] Most of the books that are banned "focus on communities of color, the history of racism in America and LGBTQ characters. In fact, one in three books restricted by school districts in the past year featured LGBTQ themes or characters."[21] To that end, in August of 2022, as teachers were returning from summer break, a national survey reported that one in four teachers was told to limit conversation about race and racism in the classroom by school officials and administrators.[22] And when book bans and legislative bills are not enough, the super predators' foot soldiers will do their bidding, erasing the educators who do the work of DEI.

In Georgia, the furor over CRT resulted in two large school districts running off Cecelia Lewis, a highly qualified educator. Lewis was a middle school principal in Maryland; due to her desire to move closer to family, she applied for a job with Cherokee County School District. The district had created a DEI position in response to calls for justice and anti-racism training after the murders of George Floyd and Breonna Taylor. Lewis, who studied Japanese and Russian in college and had recently traveled to Ghana on a fellowship for educators, was a perfect fit for the position. But news of her hiring kicked off a firestorm of protest in the district, about an hour's drive from Atlanta. Well-funded national organizations, such as the Koch-backed group Parents Defending Education, provided Cherokee County community members with tool kits, talking points, and videos to promote the idea that their schools were indoctrinating students with an anti-White, anti-American, "woke" liberal agenda.[23]

Lewis became their target in the spring of 2021 after her hiring was announced. She received emails calling her a "Black Yankee" who was not welcome in Cherokee County schools.[24] Cherokee County school administrators received approximately one hundred letters calling for Lewis's firing.[25] Lewis's critics cited the 1619 Project as evidence of indoctrination, with no proof of 1619 used by anyone in the district. The pressure and fearmongering eventually worked. At a Cherokee County school board meeting in May of 2021, an all-too-familiar angry White mob, yelled, pounded glass doors with their fists, and threatened school board members. The district's superintendent, who had previously lauded Lewis's "impressive credentials and enthusiasm for the role," now told those in attendance: "While I had initially entertained and publicly spoken to the development of a diversity, equity, and inclusivity, DEI plan, I recognize that our intentions have become widely misunderstood in the community and it created division . . . To that end, I have concluded that there will be no separate DEI plan."[26] Not only was Lewis's position eliminated before she even had the chance to begin but other efforts to broaden the district's curriculum were also cut short. Before the meeting was abruptly adjourned because of the threat of violence, the board voted to pass the anti-CRT and anti–1619 Project resolutions.

The next day, even after it was clear that Lewis would not be working in the district, a former Cherokee County student named Bailey Katzenstein appeared on *Fox and Friends,* claiming without proof that "someone from Maryland" would carry out CRT initiatives in Cherokee.[27] According to ProPublica reporting, the Fox host ended the segment, saying, "If you thought this was an elite, New York City school problem, Bailey Katzenstein just told you the exact opposite. This is spreading. It's going all over the country, and it's having real impacts."[28]

The controversy followed Lewis when she accepted a job supervising the social studies curriculum in the nearby Cobb County School District. In June 2022, as I mentioned earlier, the school board passed an anti-CRT and anti-1619 Project resolution similar to Cherokee's. Although Cobb County is 30 percent Black and 24 percent Hispanic, the school board is controlled by White, conservative members.[29] By the time Lewis started her job at Cobb, the position was under so much scrutiny that she was stripped of all power. She was not formally introduced to the teachers and staff, her work emails had to be vetted, and her job changed to reviewing courses already approved by the district—busywork.

Reflecting on her position at Cobb, Lewis told ProPublica, "It was pretty much them tucking me away . . . Every meeting was canceled. Every professional learning opportunity that I was supposed to lead with my team, I couldn't do. Every department meeting with different schools, I was told I can't go."[30] In a matter of six months, Lewis had resigned from two positions in Georgia. National and local conservative groups claimed victory for effectively eliminating both positions.

This is educational White rage. The book bans, the lies about CRT being taught in schools, and the attacks on educators' lives and careers are the culmination of decades of organized, well-funded, and cruel educational White rage. But the rage is also gendered. It is not an accident that many of the attacks are against Black women (including Jemele Hill, Michelle Obama, Shirley Sherrod, Nikole Hannah-Jones, Brittney Cooper, Angel Reese, Cecelia Lewis, and me). Lawrence C. Ross, author of *Blackballed: The Black and White Politics of Race on America's Campuses,* writes: "Because for all of the 'Listen to Black Women' T-shirts and 'Protect Black Women' social media posts, the right-wing mob knows that Black women will be left to fend for themselves, especially by the mainstream media, whose lack of action makes them complicit."[31]

The formula is the same: stoke White resentment for Black advancement or civil rights gains in and outside public education, manufacture lies blaming America's educational woes on Black people, fearmonger any resistance with the threat of violence or job loss, and finally, sow distrust through the media, think tanks, cable news pundits, and philanthropy about the dangers of public education. And the ultimate goal is to dismantle public education by selling it piece by piece to anybody buying. To accomplish this last piece, Trump looked to Michigan and found an accomplice in Betsy DeVos.

Betsy DeVos

Donald Trump took office as the most inexperienced American president of all time, and a number of his appointees were equally unqualified for their positions. Many of them, however, were skilled at promoting a far-right policy agenda. For his secretary of education, Trump tapped Betsy DeVos, a passionate charter school advocate whose pet project is privatizing public education. The former Republican Party chairwoman for Michigan, DeVos is a member of one of the country's richest families; she lobbied to deregulate charter school growth with the millions of dollars at her disposal.[32] As founder of the American Federation for Children, she worked to pass laws supporting school vouchers. According to Valerie Strauss at *The Washington Post,* her efforts have led to a "deeply dysfunctional educational landscape" in Michigan.[33] Thanks to DeVos, charter schools with some of the lowest test scores in Michigan were reauthorized and allowed to open new schools. Under the misnomer of school choice, tens of thousands of children, mostly Black, were trapped, their "choices" limited to a selection of failing schools. And, of course, at the 2018 Reagan Institute Summit on Education, DeVos told a room of the like-minded reformers, "Our nation is still at risk."[34]

For over twenty years, the DeVos family has funded and propped up the charter school industry by lobbying for little to no oversight of its schools. In 2000, the family spent $5.6 million on a ballot initiative that would have altered Michigan's constitution to allow school vouchers. Voters rejected the proposal at the polls.[35] In 2016, the family donated $1.45 million over two months to Michigan GOP lawmakers who opposed a bill providing oversight of Detroit charter schools.[36] The *Detroit Free Press* reported that "Michigan tolerates more low-performing charter schools than just about any other state. And it lacks any effective mechanism for shutting down, or even improving, failing charters."[37] In 2016, 79 percent of all charter schools in Michigan were in Detroit, a city with a predominantly Black population.[38] An investigation by the *Detroit Free Press* found that after twenty years of charter school expansion, most of the city's charter schools and public schools showed identical test scores.[39] Other research demonstrates that the price of those charter schools is paid through lowered achievement and school efficiency in public school systems.[40]

The DeVoses used their foundation, the DeVos Urban Leadership Initiative, to further its ideas. The foundation's website features Black faces, signaling that the organization supports "urban" students. The foundation's mission is to support urban youth leaders who lack leadership skills with "high-level, faith-based leadership training." The foundation has also given money to national campaigns to encourage union members, especially teachers, to opt out of paying dues—and to back groups that support family separation and oppose LGBTQIA rights.[41]

During DeVos's tenure, her campaign for school choice got an unexpected boost from the COVID-19 epidemic. With millions of children in the country suddenly moving to online learning, school choice advocates saw an opportunity to advance their cause. According to EdChoice, a research and advocacy group, thirty-four bills in fifteen states were introduced in one year to expand private education options for public school parents. Of course, the bills had the support of the Trump administration.[42]

But DeVos's legacy as education secretary goes beyond school choice. During his presidency, Obama implemented school discipline guidance intended to reduce racial discrimination. The

Trump administration rescinded it. Meanwhile, Trump's Federal Commission on School Safety focused on arming school personnel and bringing more local law enforcement into schools. The commission claimed that Obama's school discipline guidance made schools "reluctant to address unruly students or violent incidents."[43] The Trump administration also denied federal protection to transgender students and changed the directive on how universities respond to sexual assault and harassment allegations. The administration's new rule "expands the rights of the accused in part by creating a judicial-like process that gives the accused the rights to a live hearing with multiple panel members and to cross-examine accusers."[44] Women's rights activists rightly argued that the rule would discourage sexual assault victims from coming forward.[45]

Joe Biden returned to the White House with the task of undoing many of Trump and DeVos's harmful education policies. But his educational agenda at times mirrored his predecessors'.

Too Far Gone

Given all the damage done to education during DeVos's tenure, Joe Biden faced a steep challenge in restoring faith in the Department of Education. On day one, he signed an executive order blocking discrimination based on gender identity or sexual orientation.[46] He signed another executive order that day, initially issued by the Obama administration, but scaled back during Trump's tenure, demanding that federal agencies examine how their policies address and promote racial equity.[47] He also reinstated rights to student survivors of sexual assault on college campuses.[48]

In addition to restoring many of the civil rights taken under Trump and DeVos, the Biden administration had to address a raging pandemic. Some of his actions missed the mark. Despite countless conversations and panels about learning loss, teacher shortages, the lack of internet access in poor and rural communities, and the stress on teachers and students in a global pandemic, the Biden administration ended the moratorium on standardized testing requirements, which had been one of the few smart actions taken by the Trump administration in response to the school shutdowns caused by COVID-19. On the campaign trail, Biden had said he would end standardized testing requirements in public schools and that it was a "big mistake" to tie teacher evaluations to student test scores.[49] School leaders, educators, and parents from across the country were outraged by the Department of Education's decision to resume testing amid a pandemic. Georgia school superintendent Richard Woods told reporters, "I continue to believe that high-stakes standardized tests in the middle of a pandemic are not necessary, wise, or useful."[50] While the Biden administration extended flexible testing accommodations such as testing from home and shortened tests, many prominent voices, such as the former New York City schools chancellor Richard Carranza and the Massachusetts Teachers Association, encouraged parents to opt their children out of state tests during the pandemic.[51] Many states were also allowed to request waivers to suspend federally mandated testing.

In the late fall of 2021, when the COVID-19 Omicron variant hit America and exacerbated the teacher shortage, the New Mexico National Guard was called in as substitute teachers to keep schools open. National Guard members walked into class in their military uniforms.[52] In Oklahoma, police officers served as substitute teachers, arriving in full uniform, armed with loaded guns, and not wearing masks.[53] The pandemic showed how badly this nation's education system is in dire need of more funding, more resources, more teachers, more training, less testing, higher teacher pay, and a contraction of the police state.

The dehumanizing and deprofessionalization of teachers continued in 2022 when San Francisco schools declared a state of emergency after the district's $14 million new payroll system failed to pay teachers.[54] Principal Thor Boucher personally lent a second-grade teacher, Yuri Dominguez, $4,500 to pay her rent; Dominguez is one of thousands of teachers across the district who have gone months without pay and health benefits.[55] Teachers are living off their credit cards, borrowing money from friends and family, overdrafting their bank accounts, and going into debt all while teaching forty plus hours a week. To add insult to injury, many of the district's teachers can't afford to live in the very communities they serve because of steep housing prices. In the U.S., teachers make 20 percent less than other professionals with equivalent education and experience, and in many parts of the country, teachers make less than the family living wage.[56]

By 2023, American schools were, not surprisingly, facing a national teacher shortage. According to the Bureau of Labor Statistics, between February 2020 and May 2022, 300,000 public school teachers and staff left the field.[57] Miguel Cardona, education secretary under the Biden administration, attributed the nationwide teacher shortage to lack of competitive salaries, poor working conditions, and a nation that doesn't respect teachers.[58] The far right's grasp on education was tight, and anybody with a measure of critical thinking skills would question the wisdom of signing up to be underpaid for a profession under attack. To address the national teacher shortage, states began to ease the requirement to become a teacher. Florida and Arizona went as far as to lift the requirement that teachers hold a bachelor's degree—another tactic to de-professionalize educators and destabilize public education.[59]

The Biden administration has offered glimmers of hope, at least in terms of school funding. Biden's 2023 proposed national budget included $88.3 billion in new discretionary spending for schools and colleges, and in doing so, proposed a boost in education spending by 15.6 percent over the prior year.[60] The proposed budget prioritized marginalized students, calling for $16.3 billion for the Individuals with Disabilities in Education Act, a $3 billion increase, and $36.5 billion for Title I schools, the largest increase in the history of the program supporting low-income learners.[61] While doubling sounds good, it represents a cut to the tripling of funding for Title I candidate Biden proposed on the campaign trail.[62] The fact that Biden proposed tripling Title I funding highlights just how massively underfunded public education is for the students who need the most. Biden also called for $100 million to launch programs to desegregate schools almost 70 years after *Brown*.[63] Finally, the budget included $1 billion to hire more school counselors, social workers, school psychologists, nurses, and other support staff.[64] While these budget increases are needed and well overdue, this is not the administration's first ask. Biden's 2022 education spending bill proposed many of the same funding increases as in his proposed 2023 budget, because they were eliminated or reduced in the 2022 budget process. The proposed billions to increase Title I spending, increase integration in schools, and hire more teachers, school counselors, and nurses (while in a global pandemic) were purged from the final 2022 budget.

The 2022 budget highlighted the massive need to modernize the infrastructure of America's crumbling schools. Half of America's public school are more than fifty years old.[65] The America Society of Civil Engineers graded the overall conditions of 100,000 public schools a D+.[66] In 2019, there were still three quarters of a million children attending schools without even minimum internet connectivity.[67] America's crumbling schools are also doing irreparable harm to teachers' and students' health. The U.S. Environmental Protection Agency concluded there are more than 60,000 schools in which poor indoor air quality is due to "insects, rodents, dust mites, fungi, and respiratory irritants from sources of formaldehyde and nitrogen dioxide."[68] These were the conditions in schools when one of the deadliest airborne viruses of the last hundred years emerged.

Even after the closing of public schools nationwide to stop the spread of COVID-19, in 2022 Democrats simply eliminated the $100 billion school infrastructure package in Biden's budget.[69] The 2023 budget did not even mention school infrastructure.[70] While the Biden administration's funding goals are admirable, they have proven to be unattainable. Our elected officials refuse to invest in the health of schools, places in which we force children to spend tens of thousands of hours of their childhood. This country has decided low-income students of color must remain punished, sick, and underfunded. After all, there are profits to be made from the educational harm done to Black children.

The last forty years of education reform have been integral to this country's overall societal and educational assault on Black life. The next four decades will be no different for Black children unless we demand that the entire structure of public education is uprooted and rebuilt.

6

CARCERAL INEVITABILITY

There is a presumption of dangerousness and guilt that burdens Black and Brown people in this country. You can work in a prosecutor's office, you can be a law professor, you can be a teacher, you can be kind, you can be loving, but if you are Black or Brown you are going to go places where you are required to navigate this presumption of dangerousness and guilt.

—Bryan Stevenson, on the podcast *Chasing Justice*[1]

The Price of Black Girl Magic

Kia grew up in Chicago and was raised by the state for the first nine years of her life. Her mother was addicted to drugs for much of Kia's early life, and her dad was often out of the picture. A ward of the state, she was moved from foster home to foster home, a new one almost every year. She told me she lived with seven different foster families in the nine years she was in the foster care system. In our conversations, Kia recalls always being drawn to beautiful things, especially earrings. The pair she wore when we last met were big and colorful, making her brown skin glow as they caught the sun's light.

Kia had her first encounter with the carceral state because of a pair of earrings. When she was eight, she admired a pair of earrings in a local JCPenney. She remembers standing on her tiptoes so she could touch them. What she didn't see was the White police officer who was watching her. He bounded after her as she left the store, yelling, "I don't care how old you are. You ain't going to steal from here." Kia understood immediately that in his eyes, she was not a child but a criminal and that, as a ward of the state, she was at the mercy of not only the angry and scary White officer but also the system that thought nothing of moving her like a chess pawn every year. Kia froze in terror. Luckily for her, that year, her foster family was White. When her White foster sister saw what happened, she ran over and assured the officer not that Kia was innocent (which she was) but that she belonged to her. Kia remembers how the officer was easily persuaded to let her go at the request of a White child.

Her second encounter happened when she was fifteen. Kia was reunited with her mother, who worked tirelessly to overcome her drug addiction, weeks before Kia's ninth birthday. Now Kia attended an all-girls public high school, where she earned straight As and was a member of the National Honor Society. She excelled in algebra, geometry, and AP physics. One morning, the bathtub overflowed, and Kia stayed home to clean up the mess. Flustered, she eventually made her way to school but was late. Once she passed through the school's metal detectors, she had to explain her tardiness to the school resource officers (SROs), sworn law enforcement officers with the power to make arrests. Upset by the disruption to the start of her day, Kia tried to ignore the officer who followed her to class and kept peppering her with questions.

As Kia was about to sit down in her seat, the officer, a Black woman, seized her by the shirt collar and book bag, pulled her out of the crowded classroom, and threw her against the hallway lockers. She then handcuffed Kia and took her to a nearby precinct, where Kia sat in a holding cell while officers decided what to do with her. She told me that as she sat there, alone and terrified, she thought long and hard about how the officers in school weren't there to protect Black girls but to punish them. The officer, it turns out, told school officials that Kia had been the one to assault her.

Several hours later, she was finally released after two Black women, mentors of hers, came to the station to advocate for her. Eventually, the truth prevailed; the officer was fired, but not before Kia was suspended for two months and lost her standing in the National Honor Society as she awaited trial. It took her months of hard, determined work to regain what the officer had taken from her in one afternoon. When she was ready to graduate, she wanted to leave the state and remembered an Upward Bound trip she had taken to Spelman College two years before. She applied, was accepted, and not only graduated from college but went on to get her master's degree. Today, at age twenty-eight, she is working on her Ph.D. Her mother was able to rebuild her life in a time when treatment for her addiction was rarely an option, and she no longer uses drugs. The two now have what Kia describes as a beautiful relationship.

Kia has all the gifts of Black girl magic. But this magic does not come out of thin air. It comes from getting knocked down and gracefully getting back up with a determination never to fall again. Kia reminds me of Zook and myself: we all have overcome so much that White people want to tell our stories. Our stories seem to validate Whiteness, meritocracy, and the idea that reform works. Hollywood loves to make movies about people like us because we have succeeded despite sexism, racism, anti-Blackness, state-sanctioned violence, White fears, and countless attempts to deny, restrict, and even kill our dreams—and sometimes end our lives. When we win, Whiteness somehow still wins. It is the most peculiar thing: White people celebrate our triumphs as proof that the system works if Black people simply take advantage of the trail of crumbs reformers call justice.

We can all read Kia's story as one of triumph, but it's not one without lasting scars. The pain is real, no matter how magical she's made it all look. Her victory is necessary for the system to convince us that it's not a monster. As the structure of public education swallows millions of Black children, young girls like Kia—girls whose relentless drive intimidates the White world—make it possible for the Milton Friedmans of the world to tell you that the free market got it right. To them, there's no need to remove structural barriers: we just need more Kias and more reform. Her pain and trauma are important only in that they provide dramatic effect to the narrative—the end result outweighs the harm and violence. Black girls like Kia and me are labeled "ghetto superstars." And the Black girls who do not overcome their obstacles? They are deemed to be failures.

So before we celebrate Kia, we should also ask what is owed to her for the violent attack that she suffered at school, the trauma and shame of being arrested and treated like a criminal as a teenager, a ruthless foster care system that is incapable of protecting Black children, compounded by the days she was barred from school. There is, as well, the lasting emotional pain of her early life, shaped by drug reform policies that denied users treatment. And what about her classmates who witnessed the attack? So many events in her life were informed by reform inside and outside of school.

When I last spoke with Kia, we talked about Ma'Khia Bryant, a sixteen-year-old girl fatally shot by a police officer in Columbus, Ohio, in April 2021. Ma'Khia and her younger sister, Ja'Niah, had spent the previous two years in foster homes. At the time, they were being threatened by two older women who lived in their foster home. Three weeks before Ma'Khia was shot, Ja'Niah called the police, informing them of the situation and saying, "I want to leave this foster home." The night Ma'Khia was shot, Ja'Niah had called 911 again. She told the dispatcher the women were trying to fight and stab them. When Officer Nicholas Reardon arrived on the scene, Ma'Khia was holding a steak knife, lunging at one of the women. Reardon shot her four times. He was later cleared of all criminal wrongdoing.

Ma'Khia's teacher described her as "a hard worker, a sweet girl, very shy." She was an honor roll student who took her schoolwork seriously. Her TikTok videos were a testament to her love of life, filled with good music and hair care tips for Black girls.

Kia told me that Ma'Khia's death was triggering, and she planned to write about it with a few other Black women, all doctoral students. She wanted to explore how some people justified the violent end to Ma'Khia's life because she had a knife, because she was a Black girl, because she was thought of as someone unworthy of protection. Reardon shot Ma'Khia within ten seconds of getting out of his cruiser—there was no attempt to de-escalate. In 2015, after Clementa Pinckney, Cynthia Hurd, Sharonda Coleman-Singleton, Ethel Lance, Susie Jackson, DePayne Middleton-Doctor, Daniel Simmons, Tywanza Sanders, and Myra Thompson were shot and killed by a White man, Dylann Roof, at the Mother Emanuel AME Church in Charleston, South Carolina, police officers bought him Burger King because he was hungry. Police gave Ma'Khia a mere ten seconds of life.

Kia was still processing her own story and so certainly couldn't make sense of Ma'Khia's. But how could she come to terms with such atrocities? Ma'Khia was shot and killed minutes after Derek Chauvin was found guilty of murdering George Floyd. For Kia, the trauma, grief, and pain are ever present.

As Kia's experiences demonstrate, being Black in this country so often means being presumed to be a criminal, regardless of age.[2] Black girls are routinely viewed as social deviants who are "unladylike," "ghetto," "uncooperative," and "disrespectful."[3] Studies show that Black girls are perceived to be "less innocent" and "more adult-like" than White girls of the same age.[4] This phenomenon is what researchers call "the adultification of Black girls," which potentially contributes to the disproportionate suffering of Black girls in schools and in the criminal punishment system.[5] Black girls are *six* times as likely to be suspended as White girls.[6]

As a nation, we shrug when confronted with the fact that thousands of young people are pushed out of school every day, never to return. We are outraged by videos that show Black girls being assaulted by SROs—but only temporarily. These videos trend for a few days; then their pain is forgotten by the masses. But they're never forgotten by the Black girls who were attacked and the Black girls who watched in person and online.

On any given day in the U.S., millions of children attend schools patrolled by police officers but with no mental health resources.[7] During the 2015/2016 school year, over fourteen million kids—nearly a third of public school students—attended a school without a school counselor, nurse, social worker, or psychologist, and yet the school had a police officer standing guard.[8] In many states nationwide, SROs receive standard police training to work in schools.[9] Maryland and Utah provide SROs with diversity training, while only a few states require de-escalation, youth development, conflict resolution, or mental health training.[10]

The American Civil Liberties Union released a comprehensive report detailing the cost of school policing in the state of Florida. The report found that in Florida, during the 2018/2019 school year, 3,650 police officers were working in schools compared with only 2,286 school nurses, 1,414 school social workers, and 1,452 school psychologists.[11] No school in the state met industry standards for the school counselor per student ratio.[12] The report also revealed that school youth arrests increased by 8 percent while youth arrests in the community declined by 12 percent.[13]

The cost of school policing doubled after the tragic mass shooting at Marjory Stoneman Douglass High School in Florida, reaching $383 million spent on putting police or armed security personnel in the Sunshine State's schools.[14] However, research shows that police in schools is not effective in preventing or stopping mass shootings; experts tell us that the more we place police in schools, the more Black and Brown students disproportionately are punished and criminalized.[15] And of course, nationwide, schools with the most police presence and carceral technologies (e.g., surveillance equipment, metal detectors, body scanners, isolation rooms) and the least amount of relevant training in working with youth are in urban schools filled with Black and Brown students who are punished at a place they are legally compelled to attend.

Scholar Simone Browne, author of *Dark Matters: On the Surveillance of Blackness,* argues that the "surveillance of blackness has long been, and continues to be, a social and political norm."[16] So are harm, punishment, and the incarceration of Black children. This is especially clear at Orr Academy High School, on the West Side of Chicago, which hosts a police processing center to expedite booking students on-site.[17] In 2019, the Chicago City Council greenlit a plan to build a $95 million police training center right next to the school, despite outcry from community members, who pointed out that the amenities afforded to cops would far surpass those at Orr.[18]

Black students are suspended at higher rates than any other racial group. (I should note that I do not believe in suspending students, regardless of race.) Researchers found that nearly 60 percent of all Texas students between grades seven and twelve were expelled or suspended at least once.[19] Black students were 31 percent more likely to be expelled or suspended than White students.[20] An alarming 15 percent of students were suspended eleven times or more.[21] Congressional hearings have been held on the school-to-prison pipeline and the extreme, harmful disciplinary measures that disproportionately punish Black students, especially those with disabilities. Studies show that Black students with disabilities are more than twice as likely as their White peers to receive more than one out-of-school suspension, which increases their likelihood of incarceration.[22]

In the winter of 2022, Wayne Ivey, sheriff of Brevard County, Florida, stood outside the county's jail complex and told his constituents that "If you're a little snot that's coming to our classes to be disruptive, you might want to find someplace else to go to school because we're going to be your worst nightmare starting right now."[23] There should be national outrage at Ivey's statement and the rates at which this nation expels and suspends Black children, but many of our most famous and praised politicians rose to prominence by punishing Black children who were absent from school.

Suspensions and Truancy Laws

Sam is one such individual who endured a history of suspensions as a youth. He estimates that he was suspended somewhere between 120 and 140 days from kindergarten through high school, and he laughs with disbelief as he recalls the number of school days he missed because of suspensions. A school year is typically 180 days, so Sam's suspensions deprived him of the better part of a school year.

For Sam, the punishment dates to daycare, which he was kicked out of because he was deemed aggressive. (He remembers hitting a teacher with a book.) After this expulsion, Sam stayed with his grandmother while his mother and father went to work. "I was always fighting," Sam told me. His elementary school principal saw that Sam needed somewhere to channel his aggression, so he recommended football: "He never thought I was a bad child. He thought I was different and needed to be in contact sports."

Sam's middle school was filled with gangs. "Everybody was fighting everybody," he recalled. "You were fighting for protection." Because so many students were brawling (a sign of unaddressed trauma), the school couldn't suspend all of them, so they were given in-school suspension (ISS). ISS isolates students from the rest of the student body but keeps them in the school building. Typically, a teacher provides work for the student to complete in ISS, but there's no actual instruction from a teacher. "School was always like whatever to me," Sam said. "I always did good in math. I did not have to study for math, and I would get As. Reading was the problem, but I was never failing."

Sam grew up in Atlanta in a two-parent home with an older brother. His parents worked hard to provide for Sam and his brother. As a child, he was rarely outside his zip code; Sam left his neighborhood only for football, basketball, and band practices. His neighborhood was loving and nurturing, and his parents worked around the clock to provide for their two boys. Reflecting on his youth, Sam knows he could have had better grades if he had not been suspended so much.

In high school, Sam went to jail. The city's police entered a boys' bathroom at the school and arrested everyone there for selling drugs. Sam was in the wrong place at the wrong time. He was transported to jail on a school bus. He then had to go through metal detectors, "people telling me to line up on the wall, be quiet, and don't talk." After a few hours, he was able to call the principal to get him out of jail because the school's camera could prove he was not affiliated with the other students selling drugs. Sam was not released until his principal arrived to clear his name.

Sam attended a school full of security cameras, metal detectors, SROs, and city police. When I asked him to compare how he felt in school to how he felt in the city jail, he replied, "Thinking back on it, I did not see any difference." The similarities between school and jail stayed with him. "The stuff I was doing in high school, I was doing in jail," he said. "I was very much prepared for the situation . . . We even had the same lunch; the jail had the same cheese sticks as school." Essentially, Sam was being transported from one place of confinement to the next, to just another institution filled with Black bodies.

Sam is now thirty-two. He lives in the suburbs with his beautiful wife and a three-year-old daughter with soft brown eyes; he hopes for a better life for her. He is an accountant, has a nice home, and is doing fine—it shows in his gregariousness and cheeriness. However, Sam does not have this life because of the system—he has it despite it. When he was a student, instead of receiving counseling and social-emotional health and healing support, he got suspensions—too often the only consideration for Black boys. Sam told me he is trying his hardest to ensure that his daughter never walks into a school filled with cops, metal detectors, and low expectations for Black children. Suspending Black children from school is just one of the mechanisms of an educational police state. Not attending school is also criminal.

As much as we might think school districts are to blame for their treatment of Black children, they are not acting alone. In fact, the districts are joined at the hip with police departments and district attorneys' offices to fine and arrest parents and students for not attending school. In districts around the country, parents are fined and made to perform community service for an unexcused absence by their child, a misdemeanor. If the parents or students fail to appear in court, a warrant can be issued for their arrest. Truancy laws that criminalized absences were championed by Kamala Harris, who, as California's attorney general, enacted a law in 2011 that "made it a criminal misdemeanor for parents to allow kids in kindergarten through eighth grade to miss more than 10 percent of school days without a valid excuse."[24] In her 2011 inauguration speech, Harris said, "We are putting parents on notice . . . If you fail in your responsibility to your kids, we are going to work to make sure you face the full force and consequences of the law."[25]

Robert Balfanz of the Center for the Social Organization of Schools at Johns Hopkins estimated in 2012 that chronic absenteeism was "at 10 percent to 15 percent among U.S. public school students, with highest levels among poor students of all racial and ethnic backgrounds."[26] Balfanz argues that "chronic absenteeism . . . is how poverty manifests itself on school achievement. . . . It isn't an argument for making truancy criminal."[27] Truancy laws hit low-income families the hardest; courts cash in on charging truancy fines that can cost parents from $100 to $2,500. In 2014, Texas collected $10 million in truancy costs and fines.[28] As state budgets are cut, truancy fines are a way for local authorities to supplement funding. Poor Black families are funding courts and police departments, and the reach and tactics of the criminal injustice system are expanding.

Truancy laws attack the country's most vulnerable families who need health care, mental health support, reliable public transportation, a living wage, and affordable housing. Truancy fines played a part in the death of Eileen DiNino, a fifty-five-year-old White Pennsylvania mother. In 2019, DiNino was arrested and imprisoned for failing to pay $2,000 in truancy fines for her children's school absences. She complained to the prison nurse that she was experiencing breathing problems. Sent back to her cell, she was found dead hours later. After DiNino's death, there were statehouse conversations about how unpaid parking tickets and truancy fines criminalize citizens, but those talks did not lead to substantial changes.[29]

In Ferguson, Missouri, where eighteen-year-old Michael Brown was fatally shot by police officer Darren Wilson in 2014, the municipal court in 2013 issued 32,975 arrest warrants for non-violent offenses, generally driving violations, in a city of 21,125 people.[30] Ferguson is 67 percent Black, but 86 percent of motorists pulled over by police in the city were Black. By contrast, White people accounted for only 12.7 percent of vehicle stops—even though they total 29 percent of the population.[31] In 2013, these kinds of warrants generated $2.6 million in court fines and fees, the second-largest revenue stream for the city.[32] Courtrooms packed to capacity are locked five minutes after court begins; if you are late and cannot get in, a warrant could be issued for your arrest.

This is the criminal punishment system, and education is not immune—it is an indispensable segment of the carcerality. In reality, there is no pipeline: Black people's lives, regardless of location, are carceral. Schools are too often just another place where Black bodies are disciplined, tested, harmed, caged, and disposed of. For Black people in this country, protection, safety, and freedom from carcerality are tangential and, at best, temporary, even within schools. At any time, the state can, with impunity, dispose of us.

Public education's entanglement with carcerality is often linked to the "zero tolerance" policies that emerged in the 1980s in the fast-tracked war on drugs. But that explanation is too simple. Zero tolerance was undoubtedly a factor in turning schools into prisons; however, the backlash to *Brown* had already set the stage within this nation's public school system. Violent White resistance to school integration through the courts, the defunding of public education, the gutting of cities through racial zoning laws, subsidies for building all-White suburbs, tax exemptions for White people to build their own private schools, White people calling for school choice when the choices are not good enough for their own children, low wages that keep people in poverty, "targeted mass incarceration," high-stakes standardized testing, charter schools, zero tolerance school discipline policies, compulsory school laws—all of these helped transform schools into spaces that cannibalize Black students.[33]

All Black life, regardless of the setting, is susceptible to incarceration, punishment, disposability, testing, and being branded a threat by the state. Driving is carceral (Sandra Bland). Sleeping is carceral (Breonna Taylor). Shopping is carceral (George Floyd). Playing in the park is carceral (Tamir Rice). Protecting trees is carceral (Bobbi Wilson). Walking home is carceral (Trayvon Martin). Home buying is carceral (Roy Thorne). Watering your neighbors' flowers is carceral (Pastor Michael Jennings). Exercising is carceral (Ahmaud Arbery). Calling the police for help is carceral (Ma'Khia Bryant). School is carceral (Kaia Rolle).

Carcerality is inevitable because Blackness is so often understood as synonymous with criminality.[34] Therefore, we need to expand our understanding of carcerality beyond the walls of what we know as prison or jails to all Black life living under White rage and anti-Blackness. Black life is consumed with desperately trying to escape carceral inevitability because we wear the "presumption of dangerousness and guilt"—from the cradle to our premature graves. I want to be clear: prisons and schools are highly similar but also distinctly different. I don't want to erase how many prisons in the U.S. violate human rights standards, allowing cells so hot that people die, contaminated food and water, lack of medical care, and the cruelty of solitary confinement. Some are forced to endure these conditions for decades.[35] One of the most hideous stories about the conditions of prisons comes out of Atlanta, Georgia, as recently as 2022. Lashawn Thompson, thirty-five, was found dead in an Atlanta jail after being eaten alive by insects and bed bugs. We must be clear and name how brutal and inhuman prisons are. But the tentacles of carcerality are always present in Black life, including during time spent at school.

Sapping Black Children's Spirits

The stories of the Black people in this book show how punishment, testing, police in schools, and incarceration groomed so many for captivity. I draw on the insightful work of Damien Sojoyner, whose critique of the school-to-prison pipeline is necessary to understand the design of public education for Black children. As Sojoyner writes:

> Enacted through various strategies such as forced removal, benign neglect, abandonment, and incapacitation, the goal of enclosures is to blur the social vision of Black communities. That is, rather than a school to prison pipeline, the structure of public education is just as and maybe even more so culpable in the enclosure of Black freedom, which in turn has informed the development of prisons.[36]

In my previous work, I described this type of attack on Black children as spirit-murdering. Legal scholar Patricia Williams argued that racism is more than just physical pain; racism robs Black people of their humanity and dignity and leaves personal, psychological, and spiritual injuries. Racism, anti-Blackness, and carceral inevitability are traumatic because they result in the loss of protection, safety, nurturance, joy, and acceptance—all things children need to be properly educated—and to grow as healthy children.[37]

Educational reform is just one of many societal investments in White supremacy that produce dividends across multiple systems.[38] Sabina E. Vaught, who studies carcerality and schools, stresses that "juvenile prison and what we call public school are two interconnected systems—state apparatuses that enjoy compulsory relationships with youth," and with Black youth in particular. This is why, as prison abolitionist Erica Meiners suggests, we use the term "targeted mass incarceration."[39] The school system is carceral because it is designed by the state to target the disposal of Black life, Black dreams of freedom, and Black creativity. But that threat can often look harmless, even to those of us in education. My peers and I learned this lesson by way of a dare.

Dared to Turn in Our Parents

In the 1980s, Nancy Reagan's worthless advice to "Just Say No" to drugs was pounded into my head. Like many other Black kids, I was told at school to accept Officer Friendly as the neighborhood hero. This country gave me a literal dare to avoid drugs and stay in school. D.A.R.E., short for Drug Abuse Resistance Education, was created by Daryl Gates of the Los Angeles Police Department in 1983, the same year *A Nation at Risk* was released.

Gates was one of the most notorious and racist police chiefs in the war on drugs. He took the word *war* literally, bringing it to the streets of LA. Gates was known for using military-style SWAT tactics, including steel battering rams on armored vehicles, and, according to the *Los Angeles Times,* "made no apologies for declaring that casual drug users should be shot." He once said that Black people are physiologically different from "normal" people, which explained why Black people die when placed in choke holds by police.[40] Gates's extreme and widespread state-sanctioned violence toward Black and Brown communities sowed the seeds for the notorious 1992 police beating of Rodney King and the subsequent uprisings in the city.

Gates was chief of police when LAPD officers nearly beat King to death after a high-speed chase. There were more than fifteen White officers at the scene of the attack. Only four were charged with assault and excessive use of force for striking King with their batons over fifty times and tasing him with a fifty-thousand-volt stun gun. All but one were acquitted by a largely White jury empaneled in conservative Simi Valley. That same jury failed to reach a verdict on the fourth officer.

Ultimately, Black and Brown Angelenos took to the streets for six days to condemn not only the police beating of King but also the racist and military-style brutality of the LAPD—fueled by an initiative called Operation Hammer greenlit by Gates. The 1992 LA uprising ended with dozens of people killed, more than two thousand injured, and thousands arrested. Gates— once called an "all-American hero" by President George H. W. Bush—was forced to resign after the uprisings, but his legacy lives to this day.

Gates's racist ideas and his approach to crime and punishment were disseminated throughout the country, reaching my child-hood home thousands of miles away in Rochester, New York. The D.A.R.E. program, implemented at my elementary school and many other schools, is now taught in all fifty states. By 1995, the program had been taught to more than twenty-five million elementary students. Tens of millions of kids across the country have experienced a police officer entering their schools to tell them to say no to drugs or else suffer the consequence of prison. Although countless studies have found D.A.R.E. to be ineffective while others found drug use was higher among youth who completed D.A.R.E. than among those not enrolled in the program,[41] it is the nation's single-largest school-based prevention program in terms of federal funding.[42]

Teachers stopped teaching on any given day in America's schools in the 1980s and 1990s so children could learn the so-called three Rs: recognize, resist, report. Police asked children in the inner city, most of us Black, to report if there were drugs or drug users in our homes. Essentially, they were asking us to turn in our parents for using drugs. We were bribed with coloring books, key chains, rulers, and T-shirts by the D.A.R.E. mascot, Daren the Lion—a cartoon character that vaguely resembled Tony the Tiger, the kindly Kellogg's Frosted Flakes mascot.

The D.A.R.E. program, along with the over-policing and surveillance of Black communities, taught children like me to see the world through the lenses of anti-Blackness and punishment. I was told to believe that the Black boys in my neighborhood who were in gangs or sold drugs were fundamentally bad. We were told the lie that our parents, aunties, uncles, and older brothers and sisters who became drug addicts were not strong enough to live up to America's D.A.R.E. and therefore deserved to be sent to prison or to die of an overdose. People in my community started to disappear. As iconic scholar-activist Angela Y. Davis tells us, prisons serve as "a way of disappearing people in the false hope of disappearing the underlying social problems they represent."[43]

Ava, now forty-two, still remembers being terrified from age seven to ten when Officer Friendly came to her school for the D.A.R.E. program. At the time, Ava's mother had a drug addiction, a habit Ava now believes was self-medication for undiagnosed depression.

"No one told me not to talk to the police about my mother's drug use," she said. "I didn't have the language as a child to avoid a question about drugs in my home. My anxiety was high when I saw Officer Friendly, hoping he would not ask me any questions." Ava told me she remembers feeling tense at school, worried that if the officer or others at her predominantly White school learned about her mother's drug use, Ava would become disposable, no longer recognized as a prized pupil. She didn't want her mother to attend school events in case her addiction was evident to others in some way. Ava excelled at school and did well on standardized tests. But to Ava, the D.A.R.E. program threatened her sense of belonging at school and promised to put her family on a path to imprisonment.

Many of the people I interviewed remember D.A.R.E. as a harmless part of their schooling experience. But though D.A.R.E. is patently ineffective, it is far from harmless. It successfully told children to trust cops above their parents, that incarceration was the only solution for drug use, and that losing our friends and family members to drug overdose or prison was justifiable because they got what they deserved—their drug use forever defined them. D.A.R.E. taught us that Black bodies deserved punishment. And there were no second chances, no mercy, no redemption. D.A.R.E. was just one of the reforms that would steal away our childhoods. Recently, D.A.R.E. is mounting a comeback. In school districts around the country, D.A.R.E. is being rolled out as a program to fight the opioid crisis.[44] D.A.R.E., much like education reform, can be described as a form of "benevolent terror."[45] *Benevolent terror* is a phrase coined by Professor Dorothy Roberts, who studies law and social rights, to describe how governmental agencies, like the child welfare system, utilize the rhetoric of "saving children" but in fact police, surveil, and produce horrific and sometimes deadly outcomes for Black children and families.[46]

D.A.R.E. taught me that under the policies of law and order, a seventeen-year-old Black boy selling drugs for five to ten dollars a bag was an animal, he would remain so for decades, and therefore he should be banished from the community. His adolescent mistakes were cast as serious crimes that would forever determine the type of person he could be. I never questioned this thinking as a kid. I was, after all, just a kid. All I knew was that I was losing my friends and my community was under attack.

The Loss of Childhood

By the 1980s and 1990s, the growing narrative in this country was that Black children were lawless—and society needed protection from them. Despite crime dropping in schools and across communities, beginning in 1990, the nation adopted a zero-tolerance policy as an extension of the "broken window" theory. The idea was that if schools—filled with so-called thugs and Clinton's super predators—were going to prevent serious crimes, they needed to crack down on minor infractions. This method effectively made schools intolerable to childhood. Children and young adults need nurturing spaces, spaces where everyone feels safe and cared for, their needs are met, relationship and student curiosities are taken as fundamental to learning, support systems for social-emotional health and healing are vast, and there is a culture of accountability, wherein students choose to take accountability for the harm they caused.[47] A nurturing space requires adults to see children as trustworthy, which gives them room to be vulnerable and thoughtful. But Black children in this country have been seldom seen as who they are: children. They have never been shielded from White rage. Black children as young as six worked the fields during enslavement, and "before the Civil War, half of all enslaved people were under sixteen years old."[48]

On paper, zero-tolerance school discipline policies were race-neutral, but nothing in this country is truly free of racism. The Gun-Free Schools Act of 1994, signed by President Clinton, required states to expel a student for a year if they brought a weapon to school. The act also required schools to refer students to local law enforcement if they were found with firearms or other weapons at school. But the law failed to make schools any safer.[49] Instead, students were expelled and referred to authorities for bringing in such objects as butter knives (for sandwiches), plastic toy guns, or Swiss Army knives, and for swearing or engaging in any behavior considered disruptive by school officials.

As zero tolerance proliferated in the U.S., so did the hiring of SROs, heavily subsidized by the U.S. Department of Justice's Office of Community Oriented Policing Services program.[50] From 1999 to 2005, "the federal COPS programs awarded in excess of $753 million to schools and police departments to place police officers in schools." By 2009, New York City schools employed more than 5,000 safety agents and 191 armed police officers.[51] The staggering number of law enforcement officials patrolling New York City schools in 2009 made it the fifth-largest police district in the country.[52]

The crime bill that Clinton signed into law in 1994 was an example of the bipartisan tough-on-crime crusade that dominated the national conversation at the time. Clinton was eager to show the American public that it wasn't just the Republicans who could severely punish Black people. The effects of the crime bill were devastating. It eliminated the Pell Grant for people who were formerly incarcerated, effectively denying any possibility of a college education for many of those who could have most benefited from it. It put tens of thousands of police in Black communities, exacerbating racial disparities in the criminal punishment system. It imposed a three-strike law that gave automatic life sentences to people upon any third conviction. It authorized the death penalty for sixty new federal offenses. And the bill also allowed prosecutors to charge children as young as thirteen as adults; as of 2019, Black people made up two-thirds of people sentenced to life in prison as juveniles.[53]

It was in this climate that SROs became prevalent in schools—but not all schools. Studies show that Black students like Kia, body-slammed by an SRO, and Sam, arrested while at school, are more likely to attend schools with SRO programs, walk through a metal detector to enter school, and face arrest for minor infractions.[54] From 2006 to 2011, for instance, the school district in Birmingham, Alabama, used a pepper spray / tear gas combination to discipline hundreds of mostly Black high school students.[55] "The rise in school policing cannot be attributed to a rise in dangerous crime in schools," the ACLU has written.[56] "Particularly in Black communities, school police have gone well beyond addressing serious crime activity, instead targeting perceived disorder and rowdiness."[57]

Unfortunately, there is no national database for SROs. According to U.S. Department of Education survey data, there were at least 52,100 SROs in public schools in 2016, up from 34,000 officers in 2003.[58] Remarkably, SROs have all the authority of a police officer. They are often armed. And in recent years, they have been recorded using excessive force, especially in incidents involving students of color. In 2015, South Carolina students recorded their classmate, a young Black girl who refused to give her cell phone to her teacher, being violently dragged from her desk across the classroom by an SRO named Ben Fields. The video drew national outrage. In 2019, an eleven-year-old Black boy in North Carolina was twice slammed to the ground by a sheriff's deputy. In that same year, in Orlando, Florida, an officer was fired after handcuffing, arresting, and taking mug shots of two six-year-old Black girls in two separate incidents. In 2021, an SRO body-slammed and handcuffed a young Black girl on a concrete walkway outside her school.

Law enforcement also exerts its outsize power by issuing tickets for student behaviors such as using offensive words or gestures, littering, vaping, misbehavior, or fighting.[59] In 2022, an investigation by ProPublica found that school officials and local police worked jointly to issue tickets.[60] The ticket system overwhelmingly punishes Black students. At Bloom Trail High School in Illinois, the student body is 60 percent Black, but Black students account for nearly all student tickets.[61] At DeKalb High School, near Chicago,

Black students make up 20 percent of the student population but are issued almost half of all the tickets.[62]

These conduct violations result in costly fines that families must pay. To add insult to injury, students miss days of school as they file into courtrooms waiting for hours for prosecutors to call their names to pay their initial fine and court fees. According to an investigation by the *Chicago Tribune,* records show that

> DeKalb students were most commonly cited for fighting, a violation that comes with a minimum $300 fine . . . At the hearing, students can contest the ticket or plead liable, which usually results in an order to do community service. Hearings are held twice a month at 9 a.m. at the police station . . . If the students don't pay and don't show up on their hearing date, the fine increases to the maximum allowed by state law: $750, plus a $100 administrative fee. If the fines and fees are not paid, the debt can be sent to collections.[63]

In 2019, a school resource officer issued Amara Harris a ticket for theft at Naperville North High School, located outside Chicago. School police accused Amara of taking another student's AirPods. Harris and her mother repeatedly told school officials that Amara had picked up the wrong AirPods in the school's learning commons, insisting that the incident "was a mix-up, not a theft."[64]

Harris graduated high school a year early, and Spelman College, her dream school, offered her admission. She delayed beginning her freshman year to fight to clear her name. Even after two years of Harris maintaining her innocence, school officials refused to drop the charges. Her case is now going to trial. Harris is one of the 11,800 students issued a ticket in Illinois over the last three years. The pace of tickets issued for so-called violations of municipal ordinances did not let up during the pandemic.[65]

Sadly, punishment, harassment, assault, and arrest are normalized and accepted as everyday experiences of Black students' school reality.[66] Today, nineteen states still permit adults to hit children in school with canes, paddles, belts, or other objects that can inflict pain. Not surprisingly, there are racial disparities regarding which students are subjected to corporal punishment. A 2019 report by the Southern Poverty Law Center and the Center for Civil Rights Remedies found that students with disabilities are hit at higher rates than those without. Black girls are paddled three times as much as White girls. Black boys are struck nearly twice as much as White boys. Astonishingly, more than 70 percent of all students receiving corporal punishment live in four states: Alabama, Arkansas, Mississippi, and Texas.[67]

The physical, mental, financial, and spiritual punishment of carcerality doesn't just traumatize students and their families. The entire community is involved, both profiting from and being harmed by carcerality. I never understood this more clearly than when I interviewed Johnnie.

A Family's Carcerality Story

Johnnie was raised by his grandmothers in a small town about an hour's drive from Columbus, Ohio. He speaks of them with much love and admiration, and it is evident by his composure and poise that they had a significant impact on him. Johnnie seems like an old soul, even though he's only thirty-six. He's soft-spoken, thoughtful, and devoted to his job as the leader of a small school district's diversity and equity efforts. His town was the site of a race riot in the early twentieth century that resulted in most Black residents fleeing for their lives. Deeply entrenched racism remained when his family arrived in the 1960s. He is among the few Black people there. In a calm and steady voice, he revealed to me that his father and mother were incarcerated in the 1990s. The woman he calls his stepmother (a relative by marriage who is a matriarchal force in the family) was the warden at the prison where his mother was held.

At that moment, I realized just how all-encompassing the prison industrial complex was for Johnnie and his family and community. Since the 1990s, the proliferation of state prisons has boosted local economies—all on the backs of Black people living under state captivity, containment, and surveillance. Angela Y. Davis sees a link between "corporations, government, correctional communities, and media" to punish, criminalize, and incarcerate Black people for profit and the conservation of racist ideas.[68] This in turn upholds a larger political agenda and structures that render Black life disposable and dispossessed.[69]

Johnnie described to me how the prison industrial complex "incapacitated" his family. The system made them complicit due to the need for jobs in their small town.[70] "Losing my mom gave me a deep sense of loss," he said, reflecting on his mother's imprisonment. Her crime? Defending herself from a boyfriend who was assaulting her.

Sadly, there are too many Black women who are behind bars for defending themselves from their attackers or rapists. Why? The criminal punishment system refuses to see Black women as victims, instead painting them as aggressors despite overwhelming evidence to the contrary. Many Black women and other women of color "are often victim blamed when the court discovers they were involved in sex work, even against their own will."[71] No agency collects data on women who are criminalized for surviving abuse. Still, numerous studies have found that a majority of incarcerated women have experienced intimate partner violence or sexual violence.[72]

In 2019, Cyntoia Brown was granted clemency after serving fifteen years of a life sentence for killing a man who was trying to buy her for sex—she was only sixteen at the time. In 2006, a group of seven young Black women were confronted by twenty-eight-year-old Dwayne Buckle, who was selling DVDs in a park in Greenwich Village, a gay-friendly neighborhood in New York City. He threatened to make the women, who were lesbians, "straight"—by raping them—and then proceeded to attack them. Fearing for their lives, one of the women, Patreese Johnson, pulled a knife from her purse and stabbed him. The altercation lasted four minutes, and everyone walked away alive. Buckle had only minor injuries, but the media turned the women into brutal killers. Newspaper headlines screamed ATTACK OF THE KILLER LESBIANS, GIRLS GONE WILDING, and MAN IS STABBED IN ATTACK AFTER ADMIRING A STRANGER. The seven friends, also called the "Wolfpack" by the media, were charged with felonies. Three pleaded guilty and were sentenced to six months in jail and five years on probation. Four women, including Johnson, lost at trial and were given prison sentences ranging from three and a half to eleven years. In 2007, two were sent to Bedford Hills Correctional Facility, a maximum-security prison, and two were transferred to Albion Correctional Facility, forty-eight miles from the Canadian border.

Like so many other Black women, Johnnie's mother had survived assault, only to be punished and criminalized for her survival. The prison system surrounded his family, community, and school. Johnnie was suspended twice in middle school for fighting boys who called him the n-word. Taking part in D.A.R.E., the national drug prevention program, he drew flags and took pledges to say no to drugs. "At the same time I was in D.A.R.E.," Johnnie recalled, "they were building the juvenile detention center and a new prison . . . We have three prisons: one public, one private, and a juvenile detention center."

Johnnie witnessed SROs harass and "rough up" his friends

during high school. He believes he was not surveilled and targeted by the SROs because he was a football star and on an accelerated academic track. He also said, "When my mom got home from prison, she would interact with the police at school and tell them what was and wasn't going to happen with me." Johnnie's mother understood the ways that carceral inevitability targeted her son. Her communication with the police at his school let them know that she was watching their actions.

Today, Johnnie's joy is channeled into creating spaces where boys of color can be goofy and laugh, an unfortunate rarity for Black boys in schools. He went from kindergarten to high school without a single Black male teacher. The only Black men he interacted with at school were coaches. Johnnie's experience is like those of many other Black males I interviewed for this book. Black men make up less than 2 percent of teachers in this country. The need for Black male teachers is essential in the life of school-aged Black boys who need to see people who look like them reflected in their lives. It is also critically important to the lives of all children who need to see Black men as role models to combat societal stereotypes about Black men as brutes and criminals.

Johnnie did not have Black male teachers, but he had his grandmothers, both of whom passed away in his senior year of high school. His face lit up when he talked about them. Half of the children of incarcerated parents live with a grandparent. Between 1999 and 2007, the number of children aged eighteen and under with an incarcerated parent increased by 80 percent.[73] By 2015, at least five million children were estimated to have had at least one incarcerated parent.[74] And Black children are over seven times more likely than White children to have an incarcerated parent.[75]

Johnnie said his grandmothers got involved to ensure he did not end up in foster care. He attended church regularly. "When you are Black in a small town, you don't have a choice. You go to church twice a week, Thursdays and Sundays." His mother's mother was his rock, and she would sing throughout the house, especially the old Negro spiritual "Precious Lord," Dr. Martin Luther King Jr.'s favorite gospel song. Johnnie's maternal grandmother taught him at a young age not to trust White people, that there are only a few good White people, and those few still cannot be trusted. "She was always telling the truth, harsh truths, but you find out later that she was right."

Johnnie's life story reflects the last forty years of targeted mass incarceration and educational reform driven by White rage. He has an advanced degree in educational leadership. He spent time in graduate school connecting the dots between his own experience and that of other children with incarcerated parents. He also clearly sees the connection between the drug war that has ravaged Latin American countries and the domestic policies that led to his own father being incarcerated multiple times for crimes related to his untreated addiction. Johnnie identifies as a survivor of genocide. Now he is fighting to protect Black children from the same carceral systems he experienced as a student. Instead of D.A.R.E., the school district where he works has installed police officers as youth mentors through a national program called Teen and Police Service, or TAPS. According to TAPS's website, the program builds on the work of D.A.R.E. by "reducing the social distance between at-risk youth and law enforcement." Officers are assigned to youth and paid to mentor them. In Texas, students are given one high school academic credit for completing the eleven-week program. TAPS now operates across the country. While they may be perceived as benign, programs such as TAPS continue the expansion of the carceral state. Johnnie understands just how these programs can terrorize communities, families, and Black children.

Johnnie's community, White people included, deserves better. His life is shaped by the nation's inability to see Black women as victims. His mother should never have had to leave her son. She lost irreplaceable time with him because she had to fight for her life. Johnnie is a beautiful Black man who found Black feminism as a way to heal the wounds of his childhood, but the scars are still there, and so are the prisons. Johnnie's town sees prison as a way out of poverty, which means they need Black bodies in captivity. The conviction that prisons will rescue the town economically joins with the stereotypes and myths that Black people are dangerous—and criminals. Prison towns feed on these lies, White fears, and economic woes to make human captivity seem like a necessary outcome. Racism, anti-Blackness, and capitalism dehumanize White people as well.

From 1990 to 1995, crime declined in the United States. And yet, during that time, 213 new state and federal prisons were built across the country. For prison abolitionist, geographer, and scholar Ruth Wilson Gilmore, this signaled a disturbing trend: "Prisons grow in order to get rid of people of color, especially young Black men, accomplishing the goal through new lawmaking patterns of policing, and selective prosecution."[76] In recent years, Black women have doubled the incarceration rate of Black men.[77] As a "carceral geographer," Gilmore argues that geography, not just race and economics, are behind the prison industry's growth. Following the Great Depression, prison expansion in rural areas created employment opportunities for small towns throughout the United States. In the 1980s and 1990s, prison hosting became an economic development model. Rural communities saw prisons as addressing lasting poverty, "with an average of 35 jobs being created for every 100 inmates being housed."[78] Schools provided those fortunate enough to escape prison with the job training necessary to become the ones to put their classmates behind bars.

"No Fear"

So many Black people are either caged by the prison system in high school or recruited in high school to work for the criminal punishment system as police officers and prison guards—for example, the Junior Reserve Officers' Training Corps, or JROTC. The program puts army, air force, navy, marine corps, and coast guard units in schools. Today, it has more than 3,500 stations in schools.[79] The program started in 1916 with the National Defense Act, which established JROTC to "increase the U.S. Army's readiness in the face of World War I."[80] President George W. Bush's No Child Left Behind Act advanced this military goal by requiring schools to grant access to military recruiters as if they were college or job recruiters. A year after the act was signed, the United States invaded Iraq.

Recruiters are disproportionately deployed to low-income schools filled with Black students. A 2017 study found that "at public high schools with JROTC programs, 56.6 percent of students are eligible for free or reduced-price lunch, on average" and "at schools with JROTC, black students make up 29.4 percent of the school, compared to just 12.1 percent at non-JROTC schools."[81] The same study also found that roughly half of JROTC programs are based in the Southeast,[82] home to some of the poorest people in the nation. In 1993, there were about 310,000 students enrolled in JROTC; now, there are over 500,000. Many of these young people are being trained as marksmen in a program sponsored by the National Rifle Association. And yet, in their book, *Making Soldiers in the Public Schools: An Analysis of the Army JROTC Curriculum,* Catherine Lutz and Lesley Bartlett write: "The JROTC program has not shown that it reduces minority dropout, facilitates minority college attendance, or raises earnings through better job placement in the civilian or the military world."[83]

In addition to JROTC, schools in urban neighborhoods host

other recruitment programs that encourage students to become employees of the carceral state. For example, organizations affiliated with the Boy Scouts of America train young men, ages fourteen to twenty, to become Border Patrol Explorers. Through the program, students "learn survival skills, first aid, and participate in training exercises in which they play Border Patrol agents or the people they target."[84] Border Patrol Explorers prepares young men to "arrest drug runners and undocumented immigrants."[85]

Police are also granted access to classroom in an educational capacity. In Indiana, at the end of 2022, Tim DisPennett, a Vermillion Country sheriff deputy, accidentally shot a high school student while teaching a law enforcement class.[86] The student was taken to the hospital with non-life-threatening injuries, an outcome characterized by the district superintendent as "a positive ending."[87] Beyond public high schools, there are also high school police academies that teach a specialized carceral curriculum. The Los Angeles Police Academy Magnet Schools (PAMS) "simulate[s] the LAPD's recruit academy structure" and teaches "criminal law, principles of law enforcement, constitutional law, the criminal justice system and other law related topics throughout all core academic courses."[88] As of 2022, PAMS operated in seven high schools and two junior high schools, serving more than 1,300 students.[89]

One person who has invaluable firsthand knowledge of law enforcement and its effects on Black people is Officer Marcus Fox. Raised in the church—he's also a youth minister and a pastor—Marcus has wanted to be a police officer since he was a young boy. As a child, he remembers being excited to get plastic badges and stickers from officers in his neighborhood. "Some people see this as a job, but I have been called to do this," he told me. Marcus is passionate about law enforcement. He is determined to be viewed as a good cop. You can see the conviction in his eyes and hear it in his voice.

In ninth grade, the JROTC began to groom Marcus as a cadet. He said the JROTC program "planted the seed" for who he is today. When I asked what the program taught him, he said, "Discipline, self-respect, survival skills, and responsibility." Marcus entered the force when he was twenty, after completing his associate degree in criminal justice from a community college. After almost two years of field training, Marcus's dream came true. He spent his first few years as a street cop, then applied to be a school resource officer. "Policing is great," he said, "but I have a passion for helping children." He has been an SRO since 2014. He's now thirty-two.

When I asked Marcus to explain the role of an SRO, he said, "We find ourselves being counselors, fathers, and mothers. We bridge the gap between school and law enforcement." More than anything, he added, "We serve as a deterrent . . . we maintain safety." Marcus told me that students see him just as they see their teacher or principal. He is there every day, interacting with students like an educator.

Regarding whether officers should be removed from schools or defunded, Marcus said, "There are some schools that could not function without police in the building." He said there is no place for police misconduct and brutality, especially in schools. But he added, "There is a term in policing—we say, 'You can't Monday quarterback.' There are incidents where you may have to handcuff a six-year-old, but that does not mean they are going to jail." When it comes to body-slamming students, he said, "We lose our cool, absolutely. Officers lose their cool just like you and I . . . I have seen incidents that are absolutely egregious." As he spoke, his body rocked back and forth. He seemed uncomfortable remembering some of the actions of his fellow officers. As much as Marcus might believe that he and I are the same when we "lose our cool," we are not. I do not walk around with the power to take away someone's freedom or a gun that could take someone's life.

Marcus then said something that shocked me: "The biggest thing is that our children are not afraid. Even looking at police officers, they are just not afraid. . . . Let's take a cafeteria fight. People want to say you could have gone softer, but every situation is different. It's not an excuse, but the hope is that the officer will respond in a professional matter." I can't help but ask myself, how do you respond to a human being you believe has no fear? What kind of force and punishment do you exert? Do you ask yourself, "If they have no fear, do they experience pain?"

Marcus works in schools filled with Black children. He said that of all the officers he works with, only five or six are White. The overwhelming majority of his fellow officers are Black. Those officers believe that young Black children—who they were not so long ago—have no fear. I was stunned, too, by what Marcus said about his own experiences with racial profiling and police brutality. He told me he had been racially profiled several times, even as a police officer. When he was eighteen, he was pulled over by a Black officer. When he asked the officer why he had been pulled over, the officer refused to tell him. He asked a second time why he was being pulled over; the officer refused to answer. The officer then flashed his light into Marcus's car and saw a cup, which Marcus said was melted ice from a soda he had gotten at a pizzeria. The officer then asked for the cup. Marcus told the officer that he didn't have to hand it over. The officer then instructed Marcus to step out of the vehicle. Marcus complied. The officer's partner reached into the car, picked up the cup, and smelled the drink. "Smells like someone has been drinking," he said.

"At this time, you can only imagine how pissed I am," Marcus recalled—he had previously told me that he doesn't drink. Then the officer detained Marcus and put him in the back of his patrol car in handcuffs. The officer proceeded to search Marcus's car illegally. Once back in the car with Marcus, the officer started to write up Marcus's citation on the computer. From the back seat, Marcus read the screen, which indicated he was being cited for an open container and failure to stop at a stop sign. As the officer let Marcus out of the car, removing the handcuffs, he told Marcus that if he did not sign the citations, he would go to jail. Marcus knew his dream of becoming a cop was on the line. So he signed. But as he put his name down, the officer whispered, "It's your word against mine."

Marcus said that single encounter taught him that he would never become that type of officer. But there's another takeaway from that night: Marcus was able to stay calm in the face of injustice, and he believes that should be the norm for targets of police brutality. He took the high road. Marcus told me this story after I asked him how he felt about what happened to George Floyd. Marcus said he would never question the actions of a fellow officer. In doing so, he puts all the responsibility of injustice on the backs of its victims. He acknowledges this. He's aware of the contradictions. Despite witnessing "egregious" police brutality and having been racially profiled, he believes that Black children have no fear; to this, I say, their carcerality is inevitable because they are not seen as human.

7

STANDARDIZING CARCERALITY

The new lynching tool [standardized tests].

—Barbara A. Sizemore

"I Hated Coming Back on Test Day"

I met Rob twelve years ago through our shared family and social network. He's chatty and playful, with a laugh that fills a room, and he's the father of two little girls who adore their dad. Rob is thirty-four, and his chocolate skin is baby-smooth, which I joke about whenever I see him. He works odd jobs and loves hip-hop and everything Atlanta—especially his hometown's sports teams. Rob can talk for hours about Atlanta's politics, history, and how the city could be "upgraded" for its Black residents. Rob used to be a part-time janitor at an elementary school. With the biggest smile on his face, he would tell me stories about the connections he made with the students and how much he enjoyed debating with them about the future of Atlanta sports teams. Rob loved working at a school, which is ironic because, as a young Black boy, school was where Rob never felt seen.

In elementary school, a critical period of academic development, Rob was suspended roughly two months out of every year.

When I asked why, he said, "If you can't keep up with the teacher, you getting in trouble." He recalled classrooms packed with too many students and stressed-out teachers. Rob said he was a good student academically, but he was "active," always running and jumping around. And too often, active little Black boys find themselves suspended.

Studies have shown that little Black boys seldom get to be boys.[1] One research study found that White female undergraduates perceived Black boys to be, on average, 4.5 years older—and "less innocent"—than White boys,[2] a statistic particularly upsetting when paired with the reality that 3 in 4 US public educators are women and 4 in 5 are White.[3] Administrators and teachers view Black boys as potentially criminal, violent, and disruptive from the moment they enter school buildings. Federal civil rights investigations have found that Black students are punished more harshly than White students in schools across the nation, even when Black and White students engage in identical or similar behavior. Black boys are three times as likely to be suspended as White boys.[4]

Rob's early school years were marked by punishment. He did not get into many fights, yet he was punished for being rambunctious. He went to a high school filled with metal detectors and SROs. Rob does not recall any negative interactions with the SROs. However, he did not do well on most tests and found standardized tests at the end of the year to be the hardest. He felt that the tests did not address what he had been learning all year, so he didn't take them seriously. He got what he called "decent" grades, mostly Bs and Cs. Ultimately, he did not graduate from high school. He had faced chronic suspension early on. In 2005, when he was pushed out of high school by standardized tests, no school official attempted to stop Rob from leaving. "I just stopped going," he said. "No one called." Like many others I interviewed for this book, Rob did not have a single connection with a teacher while attending public school for thirteen years. Many I talked to named coaches and after-school club directors as influences in their lives, but they recall no teacher expressing to them their potential or recognizing them beyond punishment. Overall, Rob did not have many Black teachers; he did not have his first Black teacher until he was in middle school. A groundbreaking 2017 study found that having just one Black teacher in elementary school significantly increased a Black student's likelihood of graduating from high school and considering college.[5] The same study also found that having a Black teacher reduced the chances of low-income Black boys leaving school by 39 percent.[6]

After leaving high school, Rob was in and out of jail for nonviolent infractions, including petit theft and possession of cannabis. His experience is hardly unique. Scholar Monique Morris argues that students are shortchanged by "beliefs, policies, and actions that degrade and marginalize both their learning and their humanity, leading to conditions that push them out of school and render them vulnerable to even more harm."[7] Although Morris's findings are based on studying Black girls, her concept of being pushed out of school is applicable to Rob and other Black boys. Students are not dropping out; they are being pushed out. In the U.S., hundreds of thousands of students are pushed out of school every year. However, when students are suspended and pushed out of school, the school still receives funds for that student for the remainder of the school year. The teacher's pay doesn't change for the rest of the year. But what supports, resources, or funding followed him home when Rob was suspended? With each suspension, Rob fell more and more behind his peers. He would return to school and take standardized tests; inevitably, those tests would reveal he was "behind."

When I asked Rob how it felt to be suspended so often, he said, "I hated coming back on test day." Rob believes countless standardized tests and many suspensions were why he didn't graduate high school. He told me, "I liked school. It was cool. [But] just testing a kid ain't enough ... you got to be in the school to learn." After an hour-long interview, I asked Rob what he would have changed to improve his school experience. He said, "Teachers are stressed out like police are stressed ... all they care about is the test." The fact that Rob compared teachers to police officers is striking. Standardized testing in our public education system is part of the police state.

Justifying Punishment

In his book *The Condemnation of Blackness: Race, Crime, and the Making of Modern Urban America,* historian Khalil Gibran Muhammad contends that from the 1890s to the 1930s, Black people "had no monopoly on social banditry, crimes of resistance, or underground entrepreneurship."[8] At the time, White foreign-born immigrants filled America's prisons, but "progressive era social scientists used statistics and sociology to create a pathway for their redemption and rehabilitation."[9] In the early 1900s, crime statistics were interpreted differently to support the assimilation of the Italians and the Irish, on the one hand, while dehumanizing and criminalizing Black people on the other. Celebrated social scientist Charles R. Henderson of the University of Chicago declared that there was a "Negro factor" in crime. He concluded that racial inheritance, physical and mental inferiority, barbarism, and slave ancestry and culture were critical determining factors of criminal propensity.[10] Black novelist Albert Murray asserted that the "social science statistical survey [was] the most elaborate fraud in modern times."[11] He doubled down, adding that Black people "should never forget that the group in power is always likely to use every means at its disposal to create the impression that it deserves to be where it is."[12]

Standardized testing itself is inherently carceral. Standardized tests and IQ tests have been a tool from their conception used to invent Black people's inferiority and to justify our captivity. The concept of eugenics was developed by Francis Galton, a social Darwinist who used pseudoscience to advocate for the practice of selecting desirable human traits based on controlled breeding to increase a population of superior humans. Carl Brigham believed that the education system would decline as "racial mixtures" increased.[13] He argued that Black people were of lower intellectual and cultural ability.

Influenced by the work of his mentor, Robert Yerkes, who developed the Army Alpha (the first mass-administered IQ test) during World War I, Brigham was commissioned by the College Board to create the Scholastic Aptitude Test (SAT).[14] Standardized tests were used during the war to place 1.5 million soldiers based on race and test scores.[15] Brigham also developed the Advanced Placement (AP) examinations. By 1918, the popularity of standardized tests grew, and over one hundred were developed to measure students in elementary and secondary school. By 1930, multiple-choice tests, a specific type of standardized test, were being widely used in U.S. schools.[16] In 1940, W. E. B. Du Bois addressed Brigham and testing:

> It was not until I was long out of school and indeed after the World War that there came the hurried use of the new technique of psychological tests, which were quickly adjusted so as to put black folk absolutely beyond the possibility of civilization. By this time I was unimpressed. I had too often seen science made the slave of caste and race hate. And it was interesting to see Odum, McDougall and Brigham eventually turn somersaults from absolute scientific proof of Negro inferiority to repudiation of the limited and questionable application of any test which pretended to measure innate human intelligence.[17]

Regardless of many Black educators' and scholars' resistance to Brigham, their critiques fell on racist, dismissive ears.

As the Nazis rose to prominence in Germany in the interwar period, they focused on the U.S. Under Hitler's leadership, the Nazis "were looking to move quickly with their plans for racial separation and purity, and knew that the United States was centuries ahead of them with its anti-miscegenation statutes and race-based immigration bans."[18] Hitler told his followers, "I have studied with interest the laws of several American states concerning prevention of reproduction by people whose progeny would, in all probability, be of no value or be injurious to the racial stock."[19]

Fast-forward thirty years to the late 1960s in the United States, when public fears grew over a slight decline in average SAT scores. The nation was in a panic more generally, especially after Daniel Patrick Moynihan's 1965 report, *The Negro Family: The Case for National Action*. A Democrat, Moynihan argued that discrimination forced Black families into "a matriarchal structure" that "seriously retards the progress of the group as a whole, and imposes a crushing burden on the Negro, and in consequence, on a great many Negro women."[20] The report claimed that Black men's feelings of alienation led to high rates of poverty, child abuse, and low educational outcomes. In short, Moynihan branded the Black family structure as broken, then blamed it for the struggles encountered by Black children.[21] Moynihan's fiction informed generations of White Americans' understanding of Black people's lives; his work continues to be celebrated in some conservative circles.

The Moynihan report was followed a year later by the Coleman report, *Equality of Educational Opportunity*. James Coleman's 737-page report was delivered to Congress in 1966. A sociologist at Johns Hopkins University, Coleman studied education and public policy. The study argued that families were a key driver of student achievement, and integrated schools benefited all students.[22] Coleman's report presented data showing disparities between Black and White student achievement. This was America's introduction to "the achievement gap." Critically, the explanation of this gap failed to consider unequal funding, lack of resources, or the anti-Blackness and racism of the nation's public education system. The notion of "the achievement gap" would become the driver for standardized testing that would be weaponized against Black children. Thus, the minimum competency testing movement emerged, and Reagan would capitalize on it by the 1980s.

The achievement gap is not about White students outperforming Black students; it is about a history of educational White rage.[23] It is one of the fallacies of education to know that the achievement gap is due to racism, anti-Blackness, and reform, and yet never to discuss their roles as mechanisms of the achievement gap. In 2006, legendary scholar Gloria Ladson-Billings argued that as a nation we need to move our inquiry from the achievement gap to the "education debt" to understand achievement in U.S. schools. She writes that, "In the case of education, each effort we make toward improving education is counterbalanced by the ongoing and mounting debt that we have accumulated."[24]

The average student in U.S. public schools takes roughly 112 mandatory standardized tests from kindergarten to the end of twelfth grade, which calculates to between twenty and twenty-five hours a school year.[25] (These numbers do not account for the hours of test prep during a school year and the fact that "there is no correlation between the amount of mandated testing time and the reading and math scores in grades four and eight on the National Assessment of Educational Progress," a finding established in many research studies.)[26] And these are simply averages. As is typically the case, children attending urban schools are disproportionately affected by this over-testing zeal while receiving the least benefit from it. "Urban school districts have more tests designed for diagnostic purposes than any other use, while having the fewest tests in place for purposes of international comparisons."[27]

Standardized tests and high school exit exams pushed Black children into the streets, where the criminal punishment system was waiting on their scheduled arrival. According to a 2010 report by the Advancement Project:

> As a result, the practice of pushing struggling students out of school to boost test scores has become quite common. There are a number of widely used strategies for manipulating test scores, such as withdrawing students from attendance rolls, assigning students to alternative schools, coercing or encouraging students to drop out or enroll in General Educational Development (GED) programs, along with using suspensions, expulsions, and referrals to alternative schools. These practices are contemptible, but not surprising when one considers that those educators' future employment or salary may be determined by the results of a single test.[28]

A 2013 National Bureau of Economic Research study showed that high school exit exams increase incarceration rates by 12.5 percent.[29] In 2009, researchers at Northeastern University found that "about one in every 10 young male high school dropouts is in jail or juvenile detention, compared with one in 35 young male high school graduates."[30] It is a myth that test scores are used to estimate the building of future prisons, but the myth is rooted in truth. According to a 2012 study published by the Annie E. Casey Foundation, "One in six children who are not reading proficiently in third grade do not graduate from high school on time, a rate four times greater than that for proficient readers."[31] The same data showed that "22 percent of children who have lived in poverty do not graduate from high school," and poor Black and Brown students who are not proficient readers by third grade are about twice as likely not to graduate from high school compared to similar White children.[32]

Exit exams and mandatory standardized tests disproportionately push Black students out of the classroom and into a cell. A student who does not graduate from high school is 3.5 times more likely to be arrested than a high school graduate. Nationally, 68 percent of all males in prison do not have a high school diploma. Meanwhile, the test companies are making millions. The four major ones—Pearson Education, Educational Testing Service, Houghton Mifflin Harcourt, and McGraw Hill—dominate a testing market valued at $25 billion in 2022.[33] In 2021, these four companies alone spent almost $2 billion lobbying for more mandated student assessments.[34]

To be clear, the last forty years of mandatory standardized testing have produced little data on its effectiveness in closing the achievement gap created by educational White rage. These tests, backed by the reformers, are used as another justification for Black children's disposability.

1994

I started high school with a number of amazing role models I had never met before. In 1994, I heard Ms. Lauryn Hill's magnetic voice for the first time and was instantly put into a Black-girl-magic trance. I didn't know a Black woman could be the "Best Rapper Alive." The same year, Nas's first album, *Illmatic*, was released. He told me that the world was mine, and I believed him. I was also captivated by Biggie's wordplay on *Ready to Die*. I was jealous that Biggie knew the same words I did, but could put them together in ways I never imagined. Also, in that same extraordinary year, OutKast told me I needed to "git up, git out, and git something," and I wanted that *something*. In short, 1994 was a seminal year of classic hip-hop albums that taught me how to be in this world. Although I was carefree entering high school in 1994 with hip-hop as my life's soundtrack, the world around me was quite angry, loud, and filled with violence and conflict. On the TV nightly was the story out of Detroit, Michigan: figure skater Nancy Kerrigan was attacked after skating practice. I had never heard of Kerrigan before the attack, but when the news broke that her rival Tonya Harding was involved in the attack, I was captivated by the story. I thought, *These White people crazy.* I watched NFL star O. J. Simpson in his white Ford Bronco become a fugitive of the law as police followed him down the freeway for allegedly killing his ex-wife, and I couldn't believe a jury would later find him innocent. And the greatest basketball player in the world, Michael Jordan, would briefly retire from basketball to play minor-league baseball after his father's death. My eyes were glued to Dan Rather and Tom Brokaw, who entered our homes nightly with all the gossip. But there was one story I missed: the publication of *The Bell Curve.*

In 1994, Richard Herrnstein and Charles Murray's book became an instant bestseller. Inspired by "race science," *The Bell Curve* argued that the U.S. should stop trying to improve the material conditions of poor Black children because they are genetically predisposed to be unintelligent. The book sold four hundred thousand copies in its first two months, and the White supremacists of the time sang its praises. Murray Rothbard, an influential economist (whom I discussed in chapter 1), gushed at the release of *The Bell Curve,* writing,

> During the past sixty years, racial research or expression
> of views by intellectuals has been marginalized and almost
> literally driven underground by pressure from above and
> from below. But in October 1994, with incredible speed,

the entire culture did a 180-degree turn. Upon the publication by the respected Establishment, The Free Press, of Richard Herrnstein and Charles Murray's *The Bell Curve,* expressing in massively stupefying scholarly detail what everyone has always known but wouldn't dare to express about race, intelligence, and heritability, the dam suddenly burst.[35]

Milton Friedman also hailed *The Bell Curve,* writing an endorsement that appeared on its dust jacket: "This brilliant, original, objective, and lucidly written book will force you to rethink your biases and prejudices about the role that individual difference in intelligence plays in our economy, our policy, and our society."

A widely publicized and incessantly discussed book told the world in 1994 that kids like me were unintelligent from birth; we were genetically inferior, and time and resources shouldn't be wasted on us. It gave politically correct cover to those who had long been trying to dispose of us. *The Bell Curve* was an anti-Black and racist success because, as scholar Andrew S. Winston explains, although the links between IQ and race are illegitimate, the "view of Black deficiencies was a good fit with popular concerns over the role of welfare and the welfare state in promoting social decay."[36] Herrnstein and Murray's "research" expressed in *The Bell Curve* is subtler in delivery but echoed the eugenics movement in the U.S. From the early 1900s and well into the 1970s, eugenicist logic led to sterilizing Black women and women of color due to a belief that poverty, crime, and having children "out of wedlock" was largely caused by genetics. Murray is now a prominent conservative voice, *Wall Street Journal* contributor, and emeritus scholar at the American Enterprise Institute.

Wayne Au, author of *Unequal by Design: High-Stakes Testing and the Standardization of Inequality,* writes that "high-stakes, standardized tests ultimately maintain white supremacy in the U.S."[37] He adds that testing is used to "hide structural racism" and favors "a white, able-bodied norm and contributes directly to the schools-to-prisons pipeline."[38] Advancements in technology now allow tests to assist law enforcement in predicting Black disposability.

Police departments across the U.S., working with big tech companies and universities, build algorithms compiled of massive amounts of data, including socioeconomic background, education, and zip code, to predict whom they deem criminals. In Chicago, the algorithm listed 480 people "most likely to kill or be killed in street violence."[39] Police started showing up to individual homes on the "heat list" to "Hug a Thug," as police called their efforts.[40] Algorithms are also used to predict who will be accepted into Ivy League schools. A student's third-grade MAP score (Measures of Academic Progress) is used to measure their college readiness. As Professor Dorothy Roberts states, "Racism has always been about predicting, about making certain racial groups seem as if they are predisposed to do bad things and therefore justify controlling them."[41]

Brigham would no doubt be proud of how his standardized tests, and those which derive from his creations, help determine inevitable carcerality for so many Black bodies.

8

WHITE PHILANTHROPY

"Knowledge Is Power, Power Is Money"

I first learned of Harriett Ball almost twenty years ago while taking a class with Asa Hilliard, the renowned educational psychologist. One day, he showed us a video of an older Black woman in Houston who rapped for her elementary school students. She used the music not only to teach the students but to inspire them to love learning. Dr. Hilliard called her a master teacher, and he was right. She was captivating. She was six foot one, had long, bright red fingernails, and was blessed with a heavenly singing voice that evoked undeniable strength, Southern beauty, and the love of a God-fearing Black woman. Her passion and her affection for her students were infectious.

Ball had a singular talent for harnessing Black culture in the classroom to drive instruction. The proof of her skills was that her students excelled. She stressed that teachers should not simply sit behind their desks and lecture; they needed to create lessons that embraced the many ways in which students learn—what she called a "multisensory, mnemonic, whole-body teaching technique."[1] Ball had the clout to teach in this innovative way because she could in fact do it all. She could sing, write music, play the piano, and draw. She stressed the pursuit of educational excellence, and her teaching style matched her goal. Ball would tell her students: "You gotta read, baby, read. You gotta read, baby, read. The more you read, the more you know, 'cause knowledge is power, power is money, and I want it."

In 1992, two young White men, David Levin and Mike Feinberg, entered the teaching profession through Teach for America; they were straight out of college, inexperienced, and struggling as new teachers. They happened to be placed in Ball's school, and they asked her to mentor them. Ball's son, Paul Franks, and daughter, Pamela Franks, remember Levin and Feinberg at their childhood home, sitting at their mother's feet while learning her teaching methods and songs. "He was a young White guy, couldn't have been no more than 25 years old," Paul told me, speaking about Levin. "She told me he was family, a teacher she was working with." Paul said that Levin "was frustrated with the kids, that they couldn't learn, couldn't sit down, but he would pass Mrs. Ball's class, and all the kids were learning, paying attention, and he heard the music." Pamela referred to herself as her mother's test pupil; Ball would try out songs and timetable memorization chants with her before they got to her classroom. Ball would tell her daughter that she was making her into a "human cheat sheet," knowing that her songs and chants would store important information in Pamela's brain in a way that she could easily access and use. When I was interviewing Paul and Pamela, their love for their mother was palpable; they revere her and want her legacy known.

After two years of learning Ball's methods, songs, and teaching practices, Levin and Feinberg opened their own school, calling it the Knowledge Is Power Program, or KIPP. The name pays homage to Ball's classic refrain. "One of my biggest heartbreaks," Paul said, "is to see teachers and kids doing stomps and chants I grew up on, songs your mommy taught you, and they don't know these songs are my mama's." The book, *Work Hard,*

Be Nice: How Two Inspired Teachers Created the Most Promising Schools in America, documents the founding of KIPP. According to the author, Jay Mathews,

> While their chosen name, the Knowledge Is Power Program, seemed just right, they [Levin and Feinberg] fiddled with the lyrics of the song from which they had taken it. They shrank from the raw, working-class sentiment of Ball's "knowledge is power, / Power is money, and / I want it." To make their proposal more palatable to school bureaucrats, private fund-raisers, and their own values, they changed that to "knowledge is power, / Power is freedom, and / We want it.'"[2]

They removed financial success from Ball's song, but financial success is a hallmark of KIPP. By 1995, Levin and Feinberg were operating two KIPP middle schools, one in Houston and one in the South Bronx. In 2000, the Fisher family, owners of the clothing retailer Gap Inc., donated $15 million to establish the KIPP Foundation. In 2011, the Walton Family Foundation, led by the owners of Walmart—and one of the leading foundations funding the expansion of charter schools—invested $25.5 million in the KIPP Foundation. Today, KIPP has over 250 schools serving more than 110,000 students, most of whom are Black and Brown—and poor. To Paul's and Pamela's knowledge, Ball was never compensated for her ideas and songs that formed the foundation of the largest charter school network in the country. They told me that no one from KIPP has ever reached out to them to help uplift the work of their mother's legacy or compensate her children for their mother's remarkable and distinctive contributions to KIPP.

The best-known charter school network, KIPP, is characterized by longer school days, mandatory summer school, and strict student conduct rules with zero-tolerance policies. In 2016, researchers found that charter schools like KIPP suspend students at a much higher rate than public schools, with a disproportionate number of suspensions involving Black students and Black students with disabilities.[3] The same study found that 235 charter schools suspended more than 50 percent of their students with disabilities.[4] The researchers concluded that charter schools' "deep disparities in discipline practices" ultimately lead to a charter-to-prison pipeline. KIPP is also known for its infamous slogan, "No excuses." In his book, *Work Hard, Be Hard: Journeys Through "No Excuses" Teaching*, education professor Jim Horn documents the enormous amount of pressure that KIPP schools create for students. For students at KIPP, failure is not an option, and some adults have little concern for the stress put on children learning in an environment of "No excuses." KIPP officials have only recently begun to rethink long-standing discipline policies in response to growing criticism.[5]

"They took my mother's ideas and took something that was done out of love and turned it into straight profit," Paul told me. "I feel like it's been commercialized. It's all about the money." He added, "There is not one KIPP school named after my mother." To date, no KIPP school has chosen to name itself after Ball. Harriett Ball's name appears in one place in the KIPP network. Each year, the KIPP Foundation, a nonprofit co-founded by Levin to train and develop KIPP school educators and support teaching and learning in KIPP schools, recognizes ten teachers in honor of Ball. The award comes with a $10,000 prize. According to Mathews, Levin and Feinberg asked Ball to join them in the making of KIPP several times. Her reply was always the same, "I can't do it, I have four kids. I have a mortgage, and no child support. I need a salary of at least what I make now before I can do this." In response to Levin and Feinberg using the name KIPP, Mathews writes, Ball told her two mentees, "I'm going to let you use it," she said, meaning the Harriett Ball playbook, the songs, the chants, the games. It was all theirs, with one condition. "If anyone asks you where you got it, you tell them you got it from me."[6]

Levin and Feinberg received great acclaim and national attention for KIPP, even appearing on *The Oprah Winfrey Show*. Pamela told me her mother thought she was going to be on Oprah, "but she never appeared." She recalls her mother's pain and disappointment at not appearing on the show. Seeing Levin and Feinberg sitting on Winfrey's couch was especially difficult for Paul—appearing on the show had been his mother's dream. The episode included a video of Ball teaching, but she watched the show from home. Paul said his mother was "happy" to see her teaching video on the show, but he cried because he felt she should have been there. "They should have been sitting next to my mom on the show," Paul said.

In my first conversation with him, Paul said, "They took my mother's ideas, Bill Gates gave millions, and my mom is struggling. My mom's back is going out from scoliosis—she gave her life to teaching." The night after my second conversation with Paul, it was clear that he was continuing to struggle with the disconnect between his mother's ideas being used by KIPP and the lack of public recognition and compensation for her. That night, he sent me a video of a 2017 interview where Levin describes the insurmountable impact Ball made on his teaching career and KIPP. In it, Levin said, "She was an oasis, the rest of the school was a mess . . . She took me under her wing, I learned that we as teachers can always find a way, always engage the head and the heart. The other thing I learned that was so crucial to our success is that she always met kids were they were . . . The third thing I learned from Harriet was how to love . . . Everyone felt like Harriet loved them for who they were."[7]

In the video, Levin then goes on to explain why Ball couldn't join him and Feinberg at the onset of KIPP. Much of what he says echoes Mathews' book. Levin said, "Everything I know about teaching is from Harriett. Fast-forward, 18 months from then . . . Mike Feinberg and I started KIPP in 1994. We asked Harriet to come with us, but she couldn't; her kids were still at home, KIPP was high risk back then. We were not sure if we could guarantee her salary. It was very, very stressful. It was easy to do. We were young, single; if it didn't work out we would go back and be teachers. It was much more of a complicated risk, she felt like she had to stay."[8] He continues that the only request Ball made of him was to "share" her teaching methods. He ends the video saying, "There is no KIPP without Harriet."[9] In the message accompanying the video he sent, Paul sent along a question: "How can he say this and not expect to pay royalties for what they built on my mom's intellectual property?"

Books have been written about Levin and Feinberg's education model, they have won prestigious awards, and honorary degrees have been bestowed on the men. In short, they grew influential by watering down and co-opting Ball's teaching methods. KIPP's operating procedures are standard for charter schools. KIPP's national board of directors is composed of wealthy philanthropists, corporate foundations, and Wall Street hedge fund managers whose beliefs about education mirror those of the post–Civil War era, when schools for Black children focused on discipline, character education, rudimentary academic skills, and "total compliance to White economic demands."[10]

Civil rights attorney Shavar Jeffries sits on KIPP's national board and is the president of Democrats for Education Reform. This powerful lobbying group advocates for school choice and the expansion of charter schools at the highest levels of government. Reed Hastings, the CEO of Netflix, also sits on KIPP's board of directors. Hastings is a vehement supporter of charter schools and has invested millions in the destabilization of public schools. While speaking at a California Charter Schools Association meeting in

2014, he told the audience that elected school boards should be eliminated.[11] As a California State Board of Education member, he opposed bilingual education, limits to the number of new charter schools, and charter school accountability measures.[12]

Hastings is also a major financial backer of the charter school network Rocketship, which approaches student learning through what the organization calls "Learning Labs," in which students learn from computer programs while uncertified, low-paid "instructional lab specialists" supervise large groups.[13] According to Richard Whitmire, author of *On the Rocketship: How Top Charter Schools Are Pushing the Envelope,* a "school such as Rocketship Mosaic could successfully serve 630 students with only 16 teachers plus aides." In 2014, the Obama administration granted $2 million to Rocketship to expand its model.

Carrie Walton Penner, the granddaughter of Walmart founder Sam Walton, also sits on KIPP's board. The Walton Family Foundation has given more than $1.3 billion in the past twenty years to K–12 education in the U.S.[14] In 2016, the foundation announced that it would commit another $1 billion to expand charter schools and school choice. The foundation is so committed to dismantling public education that it made this investment even in an economic climate that led to Walmart closing 269 stores nationwide. Both Walmart's business philosophy and the Walton funding of school choice rest on the idea of competition.[15] Walmart's business model shuts down the competition by pricing out smaller, locally owned stores. The Walton family applies the same approach to education by funding charters that move public money to private entities and thereby close public schools.[16]

In his autobiography, *Made in America,* Sam Walton wrote that he was concerned about America's public school system and its ability to compete on the global stage. When Walton died in 1992, his son John took over the family foundation. John Walton told Philanthropy Roundtable that he read *A Nation at Risk* in 1983 and shared the influential report with his family members. "I'd like to see an all-out revolution in education," John Walton remembers his father declaring. John Walton wanted to treat parents as customers and school choice as their marketplace. John Walton and family members were also followers of Milton and Rose Friedman.[17] In the late 1990s, the Walton Family Foundation funded the Friedman Foundation, now called EdChoice. In the process, the Walton family has become billion-dollar defenders of school choice, especially charter schools.[18] The foundation has also given millions to Teach for America.

White philanthropists have thus co-opted the inspirational teaching methods of Harriett Ball—a Black woman whose life's work was to incite excitement in the hearts and minds of Black and Brown children. When Ball told her students, "Knowledge is power, power is money," she could never have imagined that the powerful would misuse her philosophy as a tool to profit from schools whose policy is punishment for Black children. She could never have envisioned that her inspiring raps steeped in Blackness would be co-opted to the point where White philanthropists who never even knew her name would utter her words as they worked to pillage public education for their own interests. And she could never have thought that under the guise of her teaching methods, an organization like the Eli and Edythe Broad Foundation would invest millions of dollars in driving market-based values like competition, efficiency, and effectiveness into the classrooms of thousands of Black children, or that billionaires like the Broads would create a two-year residency program that turns "private sector leaders" into urban school leaders and superintendents.[19]

The Broad Foundation's investments go beyond simply financially supporting charter schools; they also create a pipeline for corporate executives to run urban school districts. The idea is similar to Hastings's concept of school boards run by corporate executives, but the Broads are building the infrastructure for their takeover. The Broads are not alone in transforming the teacher pipeline: the NewSchools Venture Fund, or NSVF (which I discuss throughout this book), is also creating "teacher education academies" to train teachers outside of higher education. Their goal: to disseminate ideas of market-based education solutions within schools.[20] NSVF is also pushing for federal legislation that would deregulate the field of education, favoring educational entrepreneurs.[21] The calculated gifts and initiatives of mammoth foundations and philanthropic organizations help "sustain a crusade" to undermine and undo public education.[22]

While KIPP was gaining national attention, Ball invested her pension and borrowed against her mortgage to start her own business to help teachers improve their craft. She left teaching and she had no start-up money. Paul told me that his mother resigned when a White teacher at her school was named Teacher of the Year—school officials and teachers felt Ball had won the award too many times in a row. Paul remembers sitting in the back of his mother's green Lincoln Town Car, listening to her cry after she quit. "She slammed the door and told me, 'Baby, when you get older, you may not understand right now, but understand this: you are always going to have to work two to three times harder than somebody with brighter skin than you. I am not saying it's right. I am not saying it's fair. It's just the way it is, baby.'"

Ball died of a heart attack at age sixty-four in 2011. Paul blames her death on "stress and heartbreak." He told me, "She was happy that thousands of students were being taught with her ideas," but she faced too much financial stress raising four kids by herself, debilitated by chronic illness. After teaching for thirty-five years, Ball became a motivational speaker and was able to teach her methods to thousands of educators, despite never having received the millions of dollars in donations that two young and inexperienced White men would collect by using her ideas. One of the most infuriating details of my conversations with Paul and Pamela was the revelation that KIPP offered their mother a teaching job at one of their schools in Houston. At the time, Ball was in her early sixties, and her health was deteriorating. The offer was to teach alongside others who were using her methods at a school that would not exist had it not been for her. "My mother should have been training the teachers—Harriett Ball University," Paul said. "But no, they wanted the show, they wanted the credit, they wanted the glory." He told me his mother said she'd "rather be homeless than work for them as a teacher."

I reached out to the KIPP Foundation to give them the opportunity to respond to Paul's account of his mother not attending *The Oprah Show* in person, along with questions about compensation. I asked if Harriett Ball was compensated; if so, how much the compensation was; and if Ball ever signed anything giving KIPP the rights to her songs.[23] I was initially told by the vice president of communications of KIPP Foundation that Levin wouldn't be addressing my questions, but the KIPP Foundation provided the statement below.

> We disagree with Mr. Paul Franks' account of Harriett Ball's relationship with KIPP's Co-founder Dave Levin and the KIPP Foundation. From the very beginning, Ms. Ball was compensated for her work with the KIPP Foundation and repeatedly offered a leadership position. Mr. Levin and Ms. Ball remained close friends throughout her life.
>
> At the KIPP Foundation, we have always honored Ms. Ball, her incredible teaching talents, and the role she played in KIPP's history. She was invited often to speak at large KIPP Foundation events around the country and she shared her knowledge as a consultant with countless KIPP schools. When she passed, we established the

Harriett Ball Excellence in Teaching Award so her legacy
would live on forever. This is our most prestigious teaching award, which annually recognizes ten outstanding educators from across the KIPP Public School network with
a $10,000 prize.

After receiving KIPP's statement, I called Paul and read it
to him. He immediately replied, "This is a slap in the face. My
mother was disappointed and betrayed by David." He concluded
with a final question, raised by the statement I'd just shared with
him: "What is 'compensation' when my mother's intellectual
property built KIPP?"

KIPP Foundation's statement does not include Feinberg because in 2018, the foundation fired Feinberg after allegations
of sexual assault of a minor and two allegations of sexual harassment. The story of White philanthropists using education
to advance their racist and anti-Black agenda—while acquiring
fame, wealth, and power—is not unique to Levin and Feinberg:
it's the story of Black education in this country under the rule
of White philanthropy.

Cooling-Out Agencies

It may seem as if White philanthropists have good intentions
that are simply misguided. But the history of White philanthropy, especially in education, involves depoliticization, obedience, and the maintenance of social order. Race philanthropy
emerged in the late 1800s as foundations became "power brokers" that drove the "state's marketplace of ideas" after the Civil
War.[24] Foundations gained popularity during a time when the
U.S. government provided modest assistance to public services.[25] Foundations swooped in to support overcrowded cities
that needed "sanitation facilities, roads, hospitals." As they saw

it, newly freed Black people, particularly in the South, needed a robust industrious education to fulfill labor demands and impede social change that was not "acceptable" to the White status quo.[26] Foundations were created as supposedly egalitarian entities. Even in their earliest days, foundations did the bidding of the über-rich and government agencies of their time, whose moral and economic values throughout history have been tightly aligned without much public scrutiny.

As Edward Berman wrote in his book, *The Influence of the Carnegie, Ford, and Rockefeller Foundations on American Foreign Policy: The Ideology of Philanthropy*, foundations were created to:

> Preclude the call for more radical structural change; and the creation through education institutions of a worldwide network of elites whose approach to governance and change would be efficient, professional, moderate, incremental, and nonthreatening to the class interests of those who, like Messrs, Carnegie, Ford, Rockefeller, had established the foundations.[27]

Foundations, writes Robert Arnove, "represent relatively unregulated and unaccountable concentrations of power and wealth" that "serve as 'cooling-out' agencies, delaying and preventing more radical, structural change."[28] The Carnegie, Ford, and Rockefeller Foundations viewed Black education as a "political proposition" to control Black progress after the Civil War.[29] William H. Watkins, author of *The White Architects of Black Education*, argues that thanks to foundations, "Black education helped define and forge the race relations that shaped the entire twentieth century and beyond."[30]

After the Civil War, as the first system of taxpayer-supported schools opened across the South, White Southerners did everything possible to ensure Black education got the smallest amount of educational dollars and that Black children got the least amount of education.[31] The historical record leaves no doubt of this. In the post-Reconstruction era, the state of Alabama limited funding for Black schools to revenue collected from charging Black adults a poll tax for the privilege of voting.[32] Kentucky refused to build schools for Black children, essentially ensuring the state had no legal obligation to pay for schools that did not exist.[33] Across the South, Black people were lynched for demanding rights and equal educational funding and access. Mississippi's governor told his constituents, "Money spent today for the maintenance of public schools for the Negroes is robbery of the white man, and a waste upon the Negro."[34]

But White businessmen like George Peabody, John D. Rockefeller Sr., and Henry Ford were concerned that the South would fall behind economically without obedient and industrious—and educated—Negroes. Consequently, these men formed foundations that were part of a "political strategy" to establish order in the South.[35] U.S. representative J. L. M. Curry, a Rockefeller Foundation's General Education Board member, declared: "If you do not lift them [Black people] up they will drag you down to industrial bankruptcy, social degradation, and political corruption."[36] Race philanthropy, therefore, was about controlling Black bodies through foundations that acted as separate yet ideologically united arms of the government. The General Education Board was "chartered by Congress to shape the public education system in the United States, and . . . provide seed money to enable the construction of over 5,000 rural schools for children in the South."[37] Men with wealth and power, among them Peabody, Rockefeller, and Ford, knew that Black people "would occupy a permanent place in the socioeconomic life of the nation," and they wanted to be the architects of newly freed slaves' "socioeconomic life" by controlling the type of education they received.[38] Vocational or industrial education was beneficial and nonthreatening to White people. Vocational education for Black people in the South was promoted and heavily funded by the General Education Board. According to American studies professor No-liwe Rooks, the board "told white politicians that they should not worry about Black children gaining education, because whites would not have to pay for the buildings, land, labor, or materials associated with building 'Black' schools."[39] Industrial training institutes like Hampton and Tuskegee were viewed as investments in Black people's obedience and self-help.[40] The General Education Board endured until the early 1960s; by the end of that decade, foundations were financing social protests in the U.S. to ensure civil rights would not interfere with the status quo.

In *Black Awakening in Capitalist America,* Robert Allen documents how the Ford Foundation financially backed leaders and organizations that shifted the civil rights movement toward Black capitalism instead of liberation. In 1972, a study found that prominent foundations' philanthropic interest in Black people was a "humanitarian concern," not a "comment to the principle of racial equality."[41] By the 1980s, the "Decade of Greed" of the Reagan era, charitable giving by individuals and corporations jumped dramatically, as corporate profits were at an all-time high. Corporate giving more than doubled from 1955 to 1989, from $1.9 billion to $5.3 billion.[42] Corporate America was more generous in the 1980s partly because Reagan froze the minimum wage at $3.35 an hour during his tenure; as a result, the number of Americans living in poverty rose from twenty-five million in 1979 to thirty-two million in 1988. Reagan also deregulated the savings-and-loan industry, which allowed banks to provide adjustable-rate mortgage loans, creating subprime loans. The wealthy, meanwhile, benefited from tax cuts, and spending for programs that aided working-class families was slashed. In corporate America, the fact that CEOs were making thirty times more than their employees was celebrated as an achievement. Despite Reagan's theory of "trickle-down economics," most Americans did not benefit from wealthy people accruing yet more money. The Decade of Greed also launched an era of conspicuous consumption. The appeal of its propaganda was so powerful that the justice movement suffered; rather than being urged to rebel, Black inner-city kids were seduced by dreams of getting rich and famous—and aspiring to Whiteness.

"Champagne wishes and caviar dreams" was the mantra of the popular TV show *Lifestyles of the Rich and Famous,* and it captured the mood of the times. Debuting in 1984, the show let everyday Americans gawk at the extravagance of the very wealthy. Robin Leach, an English entertainment reporter, narrated the show. His English accent was meant to add an air of sophistication that made the opulence even more unattainable and desirable. The program was a garish spectacle of riches, including million-dollar yachts, luxury hotel suites, and mansions lined with gold bricks. Joan Collins, Brooke Shields, and Donald Trump were among those flaunting their wealth. *Lifestyles,* writes Michael Grasso, was "pure envy-bait, a goal with no visible pathway to achieve [it]."[43] I, along with many other Black inner-city kids, watched the show. We dreamed of one day accessing the privileges of the wealthy, still believing the lie that we could have a piece of what Leach was selling.

Kids in my neighborhood also dressed head to toe in the flashy clothes of fashion designer Ralph Lauren, born Ralph Lifshitz to Jewish immigrant parents in the Bronx. Lauren's Polo brand satisfied our aspirational cravings, making us feel rich as we sipped Kool-Aid and dreamed hood dreams. The Polo logo on our chests was a symbol of status that spoke to our desire to get rich, to fulfill the American dream. All this yearning for wealth came at a time when the Reagan administration was cutting funding to public libraries, public schools, public housing, public transportation, public hospitals, and basically any anti-poverty program funded by the federal government—and while corporate America was rebranding Ford's, Peabody's, and Rockefeller's ideas of philanthropy to what they now called *strategic philanthropy.*

In 1999, Reynold Levy, the first president of the AT&T Foundation, published *Give and Take: A Candid Account of Corporate Philanthropy,* which detailed his thinking on strategic philanthropy. He wrote:

> The best way to keep philanthropy vibrant, well regarded, and well funded in a corporation is to demonstrate its regular contributions to business success. That means that good corporate philanthropy incorporates both business interest and societal need.[44]

Reports surfaced in 2018 that part of the Koch brothers' strategic philosophy involved funding a social studies curriculum from the Bill of Rights Institute; the group promoted "limited government, religious freedom, free-market economics and—worst of all—a revisionist version of the history of slavery that paints it as a necessary evil to further freedom and democracy," which would serve as a foreshadowing of the banning of AP African American history, book bans, and critical race theory legislative bans.[45] At that time, more than five million students and fifty thousand teachers had interfaced with the curriculum, according to the Bill of Rights Institute.[46]

Frustrated with the scraps of school choice, many Black families have decided to leave public education, opting to homeschool their children. *The New Yorker* documented the trend in a 2021 piece, uncovering disturbing details.[47] For instance, a parent applied for a $25,000 grant from the National Parents Union (NPU), a parent organization dedicated to empowering parents and purchasing supplies for their homeschooling network.[48]

The money was granted through the NPU, but it came from the Walton Family Foundation and the Charles Koch Institute, two families who have donated billions to weakening public education. The Waltons and Kochs invest in Black homeschooling to advance the erosion of public education, even if it means funding Black people. When asked if she was bothered by receiving money from the Kochs, a Black mother replied, "I guess the bigger question is, why don't we have enough resources so that we don't have to get money from them? It bothers me, yes—but why do they have so much money that they get to fund all of our shit?"[49]

By the 1990s, as personal computers, TVs, VCRs, and technology once thought of as accessible only to big companies became universal items in American homes, a strategic philanthropy leader emerged who would wield his power and wealth on a global stage like no other: Bill Gates.

The Ringmaster of Education Reform

Like the billionaire philanthropists who came before him, Bill Gates got into philanthropy out of self-interest. As Rob Larson writes in *Bit Tyrants: The Political Economy of Silicon Valley*, Gates needed to repair his image after Microsoft's antitrust trial in the late 1990s. Gates was seen as "ruthless" and "predatory," using "monopolistic" business practices.[50] During the trial, video depositions showed Gates as "arrogant, evasive and sullen."[51] Rebranding himself as a social justice savior, Gates stepped down as CEO and contributed $20.3 billion to the Bill & Melinda Gates Foundation during the trial, making it the world's largest private charity.[52] The foundation's strategic philanthropy is so well funded that it has come to serve as a power broker for the wealthy engaging in what John D. Rockefeller III termed "venture philanthropy."[53] The Gates Foundation, like those of the

Kochs, Waltons, and Broads, has great influence over public policy, public health, and public education, which in turn weakens our democracy, reduces civic life for the most vulnerable, and furthers the dismantling of the public sector—especially public education. Through the movement of school choice, the Gateses and Kochs—Democrats *and* Republicans—have become one coalition auctioning off public education through venture philanthropy.

Regardless of political affiliations, major foundations are investing in the same educational venture: to advance the privatization of public education backed by the U.S. government.[54] The grants they give out to charter schools, Teach for America, and other educational entrepreneurs encroach on public education by shifting public funds to the free market. Venture philanthropy is a way the reformers can attack public education with no government oversight and little public scrutiny—they are allowed then to apply their ruthless business approaches to their philanthropy.[55]

Of the major foundations funding venture philanthropy, the Gates Foundation receives the lion's share of attention because of its size and scope. The foundation spends billions of dollars annually on global health initiatives, global economic development, and education in the U.S. The Gates Foundation has also become a driver of educational policy and reform, especially during the Obama administration, as I outlined in chapter 4. The foundation operates as a tangential arm of the U.S. public education system, informing education policy and curricula, as well as the expansion of charter schools from multiple entry points. Gates may be a tech whiz, but he has no teaching experience. However, he is viewed as an educational leader because of his vast wealth and the belief that extremely rich people, through philanthropy, have all the answers.

What is astonishing about Bill and Melinda Gates's record on educational reform is that they have failed time and time again. Their foundation has spent billions of dollars in failed educational initiatives. According to *The Washington Post*, "For years, they [Bill and Melinda Gates] have spent a fortune trying to shape public education policy, successfully leveraging public funding to support their projects, but never having the kind of academic success they had hoped for."[56] For example, the Gates Foundation bankrolled the Common Core movement that was popular during the early years of the Obama administration. The foundation spent $200 million and pulled significant political weight in convincing state governments to make costly systemic changes to state standards.[57] Bill Gates himself played a leading role in revamping the country's teaching standards.[58] He provided the money and operational structure to bring states together to work on the standards; he also funded teachers' unions, business organizations, and think tanks on both sides of the political aisle, including liberal groups like the Center for American Progress and conservative organizations such as the American Legislative Exchange Council. Ultimately, those disparate groups "who routinely disagree on nearly every issue accepted Gates money and found common ground on the Common Core."[59]

The Common Core movement was colloquially referred to as "Obamacore," but it was the brainchild of Gates; many educational insiders at the time viewed the billionaire as the de facto secretary of education. The Obama administration attached the quest for Common Core standards to its Race to the Top initiative, calling it "college and career ready" standards. Gates spent another $2.7 million to help states write their Race to the Top applications for the $4.3 billion in federal grant money.[60] Some applications even included Gates-funded research. Right in line with venture philanthropy, Gates told supporters that classrooms as digital learning spaces were a benefit of the Common Core. Microsoft then partnered with Pearson, the world's largest educational publisher, to build Pearson's Common Core classroom materials, which could be loaded onto Microsoft's tablets.[61] By 2018, 22 percent of all laptops and tablets in K–12 classrooms came from Microsoft.[62] *Washington Post* reporter Lyndsey Layton noted that in 2014:

> Bill and Melinda Gates, Obama and [Secretary of Education] Arne Duncan are parents of school-age children, although none of those children attend schools that use the Common Core standards. The Gates and Obama children attend private schools, while Duncan's children go to public school in Virginia, one of four states that never adopted the Common Core.

Once again, these educational reforms were good enough for poor Black children, but not the children of the reformers.

After more than forty states signed on to the Common Core, and millions of Gates's money was spent, the initiative fizzled out in 2019 as the conservative right made it a wedge issue, calling it a "federal takeover of schools" and "the silent erosion of our civil liberties."[63]

Before pushing for Common Core, the Gates Foundation funded a $650 million initiative to create small high schools, which they believed would increase student achievement and graduation rates.[64] In 2007, the Gates Foundation gave Atlanta Public Schools $10.5 million to transform all its high schools into small learning communities. While Arne Duncan was CEO of Chicago Public Schools, the Bill & Melinda Gates Foundation invested nearly $20 million in the small high school model and millions more on efforts to revamp the Chicago Public Schools' curricula.

Ultimately, the Gates Foundation acknowledged that its small schools experiment was a bust. The model led to only a "modest increase in graduation rates."[65] Bill Gates wrote in his 2009 annual letter that the small school model "fell short" of expectations.[66] The foundation decided to turn its attention to teacher evaluation systems and assessments. In collaboration with three public school districts and four charter management organizations, the Gates Foundation and its partners spent $575 million on a project that used student test scores to evaluate teachers. After millions spent and countless hours of students' learning time wasted, the assessment tool failed to improve student achievement. The Gates Foundation pursued the project despite warnings from assessment experts that tying student test scores to teacher evaluation presented serious problems.

The foundation subsequently released a 526-page report outlining failure after failure—equivalent to more than a million dollars a page. In 2013, Bill Gates acknowledged that the Common Core initiative was not successful, and in 2018, he conceded that the teacher evaluation project had also failed.[67]

While Bill and Melinda Gates were telling the education world what is best for Black children, the Gates Foundation Trust, which manages the foundation's endowment, invested millions in the private prison industry. In 2012, they had $2.2 million invested in a Florida-based prison company, the GEO Group.[68] Activists rallied outside of the foundation, demanding transparency and calling out the foundation for investing in communities of color and the prison industrial complex at the same time, which flew in the face of the foundation's stated commitment to social justice and human rights.[69]

There is, however, one initiative that Bill and Melinda Gates got right: the Gates Millennium Scholars Program. In 1999, the foundation committed $1 billion to finance the college educations of twenty thousand high-achieving, low-income students of color. After completing their undergraduate programs, Gates Millennium Scholars could receive support for a graduate degree in one of the following disciplines: computer science, education, engineering, library science, mathematics, public health, or science. The program has awarded $1.2 billion in scholarship money, selected one thousand students a year, and has a 96.2 percent average first-year retention rate.[70] Unfortunately, the 2016 cohort is the last group of students that will be granted funding. But I was fortunate to have the opportunity to discuss its impact with one of its earliest participants. Joe graduated high school in 2000 as one of the first Gates Scholars. He told me that he would be dead without the Gates Millennium Scholars Program.

The "Golden Child"

Joe jumped right into our conversation with surprising ease. I have known him for more than ten years. He's a loving father and husband, a proud Morehouse man, but we have never spoken about his childhood. "My family's story is around crack," he began by saying. "My father died when I was ten from a crack addiction." His father was a Black veteran who had post-traumatic stress disorder. Joe said his father took many prescription pills daily to deal with his condition. Joe was only in fifth grade when his father died. In trying to cope with the loss, Joe began to lash out at school. His behavior was so violent that he was asked to leave for the last month of school. Forced to care for six children without a father, Joe's mother moved the family to the poorest neighborhood in Columbus, Ohio.

Joe attended a high school full of poor Black and White kids. He told me that poverty proved a common ground even amid racial tension: "We were all in this melting pot," he said. "Clearly, there were racial dynamics, but we were all so poor it didn't matter. Summertime, we would all just go outside, knock on each other's doors, and walk to get free lunch, then we would go to the swimming pool because it cost twenty-five cents, and we would stay there from 11:00 a.m. to 7:00 p.m. That was our lives. . . . we were so poor everybody linked up." Joe's school had one "overworked" resource officer, but he joked that the school was too poor for metal detectors. "People brought guns to school; there were stabbings at our school," he said. "There was no real opportunity to learn. . . . For me, it was a place to eat. I would eat breakfast and two lunches."

Academically, Joe soared above his peers. Many of his siblings never finished high school, and his younger brother stopped going to school by middle school. "I looked around, and all my brothers and sisters had dropped out," he said. "They were either in jail, prostitution, or drugs. . . . My whole family were sex workers and drug addicts. . . . Teachers felt horrible for us. . . . They looked and said, 'Here is one kid, Joe, who actually still comes to school.' So many people had sympathy for me. Teachers were willing to do anything. They would give me rides to school, give me food, take me out to restaurants, show me how to tie a tie. Education was the only thing in my life I got attention from an adult where someone was not trying to molest me or rob me. That's what made me get so doubled down on education. I was not a nerd or Rain Man with all these abilities or a grand chess master—I had adults that cared about me."

Joe was hooked on all the attention he received for being a good student, which made him want to excel even more. He didn't care that the attention was out of pity—he loved it. "I did whatever it took to continue to have people talk to me at school. I wanted that positive feedback loop." Joe needed the teachers, but he felt like they also needed him. "My entire education was surrounded by these people who have been teachers for twenty-five to thirty years—decades—and many had never seen success. They didn't see kids who made it out of our school. My high school started out with four hundred kids—eighty graduated." Joe felt like he was living in a *Lifetime* movie. He became the "golden child." He was a star athlete and a straight-A student at a failing school. The city newspaper wrote articles about him because no one expected a student from his school to excel.

In sixth grade, his life changed, thanks to Ohio State University's Young Scholars Program (YSP). Founded in 1988 and funded by the university, the program helps "academically talented, first-generation students with high financial need to advance their goal of pursuing higher education." YSP recruits low-income students from Ohio's nine largest urban public school districts (Akron, Canton, Cincinnati, Cleveland, Columbus, Dayton, Lorain, Toledo, and Youngstown) to be the "first in their family to receive a bachelor's degree." During summers, Joe and thousands of other low-income kids from around Ohio would spend two months on the Ohio State University campus in Columbus—for free and with a monthly stipend. Students who meet program requirements and maintain good grades receive a scholarship to OSU.

"Black, White, Asian, Latino—you just had to be extremely poor," said Joe. "I got to leave my neighborhood for a couple of months with kids who wanted to leave their environment, too, and now we have created this pure community of love and education." The Columbus chapter of YSP employed roughly thirty staff members who would visit high schools and check on students monthly. "You couldn't get lost," Joe said. "They would find you."

The sense of community was a welcome contrast to Joe's home, where the pain and trauma of drugs, loss, and poverty weighed heavily on his family. Joe said his brothers and sisters would fight almost every day in "a way where we were trying to kill each other." He believes the only reason his family was not separated and put into foster care is that his mother is White. "My mom would always call the cops to break up these huge fights, like brawls, and child services never stepped in." Joe recalled that his mother worked a minimum-wage job, but she could still secure a car and home loan. "She was just a White country lady, and no one thought differently until her Black kids showed [up]."

Joe had another gift that set him apart from his siblings: he was a good standardized test taker. "I was neurotic about education. This was the one thing opening up for me. I wanted to get ninety-nines and one hundreds on everything, and I did well on tests." In his senior year, Joe was set to go to OSU, but another program that helped high school students complete their college applications and financial aid paperwork told Joe about HBCUs. "These two Black women started naming all these colleges I had never heard of and told me I would be great at Morehouse," he said. "A week or two later, they did a fundraiser, got me a plane ticket, and sent me to Morehouse for a one-week program for high school seniors." After his trip to Morehouse, a teacher approached him with an application for the Gates Millennium Scholars program, which would allow him to attend Morehouse. Joe did not understand the gravity of the decision these teachers were making for him, but he trusted them. "All of a sudden, teachers were sitting me down to write these essays for this scholarship," he said. At one point, the entire high school English department reviewed Joe's essay.

When it was announced that Joe would be a Gates Millennium Scholar—among the first in the nation—he said it felt like *Charlie and the Chocolate Factory.* "I started applying to colleges all over the country because I now had the money to pay for it. But my teachers told me, 'If you get into Morehouse, you are going there.'" He was accepted into Morehouse, where his roughly $40,000 tuition would be covered in full; he'd also receive another $10,000 a semester for living expenses. The morning after his high school graduation, teachers put Joe on a plane to Morehouse for a summer program so he could start college classes early. "They put me on the first flight to Atlanta, 6:00 a.m. . . . I got to Morehouse, and my school is paid for, my books are paid for, my computer is paid for, and I have money to live." When Joe came home for winter break, he paid his mother's bills with his Gates money.

The Gates Millennium Scholar Program routinely checked on Joe, just as YSP had. He attended national symposiums of the Gates Millennium Scholars, where he realized he was "a part of something more than just an injection of cash." The Gates scholarship, he said, made all the difference in his life. After graduating from Morehouse with a bachelor's degree in finance, Joe also used the Gates scholarship to get a master's degree in education. "Bill Gates let me live six years without any bills while I was getting my education," he said.

Joe does not doubt that if he had stayed in Columbus for college, he would not have graduated. To Joe, Morehouse is his mecca. The college saved his life, he said. "How do I verbalize how an institution with all these different Black men stopped me from dying? I would have died, I know that, or become a crackhead like my father. I met all these other Black boys who were straight-A students like me. . . . I still get goose bumps thinking about how that place put its arm around me and would not let me leave. I am indebted to that place." When I asked Joe if he has survivor's remorse, his answer was poignant: "Oh yes. I cry a lot, I am crying in the middle of the day in front of my kids, and they are like, 'Dad, what's wrong?' and I am hugging them because they did something amazing. . . . I am so sad for all the people who did not get out of my high school. That shit breaks my heart. I am about to cry now. I miss those people. I do not deserve this. Imposter syndrome, survivor's remorse, yes. People meet me and think I am polished and went to private schools. . . . No, I am hurt and broken, and I feel guilty as hell that not only did my family not make it out but [neither did] my best friends. It's a great horrible feeling."

To the outside world, Joe's life is a success. He lives in one of the most expensive neighborhoods in Boston, has an impressive résumé, and has a beautiful wife and four amazing sons. But in many ways, Joe's life in Columbus haunts him. Joe told me Columbus is the "fire in my belly to even make me pursue success." But that success has come with a heavy mental price. Joe often walks into power rooms feeling like an *imposter*. Joe and I ended our interview with me sharing that I, too, suffer from survivor's guilt. I have been in therapy for seven years, and I hope Joe one day takes up my recommendation to seek help, too.

Extraordinary to Be White Ordinary

Joe's story is heartbreaking, but the feel-good ending makes us all sleep better because we can point to Joe as a success story of public education. Joe survived an educational system made for poor Black children to achieve not because of the system but despite it, and he lives with the guilt of surviving. It takes a village of loving, caring, and committed individuals working for well-funded programs to get one Joe off to college. But there are countless Black students in low-income neighborhoods that will never get the opportunity to go off to college and, if they do go to college, leave debt-free like Joe. The friends Joe left behind were just as deserving as Joe, but opportunities for kids living in poverty created by policies of divestment are few and far between. Reformers will highlight one or two Joes a year, while thousands of Joes are left behind because they have to be extraordinary to be White ordinary. Reform tells us that poor Black kids are left behind because of merit, but merit is another myth to preserve White mediocrity. Black children work twice as hard and have to be three times as good to get not even half of what Whiteness affords.

Data from 2012 showed that four years after graduation, Black college graduates, on average, owe $52,726 in student debt compared to White college graduates, who owe closer to $28,006.[71] Nearly 90 percent of Black college students take out loans to attend college.[72] Not to mention that Black parents are more likely than parents of any other racial group (with the exception of "Other," which often includes folx from the African diaspora) to take on Parent PLUS loans.[73] Many of these Black parents still have their own student loans to repay, while taking on portions of their children's college debt. Due to centuries of racist and anti-Black housing, banking, and labor policies, Black families have substantially less generational wealth than White families. Another reason Black college graduates have more debt is that they are lured into for-profit colleges. Professor Tressie McMillan Cottom, author of *Lower Ed: The Troubling Rise of For-Profit Colleges in the New Economy,* writes that for-profit colleges are "predicated on inequality."[74] For-profit colleges prey on economically unstable people seeking upward mobility through higher education. Flashy and strategically placed online ads and commercials target Black folx aspiring to be first-generation college students who need flexible, on-demand education. For-profit colleges capitalize on these conditions and poor folx' dreams of social mobility by charging more than traditional colleges and pressuring students to take out private loans with higher interest rates and none of the protections that come with federal loans. In 2018, former president Trump paid a $25 million settlement to the students of Trump University for using "false advertising and high-pressure sales" tactics to entice people into purchasing expensive seminars that "promised to teach them the 'secrets of success' in the real estate industry . . . A 'one-year apprenticeship' at the educational institute cost $1,495; a 'membership' over $10,000; and 'Gold Elite' classes ran $35,000."[75]

On average, in 2020/2021, a four-year for-profit college costs $15,780, compared to a public four-year college that costs $10,570 a year.[76] Moreover, Black college graduates make less than their

White coworkers with the same level of education. Even America's solution to college affordability, merit-based scholarships, is undergirded by racism, White privilege, and the lies of fairness and equal access. Researchers found that many states awarded broad-based merit scholarships that do not consider financial need.[77] White students make up 72 percent of all scholarships, although they represent roughly 66 percent of applicants.[78] Merit-based scholarships assume that all students have equal access to educational learning environments that lead to academic success (extracurricular activities, experienced teachers, SAT and ACT preparation, and Advanced Placement classes). In reality, Black students are more likely to be taught by a first-year teacher and attend schools with a higher percentage of uncertified teachers. For example, "in Massachusetts, 32 percent of Black students attend schools with high percentages of uncertified teachers compared to 13 percent of non-Black students. In Mississippi, 25 percent of Black students attend schools with high percentages of uncertified teachers compared to 7 percent of non-Black students."[79] Black students attend underfunded schools with more police officers than extracurricular activities. Merit-based scholarships help the rich stay rich. The poor and Black are stuck with inflated tuition and high-interest loans with degrees from unaccredited colleges that employers are not moved to recognize. Between 1995 and 2004, the amount colleges awarded in merit-based scholarships more than tripled, while need-based scholarships saw only a marginal increase.[80] Joe's story is why we should cancel student debt, make college free, and provide funding while students are in college to ensure their well-being and retention.

In 2020, the Bill & Melinda Gates Foundation released its annual newsletter. In it, they told supporters, "We certainly understand why many people are skeptical about the idea of billionaire philanthropists designing classroom innovations or setting education policy. Frankly, we are, too." The letter continued, "The fact that progress has been harder to achieve than we hoped is no reason to give up, though. Just the opposite. We believe the risk of not doing everything we can to help students reach their full potential is much, much greater. . . . But one thing that makes improving education tricky is that even among people who work on the issue, there isn't much agreement on what works and what doesn't."[81] The Gateses' candor is admirable. But it assumes that money aimed at improving education—bypassing traditional public schools, years of community grassroots organizing, and the history and methods of Black educators—is the solution.

Joe's experience is an example of effective philanthropy. Philanthropy that addresses systemic barriers should not be phased out; it should be turned into public policy. But much of philanthropy is instead determined to invest in infrastructure, think tanks, research centers, advocacy organizations, and political action committees to advance an agenda and seize power. Foundations founded and funded by the super predators work in unison to promote the destruction and sale of Black education. In the name of philanthropy, these foundations betray the egalitarian undertaking of altruism and sacrifice Black children and pioneering Black educators to absolve themselves from public relations crises, and always, first and foremost, maintain their power.

9

THE TRAP OF DIVERSITY, EQUITY, AND INCLUSION

> The possessive investment in Whiteness can't be rectified by learning "how to be more antiracist." It requires a radical divestment in the project of whiteness and a redistribution of Whiteness and resources. It requires abolition, the abolition of the carceral world, the abolition of capitalism.
>
> —Saidiya V. Hartman[1]

Waiting on Hearts and Minds

The field of education saw a resurgence in calls for anti-racism and equity in the spring of 2020 when the world watched George Floyd die at the hands of police officer Derek Chauvin. A few months earlier, police in Louisville, Kentucky, had shot and killed Breonna Taylor in her own home. School districts and colleges around the country rushed to tap diversity, equity, and inclusion—or DEI—leaders to form task forces, committees, and working groups to tackle the issue of racism. But they did not address the real problem: that despite good intentions, the work of racial justice is at best elusive without substantive commitments from institutions.[2]

DEI approaches that leave intact harmful structures are window dressing for Whiteness.

Rather than addressing harmful structures head on, the work of DEI in education is often predicated on the belief that unless White people can be convinced of the need for change, change cannot occur. In 1965, Dr. King delivered rousing speeches calling for the end of "Old Man Segregation" and the social systems that maintain White supremacy. In his addresses to crowds of thousands, he said, "It may be true that the law can't change the heart, but it can restrain the heartless."[3] Waiting for a vast majority of White people to have a change of heart before Black people can have justice is an empty endeavor. We need policies that will atone for the centuries during which Black people have endured "disparities in wealth, income, education, health, sentencing and incarceration, political participation, and subsequent opportunities to engage in American political and social life."[4] As King emphasized, policies and laws are fundamental to offset and counter the ever-present, dogged, and harmful practices of racism and anti-Blackness.

In practice, the work of DEI and anti-racism amounts to attempting to help White people learn to be less racist. In prioritizing this as the goal, the work of changing policy is put on hold. It's easy to see why. Those in power must approve policy changes; until those in power are unbound from Whiteness, policy change remains unattainable. Until then, DEI directors create reports that tell the stories of racism, anti-Blackness, and harm at their workplaces. Under these conditions, the promise of equity is ultimately hollow because White people can use the language of justice while remaining deeply committed and invested in Whiteness—thereby devaluing the work of DEI as a "symbolic commitment." Feminist writer and scholar Sara Ahmed argues, "Equality and diversity can be used as masks to create the appearance of being transformed."[5] These empty commitments leave the work of DEI trapped by the very structure it seeks to transform. Real equity work attempts to repair, undo, heal, and atone for generations of violence, trauma, and racial, educational, and economic inequities while recognizing Black people as a mighty people with a beautiful history of resistance, refusal, strength, and creativity who also deserve ease and grace.

In the current environment, however, equity work relies heavily on the ingenuity and brilliance of Black people to "fix" problems of racial inequalities with limited to no financial or material resources, institutional power, and/or commitment beyond buzzwords and their superiors' savior complex and desire to be perceived as a social justice ally. Black DEI leaders are asked to chair diversity committees and fix the problems of racism, as if one person with no real power could. DEI is seen as a compelling theme for a conference, while the institutions that host and send their staff to attend such conferences do not embrace it as the foundation of their work. Their voices are valued, but only, it seems, in conversations about DEI—to make the institutions appear justice-centered. The work of DEI is included but not essential to the organization. Therefore, when budget cuts routinely occur and political winds blow right, DEI will be left behind with the promise that the work will be picked up at a later date. As Ahmed reminds us, "The diversity worker has a job precisely because diversity and equality are not daily practice."[6]

Workers of color, especially women of color, are the backbone of equity work and anti-racism in education. Their work is laid against a backdrop of anti-racism and DEI on an institutional, individual, and societal level that is too often made painstakingly ornamental.

In June 2020, a Pew Research Center poll found that 67 percent of American adults supported the Black Lives Matter movement— six in ten White people and nearly 40 percent of Republicans.[7] By

September, that figure fell to 55 percent—and 45 percent of White people. A *USA Today*–Ipsos poll showed that trust in law enforcement, meanwhile, rose from 56 percent in June 2020 to nearly 70 percent in March 2021, even though no federal action was taken to reform legislation on policing.[8] By contrast, the poll showed that 75 percent of Black people supported Black Lives Matter, while their confidence in police never reached 50 percent.[9] For many White Americans, the work of racial justice is to be carried out by Black people while White people use Black bodies and intellect as fronts for their performative justice.

Teaching White People How to Be Less Racist Ain't Justice

Lia knows all about the work of DEI and feeling like a prop in a futile process. As a DEI leader at her school in Virginia, she is responsible for creating and implementing structural changes to address inequalities, promote diversity, and help teachers grow to be anti-racist. She moved to Virginia from Ohio when she was twelve years old. She does not consider herself a Southerner, but she tells me sincerely, "I love Black people, I love Black women, and I love the South." This love for Black people was instilled in Lia early on, and the move to Virginia only reinforced it. In her new state, she was surrounded by HBCUs. Her parents took her to homecoming events at HBCUs every year until she went to college—not surprisingly, she chose to attend an HBCU. HBCU homecoming is part football, part family reunion, but everything about it is a celebration of Black life. Because of COVID-19, Lia, who is thirty-five, missed homecoming in 2020 for the only time since she was twelve. She told me that growing up with so many Black colleges and Black people made her childhood special.

Lia now works as the director of equity and inclusion at Wilson Academy, a predominantly White private school in Virginia.

When I asked her to tell me about her work, she chuckled. "It's messy," she said. Her job, is "essentially teaching White teachers and parents how to be less racist." She explained that roughly 90 percent of her job is supporting students of color who deal with racist incidents in school and helping White teachers, donors, and parents understand why equity and inclusion are important. But Lia's daily responsibilities have little to do with equity. Equity seeks to systematically address oppression with meaningful and community-driven solutions that disrupt the status quo and re-distribute resources to those who have been historically denied access to education. Lia's top equity goal is diversifying the teacher population at her school—she would like teachers to reflect the student body and the world at large. In reality, she has neither the time nor the resources to tackle her equity goal. Instead, she is consumed by protecting students of color, especially Black students, from being spirit murdered.

In her role, Lia helps teachers create lesson plans that are not filled with assumptions, stereotypes, and anti-Black references. Lia said that in the wake of 2020's Black killings and uprisings, White teachers are often afraid to say the wrong thing. Much of Lia's job has therefore been helping these teachers navigate conversations about race. Lia's work is vital not only to the school's culture but to her Black students. She knows that racist and anti-Black incidents "break" Black students. When I asked how her students manage the trauma of racism that their teachers and peers inflict, she told me they see the educational opportunity as a ten and the overall school experience as a three to four. For them, she said, "the trauma outweighs the diploma." This is a sobering statement for someone who has worked in independent schools for over a decade, but Lia is realistic, and educational anti-Blackness takes no days off.

Lia is just one of nine Black equity leaders in K–12 settings that I interviewed for this book. Invariably, these leaders told me they felt White educators had little to no trust in Black equity leaders tasked with training them to implement DEI goals. DEI leaders, in turn, have little to no trust in White educators. This is made clear in a letter that Lia shared with me. A White teacher wrote the letter to the school's administration after she and Lia were refused entry to a staff meeting.

I am writing to express my concern about an incident that occurred yesterday. Lia and I were entering the High School faculty meeting, along with Jane Smith, when we were abruptly turned away by Julie in front of the entire High School faculty. She looked at Lia first and explained that she did not want us present because it was her "last meeting with [her] faculty" and that she was mostly just going to be recognizing various teachers. She repeated this several times. Unless we had something specific to share, we were uninvited. This is the second occasion this has occurred this school year. In the first case, I was also with Lia.

I have attended almost all of the High School faculty meetings since beginning my role at Wilson Academy due to the cross-divisional nature of my job. Lia has also attended the meetings when available. As shared with Julie yesterday, she and I both were hoping to join the meeting to be a part of the last faculty meeting of the school year and learn about any important updates or information that may have been shared. I am almost certain that if I had been attempting to enter the meeting alone, I would not have been turned away. I have witnessed other instances of hostility toward Lia by Julie and find it extremely concerning, especially given that Lia is often the only woman of color, and specifically the only Black woman, in the room. The fact that we were unreasonably denied entry to a meeting, where attendance is indicated by our roles is unacceptable to me.

> I feel it is my responsibility to share this with you as I
> am actively and continuously trying to hold myself and
> others accountable, especially when it comes to instances
> of racial and other microaggressions that potentially cause
> harm to my colleagues and others, and because I know
> that Wilson Academy is a place that embraces diversity
> and equitable treatment.

And so Lia was an outcast at the school where she oversees inclusion. Reflecting on this incident, she said she felt emotionally and professionally trapped. As a Black woman, she had no mechanism to respond. Her gender, race, and position rendered her powerless in this face of this expression of White rage. "When I got home, I cried because I was also embarrassed," she told me. "I was embarrassed to be shunned in front of all those people, embarrassed because I felt like I couldn't stand up for myself in front of my team, embarrassed because other people of color saw this. But deep down, I knew that I couldn't react. I had built too much social capital with the White people in that room. If I cracked, they could use it against me: 'She is just angry . . . she can't handle her emotions . . . we don't feel safe with her—she might blow up at us.'"

Lia's work was undermined and devalued by faculty members who see DEI work as a threat to their institutional power and Whiteness. Lia told me that the woman who refused her entry into the meeting had been at the school for twenty-nine years. She said, "I remember thinking she has been allowed to do this for over twenty years, and I am her peer colleague—what has she done to those who report to her?" She added, "I was exhausted having to be on guard anytime I was in her space. . . . She was mean, and she was spiteful, but I always had to rise above. It is this constant struggle that would give me heart palpitations. I always had to present well. I could never do or treat people the way she did. I always had to have my composure, and I knew for sure, had I not had witnesses, she would look me dead in my face and tell me that what happened didn't happen."

The harm that is being done to Lia is also being done to Black students. Because of the failures of public education, Black parents are led to believe that private school may be the best option for their children. But as Lia observed, the educational opportunity may be a draw, but students suffer socially and psychically. When "the trauma outweighs the diploma," what kind of choices do Black parents have, even those who can afford private school?

In the summer of 2020, amid the uproar over yet more Black death at the hands of police, Black students attending some of the most prestigious private schools in the country used social media to share how their teachers, administrators, and fellow students caused them racial trauma. For example, at a private school in Connecticut, Black students posted detailed stories on an anonymous Instagram account about how school faculty were "completely obsessed with policing Black women's bodies" and "sexualizing" Black students.[10] One post, allegedly from a former teacher, claimed that White faculty members would comment to other White teachers that the school's director of equity and inclusion was "pushing that agenda again."[11] "That agenda" includes justice, a disruption of power, educational opportunities for children of color, diversity in hiring and curricula, and ensuring the school is inclusive to all. Black students and alums from private schools used social media to expose the racism they endured and gain a sense of validation, social support, and community after experiencing racial harm.[12] According to one report, over forty different Instagram accounts were created by students at private schools in a dozen states; using the handle "Black@[insert name of school]," they told of their pain and trauma.

A year later, at one of the most elite private schools in Atlanta,

White parents submitted a five-page letter—"written on behalf of thousands of parents, alumnae, community supporters, and financial donors"—attacking what they called the "holy trinity": "Equity, Diversity, and Inclusion."[13] The letter expressed frustration with the school administration "supporting" Black Lives Matter, and referred to "social justice," "oppression," "equity," and "inclusion" as "garbage."[14] The letter was signed, "The No Longer Silent Majority."[15] I am not sure when the majority was ever silent. Still, without firm policies, justice for Black people is predicated on White people's hearts and minds, which, historically, have been sadly predictable. Black parents have a lousy set of options that create a no-win situation.

"It Means Nothing"

All the other DEI leaders I interviewed work in the public school system. Among them is Mya, who lives in Kansas. When I first spoke with her in the spring of 2021, she had recently been hired as the DEI leader of her district, in which more than thirty home languages are spoken. I asked Mya how much of her day-to-day was spent on equity, and she reared back in her seat, letting out a deep laugh tinged with cynicism and disappointment. After she stopped laughing, she said, "On a good day, twenty-five percent. [On] the average day? About ten to fifteen percent."

I wondered: Why were so few resources and so little time and energy spent on equity in a district that's one of the most diverse in the state? Her answer: "We are not working with anyone or the school to ensure our practices are equitable. It's a lot of go and find." Mya's district viewed DEI as additive information she should bring to the district but never important enough to be integrated into the school's foundation or structure. I told Mya that in my interviews with other equity leaders, a word that often came up was *fixer*. Again, she laughed knowingly. She told me her work was "completely reactive, never proactive—the days I do the most work is when there is an explosion in the building—that I need to go now and mediate so it does not hit the news and we are not in trouble." The "explosions" Mya is charged with responding to were acute instances of racism. However, Mya's school district does not like to use the word *anti-racism* because, she said, it "offends people, and we don't want to make anyone bad, but we are okay offending our [Black and students of color] kids and parents." She added that White women in particular, who make up the overwhelming majority of teachers in her district—and the country—feel attacked by the word *anti-racism*. Mya did not have a budget for her DEI work. She was one of only two people tasked with DEI for the entire district. She suspects she was hired because the district needed to "check a box" to comply with the state mandate to fund DEI work. Mya added that she often did not feel safe speaking about racism and did not fully trust White teachers she was supposed to support, because she could have been fired at any time—and she has a family that relies on her income.

As I wrapped up my first interview with Mya, I asked her about *Brown v. Board of Education*. The case, after all, was rooted in Kansas. "No one in the district talks about *Brown*," she said. As an educator and child of a mother who attended school during the trial, I asked her how she understood *Brown* today. "It means nothing," she said, explaining that school funding is still unequal and that White schools in the suburbs get more money than inner-city schools.

Still, Mya was upbeat. Despite her job's obstacles, she seemed motivated to keep going. But when I spoke with her just five months later, she had quit and taken a job as a principal at a school in the district. When I asked her why, she said, "All the resistance you face—you can't fight battles all the time. It was exhausting. . . . I felt I could get more things accomplished as a building leader than a district leader." Mya told me she was simply tired of fighting and worrying. "I am worried about COVID. I am worried about existing as a Black person in society and also worried about who I am going to get into an argument with at the central office." A colleague summed up Mya's resignation: "She is leaving simply because we're not putting in the work required." Mya said silence was a big reason she walked out the door. People, including those at the top, knew the harm they caused but were more concerned about not making White teachers or parents uncomfortable than striving for justice. No conversation could even be had because of the overpowering fear of White rage.

Mya shared that there were surface-level conversations about opening schools during the pandemic before she left her position. The discussions focused on equity, but they never moved into action. This is especially disheartening because Black and Brown people suffered the most during the pandemic. Black people make up roughly 13 percent of the population of the states that report the race and ethnicity of residents who die of COVID, yet in May 2020, they accounted for 27 percent of COVID-19 deaths in those places. One study found that "counties with higher populations of black residents accounted for 52 percent of coronavirus diagnoses and 58 percent of Covid-19 deaths nationally."[16]

Meanwhile, in her new position as a school principal, Mya has not even been able to address the hot-button issue of critical race theory or book bans. "I *wish* I was having conversations about CRT," she said. "I am trying to keep Black bodies in schools with White teachers. Right now, I have a kid who was put out of class for laughing. . . . I am spending my time talking to kids about misbehaving when they really are not misbehaving."

The Big Apple's Big Problems

New York City might well be the cultural and financial capital of the United States, but it also has, in the words of author Sheryll Cashin, "the most segregated school system in the country."[17] The city's public school system—the largest in the nation, serving one million students—has long been beset by racial and socioeconomic segregation. According to the New York City Council, almost three-quarters of the city's Black and Brown students attend public schools with fewer than 10 percent White students; more than a third of White students, meanwhile, attend schools where most of their classmates are also White.[18] New York is home to some of the wealthiest people on the planet, yet New York State has the least equitable funding system in the nation.[19] This disparity is due to its property tax funding system, which privileges the wealthy. As Cashin writes in *White Space, Black Hood: Opportunity Hoarding and Segregation in the Age of Inequality*:

> Differences in local taxes . . . result from the architecture of segregation that America intentionally created. It does not have to be this way. A report by the Organization for Economic Co-operation and Development notes that . . . OECD countries with high-performing education systems put their most talented teachers and extra resources in disadvantaged schools and finance education at the state rather than the local level. The vast majority of US states do the exact opposite.[20]

In her book, Cashin succinctly lays out how a liberal city, known for its diversity, continues to operate a Jim Crow school system sustained by educational White rage. It's a system in which educational policies and specialized public middle and high schools that focus on math, science, technology, and the arts operate as elite private institutions for White and Asian American children.

On February 3, 1964, ten years after *Brown,* thousands of Black parents and students took to the streets of New York City to demand that the city's schools fulfill the promises of integration.[21] They held signs that read FIGHT JIM CROW, BOYCOTT SCHOOLS, and INTEGRATION MEANS BETTER SCHOOLS FOR ALL.[22] Weeks later, White mothers marched across the Brooklyn Bridge, yelling, "Please, oh, please, leave us alone / Stop zoning, zoning, zoning."[23] Amid this tension, the city proposed busing to merge the racially divided school system, but White parents were not having it—the proposal went nowhere. Today, Black and Brown students in New York pay the price: the actions of those White parents from decades ago have kept the city's schools separate and unequal, depriving low-income students of the educational resources and funding they are due.

Ivy is one of the countless Black students who had to learn how to navigate the educational White rage of New York's highly segregated public school system. She's now twenty-seven. As a child, she and her siblings were often moved from school to school. Their mother and father wanted to ensure they got the best education and constantly searched for options better than the ones they were zoned for. Schools in Ivy's neighborhood lacked "access to good education," she said, so she ended up attending schools filled with White and Asian students.

To access options outside of her zoned school and navigate New York's racially segregated schools, Ivy needed to be a good test taker, and she honed that skill from a young age. "I would say at least three out of my five days were focused on tests," she told me. "You want to have a certain type of education? You're going to get drilled to take a test . . . I have been taking tests since I was, like, six." She told me that without an aptitude for taking tests, her life would have had a "completely different trajectory."

One must take an entrance exam to attend one of New York City's specialized public middle or high schools or high-performing schools. Of the eight specialized high schools in the city, three were founded as all-boys schools; the oldest, Stuyvesant High School, was founded in 1904. In 1934, entrance exams were mandated for all applicants. Stuyvesant did not admit girls until 1969. Today, it is one of the top schools in the country—private or public—and has four Nobel laureates among its graduates. Stuyvesant is not alone; the city's specialized high schools are all highly coveted—several have educated multiple Nobel laureates—and serve as national models for elite public education. Forty years ago, these specialized schools were filled with Black and Brown students. They were sanctuaries for Black and Brown students from low-income, impoverished neighborhoods throughout New York. In 1982, Brooklyn Technical High School's student population was 51 percent Black; by 2016, that number had plummeted to a mere 6 percent.[24] In 2019, out of 895 spots, only 7 Black students were accepted into Stuyvesant.[25] In 2021, that figure rose by just the bare minimum: Black students accounted for only 8 of the 749 spots. At Staten Island Technical High School, only 1 Black student was accepted.[26] Overall, the city's Black and Brown students represent 70 percent of the school system and a mere 10 percent of the student body at specialized schools.[27]

Students whose parents can afford it pay test prep chains like Kaplan for services starting at $1,000 for eight sessions on specialized school entrance exams, further exacerbating inequalities.[28] To diversify the city's specialized high schools—yet keep the admission exam and White people's ability to control Black children's schooling choices—billionaire cosmetics heir Ronald S. Lauder and former Citigroup chairman Richard D. Parsons spent over $750,000 on test preparation for low-income students. Their efforts did not change the racial makeup of the schools.

"Black and white students made up the same percentage of test takers—about 18 percent each—less than 4 percent of Black students received offers, compared with nearly 28 percent of White students."[29]

The admission test is not the only way Black students are denied access to elite public schools in New York City. For example, students from Manhattan's District 2, one of the Whitest and wealthiest of the thirty-two school districts, receive priority placement in the city's highest-performing elite high schools.[30] District 2 students fill nearly all the seats before other students are even considered.[31] This policy blatantly privileges the White and the wealthy and maintains Jim Crow schools.

Ivy's acceptance into one of the city's top schools almost did not happen because she is Black: "I was tested to get into elementary school. They thought I was White—they were surprised when they saw my mom." School admission personnel thought Ivy was a "White girl" because of her last name, which is Irish. Ivy says her mother loves to tell the story of when they walked into the school, and the admission officer actually blurted, "I thought you were White!"

Leaving her neighborhood and testing into a top-performing public school, Ivy felt isolated as a Black girl, not unlike Aja in Rochester, from whom we heard in chapter 3. Ivy was one of about twenty Black girls in the school; there was only one Black boy in the graduating class. "Everybody else was White," she said. Ivy witnessed the preferential treatment of White students at the school. "I mean, the institutions that are put in place that are in favor of anything that has to do with White, like White privilege—and just want them to succeed." Attending a school set up to maintain the dominance of White children is something that Nikole Hannah-Jones has described with striking simplicity: "Hitching a ride to the white majority, with the understanding that in a country built on racial caste, they get an inordinate amount of the resources. Things that are acceptable for Black children are never acceptable for white children."[32]

Many people blame modern segregated schools, what researchers call "apartheid schools," on housing segregation policies and individual choices about where we live.[33] But such segregation exists within racially integrated communities, too.[34] Neighborhoods around the country are experiencing rapid gentrification, but "the gentrification stops at the schoolhouse door."[35] Hannah-Jones makes it plain: "White communities want neighborhood schools if their neighborhood school is white. If their neighborhood school is black, they want choice." White parents will routinely use school choice to mask their racism and anti-Blackness while telling Black people and White liberal friends that they value diversity and inclusion. As *New York Times* education reporter Dana Goldstein writes, "White and privileged parents who go into diverse spaces without believing that it is important to be part of an equal, diverse community of parents and students end up trying to mold these schools to the benefit of their own kids above all others."[36]

Researchers interviewing White parents in New York City found that many were "bothered" by school segregation but remained committed to their children gaining access to mostly White schools, which they perceived as the "best" schools.[37] White parents may be uncomfortable with school segregation, but the worries, anxieties, and fears of losing their privilege supersede any desire for racial justice and impede Black children's educational choices. In this hypercompetitive, market-driven education system, White parents push aside integration, diversity, and inclusion to hoard educational opportunities and resources that ensure their already-privileged White children attend elite colleges and secure high-salary jobs to retain their lofty place in society.[38]

New York City schools have taken some steps toward integration in recent years. District 15 in Brooklyn eliminated the admissions criteria for middle schools and prioritized low-income students in the lottery.[39] Predictably, this small-scale change was met with White rage. However, many White parents did help push for the change in District 15, some indicating they felt compelled to do something after Trump's election.[40] In 2018, New York mayor Bill de Blasio proposed a bill to end admission exams for the city's specialized high schools, but the bill had little political support at the state level.[41]

Under New York State law, neither the mayor nor the city's school chancellor has control over admission standards to the city's elite public high schools, a law that dates back to 1971. At the time, the city's chancellor announced an investigation to determine if the admission exam discriminated against Black and Brown students. Burton G. Hecht, a Bronx Democrat, wrote: "The political pressure groups who continue to attack the four specialized high schools intend to eventually destroy these schools and their specialized status in science, mathematics, music and art."[42] Hecht cosponsored a bill with Bronx Republican John D. Calandra, known as the Hecht-Calandra Act, which required a single test for admission to the city's specialized high schools, effectively maintaining Jim Crow schooling. Again, educational White rage was baked into the system on a state level to ensure school segregation.

In the fall of 2021, with just three months left in office, de Blasio released a plan to abolish the gifted and talented program in elementary schools. This program exacerbates the already highly segregated school system[43] and is a pipeline into the city's selective high schools. Of the rising kindergarteners who test into the program, approximately "75 percent of the roughly 16,000 students are White and Asian American."[44] Black and Brown students are essentially railroaded from the program as soon as they start formal schooling. Gifted programs and magnet schools were created after *Brown v. Board of Education* to appeal to White families fleeing inner-city schools because they feared integration.[45] White gentrifiers cling to these programs as a way to stay in public schools—but segregate their children from Black and Brown children. The mayor's plan would have extended accelerated learning education to all students in regular classrooms.[46] Not surprisingly, there was pushback and resistance. De Blasio's successor, former police captain Eric Adams, campaigned on keeping the gifted program intact and has instead proposed eliminating the admissions exam and expanding the number of seats available.[47]

As of fall 2022, New York City school's chancellor, David C. Banks, left the decision as to whether middle schools could select incoming students based on academic performance to lower-level superintendents. In Manhattan's District 3, which includes parts of Harlem, twenty-four out of thirty school principals signed a petition against middle school admission screenings. Their petition read, "Ranking and sorting our students goes against a celebration of the rich diversity of cultures and races our students bring with them to the schools across District 3."[48] In addition, changes were also made to allow more access to the selective high schools in the city. As of fall 2022, eighth graders with course grades in the top 15 percent will have priority to the city's selective high schools, but not the city's eight highly coveted specialized high schools. Students will still need to test into those schools. Access is moving in the right direction, but the systemic change necessary to integrate schools and provide Black and Brown children with educational opportunities available to their White peers will always face White rage. Like clockwork, privileged parents contest DEI and school integration fearing the loss of a competition that's already been rigged and allows them to win uncontested.

The Toll on Black Bodies

Changing hearts and minds for meaningful DEI work leaves pain, scars, and trauma for Black people. As a renowned trauma expert, Bessel van der Kolk writes, "The body keeps the score."[49] The pressure of racism takes a toll on Black people's overall health. It slowly kills Black people—death by reform. The stress of systemic racism, compounded with everyday personal interactions with racism, has biological consequences.

Racism has finally been acknowledged as a public health crisis. By the summer of 2020, more than fifty municipalities and three states (Michigan, Ohio, and Wisconsin) declared racism as the reason for the health gap between Black and White Americans. For example, research shows that Black women are three to four times more likely to die of pregnancy-related complications than White women.[50] Put another way, Black women are 243 percent more likely to die from childbirth than their White counterparts.[51] When controlling for income and education, "a Black woman with an advanced degree is more likely to lose her baby than a white woman with less than an eighth-grade education."[52]

Black infant mortality rates, unfortunately, parallel Black maternal health outcomes. This particular health care disparity is not new. As early as 1899, W. E. B. Du Bois wrote about the racial disparities in infant mortality in *The Philadelphia Negro*. And in *The Souls of Black Folk,* he documented the personal tragedy of his baby son's death.[53] Generations later, in 2018, Black people still suffer enormous heartbreak: "Black infants in America are now more than twice as likely to die as white infants . . . a racial disparity that is actually wider than in 1850, 15 years before the end of slavery, when most black women were considered chattel."[54] Arline Geronimus, a professor in the Department of Health Behavior and Health Education at the University of Michigan, refers to the toxic stress triggered by racism as "weathering," which prematurely deteriorates the body.[55] The average life expectancy of Black people is five years less than the rest of the U.S. population. And there are harrowing statistics like this: one of the leading causes of death for a young Black man in this country is being killed by police.[56,57]

Black people are confronted daily by a world in which the systems of education, health care, criminal justice, social services, housing, transportation, climate change, and the economic development of urban areas cause racial health disparities. Imagine facing these deadly disparities—and your job is to heal this nation's schools as a DEI worker. Lia, for instance, experienced heart palpitations when interacting with her racist coworker. Medical experts call the condition "sympathetic overactivity"—when your body senses a social threat. The chronic menace of racism stresses the body and can lead to depression, anxiety, headaches, back pain, high blood pressure, cardiovascular disease, and diabetes.[58] Bridget Goosby, a professor of sociology at the University of Texas at Austin, writes: "Being a minority in predominantly White spaces adds additional burdens that impact bodies and negatively affect long-term health."[59] Racism is an ever-present trauma to the body because the "most important job of the brain is to ensure our survival."[60] Thus, the body suppresses the "inner chaos" of racism, which can result in "fibromyalgia, chronic fatigue, and other autoimmune diseases."[61]

Moreover, the stress of racism on Black women is a risk factor associated with uterine fibroids, which are painful and can lead to "anemia, bleeding, increased urinary frequency, fertility problems and pregnancy complications."[62] Black women are three times more likely to have fibroids than White women, and 80 percent of all Black women will develop them by age fifty. Several Black women in my family and circle of friends have fibroids. I also have them. I was diagnosed in 2016. In the summer of 2021,

I underwent a procedure called *uterine fibroid embolization,* which is a minimally invasive treatment. I am fortunate to have high-quality medical insurance that covered the procedure; the hospital bill totaled an astounding $80,000. Although the procedure successfully shrank the fibroids, there is no guarantee that new fibroids will not develop.

As a queer Black woman, a mother of two Black children, and a professor who teaches and researches the topics of racism and anti-Blackness in education, I have been in survival mode for decades. Being Black—and being a queer Black woman—each carries its own histories of abuse and stress. Black life in America is itself a trigger, from the moment you open your eyes in the morning until you close them at night—and even then, your nightmares are White rage and violence.

Elite Capture

This chapter began with a quote by Saidiya V. Hartman calling for the abolition of the carceral world and capitalism by divesting "in the project of Whiteness." DEI work is not interested in atoning or divesting from Whiteness. DEI is the language the reformers and White liberal parents use to make the slow death of Black children in education seem less harsh—and to forgive acts of harm by deploying the words of justice without real action toward dismantling institutions that are carceral, anti-Black, and "death-dealing." Olúfẹ́mi O. Táíwò, a professor of philosophy at Georgetown University, calls this phenomenon "elite capture." He writes that through the seizure of the language of identity politics, elites, or what I would call *super predators,* capture the ideas of social justice, unity, and inclusion to steer resources and institutional power toward their interests instead of serving the interests of the public.

Leland Saito, a sociology professor at the University of Southern California and author of *The Politics of Exclusion,* highlights how race-evasive policies—even if implemented by people with good intentions—will erase and omit Black and Brown people's financial and social needs, history, and culture. Amy Stuart Wells of Teachers College at Columbia University makes it plain: "Even when education policies are 'colorblind' [race-evasive] on the surface, they interact with school systems and residential patterns in which race is a central factor in deciding where students go to school, what resources and curricula they have access to, whether they are understood and appreciated by their teachers and classmates, and how they are categorized across academic programs."[63] DEI work coddles Whiteness, is race-evasive, and upholds White supremacy.

Instead, we need radical change. The field of education must abandon DEI work for educational reparations—a bold national policy that would establish a "societal obligation" to repair and atone for the harm of legal racial segregation, divestment, standardized testing, and the carceral inevitability of schooling.[64] Educational reparations, as I will explore in chapter 12, alone will shift power and resources to heal and transform education. The essential concept of reparations means that the *value structure* of the nation must strive toward justice. Reparations is not a race-neutral policy—it is an affirmation, pure and simple, that Black Lives Matter, harm has been done to those lives, we are owed compensation for that harm, and our nation is working toward repair.

10

WHITE PEOPLE: SAVE YOURSELVES

> If you can only be tall because somebody is on their knees, then you have a serious problem. And my feeling is White people have a very, very serious problem, and they should start thinking about what they are going to do about it. Take me out of it.
>
> —Toni Morrison[1]

Duped

"Dr. Love, Sandy Hook didn't happen. It's all a hoax." This statement shook me to my core and has haunted me for the past decade. It was the moment I understood how deeply pernicious Whiteness is. I was with a group of White teachers in a graduate-level class at my former institution. A number of them were trying to convince me that the massacre at Sandy Hook, in which a twenty-year-old White man killed twenty-six people, twenty of them children, was a government-orchestrated con. They were seduced by the misinformation tactics of Whiteness and its lure—not only to oppress Black people in exchange for White power, no matter the degree of power, but to believe myths and conspiracies that attack their morals, humanity, and religious beliefs, even if it imperils the lives of their own children.

"Dr. Love, have you seen the videos?" one student passionately asked me. "The kids are not dead." I had no response. My silence seemed to give them permission to keep talking. "Those were actors, kid actors, too."

My mind was racing as I struggled to understand exactly what my students were telling me and how I should respond. This was a master's class, after all, and so many, if not all, of the students, were full-time teachers in their thirties and forties, working with children in schools every day. I remember saying to myself: *This horror could have happened at their very schools, to the children they teach. How can they not see themselves and their students in this tragedy?*

Once I was finally able to speak, my reply was spineless. All I managed to say was, "Really." I am sure my facial expression betrayed me, but I was dumbfounded in the moment. I was shocked by this group of students I respected, enjoyed, and found to be thoughtful educators. I clearly remember the stillness of their bodies and how matter-of-fact their words were. They seemed taken aback that I was unaware of their "truths."

Until that day, White people who believed in conspiracy theories lived in my imagination. I believed them to be racist, poor, uneducated White folx I had never met but thought I knew. These students shattered my mythology. I had heard outlandish conspiracy theories before—I remember them after 9/11—but I had never actually met someone who believed such claims. In my naivete, I imagined they existed only online. In truth, I never saw them as real people. Now I was face-to-face with a group of conspiracy theorists, my own students, and the topic was the killing of children—White children. My reality shifted as the realization slowly sank in that I was embroiled in a live conversation about such theories with highly educated and respected teachers.

I allowed the conversation to continue for about ten minutes as these teachers calmly explained an array of details supporting their theory that those poor children were still alive. Finally, I shut it down by agreeing to "look into it" and report back. I was deeply uncomfortable, many of my students were visibly uncomfortable, too, and I needed to say something to end the conversation. I was not equipped to argue that these schoolchildren were in fact dead. I never knew I needed such an argument. I was unaware that *teachers* could believe such an outlandish lie that hit so close to their own lives.

After class, I went back to my office, astonished that a group of White teachers at one of the top schools of education in the country believed that innocent White children were somehow still alive and that their parents were faking their own children's deaths. I know the stories of Black death and deprivation all too well. I have lived that story. I research that story. But this was different. I can comprehend Whiteness when it convinces White people to vote against their best interests or deprive their children of a proper education in order to deny the same to Black children. But White people being unmoved by, and downright defiant of, the deaths of White children? I had no frame of reference. I have spent my professional life working to persuade White teachers that Black children matter. I was now being asked to convince a group of White teachers that young, innocent White lives also mattered and were stolen away. Not to mention that White teachers also lost their lives that day. I was in such an unfamiliar emotional and intellectual space that I ultimately panicked and retreated.

I decided to investigate this idea to attempt to understand the perspective of my otherwise thoughtful students and how they could have been so easily misled. Each far-right website, infused with media personalities spreading misinformation and false claims about Sandy Hook, took me down a terrifying path. I had never before heard of Alex Jones, a far-right radio show host and conspiracy theory purveyor, who was one of the leading voices spreading the lie that Sandy Hook was a hoax. The more I read from Jones and others, the more I felt as if I were trespassing on my own humanity. I knew the truth, I felt, and the truth had to stand on its own. I was more emotionally prepared to address the issue by the next class session. Although I do not remember my exact words, this was the substance of them:

> I know we had a discussion last class about Sandy Hook being a hoax. I want you all to know I tried my best to listen to you all. I really did. But I want to say this: I believe Sandy Hook happened. I believe those children and teachers are dead, unfortunately. I just believe it. I don't have evidence to prove they are dead, but my humanity won't let me comprehend anything else. I am not trying to disrespect anybody's views, but I believe Sandy Hook happened.

After my remarks, we never spoke about Sandy Hook again as a class. Looking back, that ten-minute conversation was a foreshadowing of so many things: the 2016 election laced with lies and misinformation and unsupported claims of voter fraud; the violent mob that stormed the Capitol Building in an attempt to overturn the 2020 election as they chanted for the vice president to be hanged; White parents demanding that their children come to school unmasked during a global pandemic; White parents at school board meetings verbally attacking and threatening physical violence toward health officials who promoted mask wearing and vaccines; White parents angrily proclaiming that COVID-19 isn't real; White conservatives banning drag shows and claiming they are protecting children. In the fall of 2022, a Connecticut court ordered Alex Jones to pay nearly $1 billion in damages to the families of the eight victims of the Sandy Hook shooting.[2] Families testified that lies spread by Jones led to harassment, threats, and feeling unsafe in their own homes.[3] Earlier in the same year, a Texas jury awarded the parents of the children killed $45.2 million to be paid by Jones. Jones eventually admitted that he lied about the massacre not happening and filed for bankruptcy.[4]

In short, the Sandy Hook conversation was my wake-up call. The far right had convinced even some educated White teachers to believe twenty murdered White children were actors pretending to be dead, living underground for reasons I still do not understand. I relate this story to frame an essential question: How can White people be trusted with racial justice and Black lives when they can't save themselves from themselves? How many times are White folx going to be duped, fooled, and bamboozled by Whiteness? When are White people going to love themselves enough to learn the truth? Throughout the history of this nation, White folx have believed the lies of Whiteness and in turn have perpetuated violence toward Black people, queer people, and people of color. If racial justice is ever going to be achieved in this country, we need White people to wake up and understand they are being duped. The lies of Whiteness undermine White people's humanity.

White folx who do the work of racial justice need to get their people because Black folx are tired. And it's not our job to save White people from Whiteness; we are trying to save ourselves from Whiteness, too. As Patty would say, "Sweep outside your own front door." I cannot stress this one point enough: if Black people have shown this world anything, it is that we will make a way. White people need to stop trying to save Black people; instead, they need to focus on saving themselves. Black people don't need saving. We need the removal of the institutional barriers that prevent, stop, and aim to kill Black progress, Black freedom, and Black joy. We need White people to love themselves—enough to let go of the need for power and conquest that is killing them and their children, enough to stand up to the super predators who tell them lies to keep *all* of us oppressed, and enough to take responsibility for their community. Enough to end the racial contract.

Invisible Ink

Philosopher Charles Mills defines the "racial contract" as an unwritten social pact with implicit rules and agreements that grant life, liberty, and the pursuit of happiness to all White people. Black people are systematically and intentionally excluded from these principles. As Mills argues, "Whites' dominance is, for the most part, no longer constitutionally and juridically enshrined but rather a matter of social, political, cultural, and economic privilege based on the legacy of conquest."[5]

The law, of course, states that murder is illegal. Throughout history, however, and to this day, the sanctioned murder of Black people is written into the contract with permanent invisible ink. The contract justifies the killing of Black people if White people feel scared. White people can shoot rounds into a Black person's car if their music is too loud. They can kill a Black boy for walking in a neighborhood that "belongs" to White people. They can bring a lightweight semiautomatic rifle to a protest for Black lives, fatally shoot two men and wound another, and be acquitted of all charges. Under the contract, Black people can be massacred for triggering White rage with Black achievement. In 1921, White mobs invaded the Greenwood District in Tulsa, Oklahoma. Known as Black Wall Street, the Greenwood District was a thriving Black community considered the wealthiest Black enclave in the country. The district was filled with vibrant and upscale Black-owned nightclubs, restaurants, movie theaters, pool halls, and luxury hotels. The Black people of the district carved out a piece of America for themselves and played by America's rules of capitalism. And yet, on May 31 and June 1, 1921, White people beat and killed hundreds of residents of the Greenwood District, destroying Black progress and leaving more than ten thousand people homeless. The massacre ended only when the Oklahoma National Guard imposed martial law, though, by some accounts, guardsmen took part in the mayhem before restoring order. No one was prosecuted for the killings of the Black residents, and insurance claims were denied—all legal under the racial contract.

In 1985, amid mounting tensions between the Black liberation group MOVE and the Philadelphia Police Department over housing code violations and a 1978 standoff that killed a police officer, a city helicopter dropped a bomb—meant for combat—on row houses occupied by MOVE.[6] Eleven people were killed, including five children. Sixty-one homes were destroyed, leaving hundreds homeless.[7] In 2005, residents were awarded $12.8 million in damages. In 2020, the city officially apologized for its decision to bomb MOVE. A year later, the Penn Museum and the University of Pennsylvania also issued official apologies to the families of the children who died in the bombing after it was disclosed that the remains of two of the children recovered from the site were used for research and training without the families' awareness or permission. Under the racial contract, the bombing and the theft of the remains were justified because Black life is disregarded and valued only as the property of White people.

In education, the racial contract functions as it was intended through segregated schools that are deliberately under-resourced and policed by state-sanctioned violence. In the words of James Baldwin, "It has allowed White people, with scarcely any pangs of conscience whatever, to *create*, in every generation, only the Negro they wished to see."[8] The racial contract allows White people to explicitly characterize Black people's "unfortunate" plight as the result of criminality and laziness, thereby maintaining White innocence, White supremacy, and the arrogance of White privilege. Adam Serwer of *The Atlantic* sums it up well: "The racial contract is not partisan—it guides staunch conservatives and sensitive liberals alike—but it works most effectively when it remains imperceptible to its beneficiaries. As long as it is invisible, members of society can proceed as though the provisions of the social contract apply equally to everyone. But when an injustice pushes the racial contract into the open, it forces people to choose whether to embrace, contest, or deny its existence."[9]

The racial contract demands White people deny accountability for the harm of Whiteness out of a fear that they will also be disposed of. A major piece of the foundation that upholds the racial contract is disposability, built on White people's fear of losing their community. The racial contract is not just about Black disposability but White disposability, too.

Some of my White students at my former institution, who are already teachers or going to be teachers, frequently describe their hesitation in challenging their White family members or classmates as rooted in fear of being an outcast or labeled a race traitor. The work of racial justice is a hat they wear from 8:00 a.m.–3:00 p.m., but once they get home, they take that hat off. To most of my White students, racial justice is only for work. It is not how they live their life, because the fear of being disposed of is real and always present.

On the flip side, it concerns me when White liberals, who are outspoken about racial justice, dispose of their far-right family members. I often hear them speaking proudly of disinviting such relatives to family dinners, essentially disowning them. In actuality, what these White people are doing is removing themselves from the obligation of how community accountability functions.

Of course, there are healthy boundaries, but we need White folx who have the ability and capacity to lovingly help their family members interrogate their harmful and at times violent beliefs. Sometimes that work is first helping people recognize they have racist and anti-Black beliefs before trying to change those beliefs. It is a delicate tightrope of balancing the emotions of shame, guilt, and anger while realizing you have been duped. It is a journey of countless conversations, where some conversations make inroads and others fall apart, but we need each conversation because justice work is emotional labor work. It is a beautiful struggle in which we fumble toward creating a community that, in Mariame Kaba's words, is "not grounded in punitive justice, and it actually requires us to challenge our punitive impulses, while prioritizing healing, repair, and accountability."[10] The work is creating "a culture that enables people to actually take accountability for violence and harm,"[11] which is the undoing of the racial contract. In other words, when our process is grounded in a culture of accountability rather than punitive justice, it permits us to work toward healing—not just for the victims of harm but for our communities because no one is disposable.

Co-conspirators (Revisited)

In my previous book, *We Want to Do More Than Survive: Abolitionist Teaching and the Pursuit of Educational Freedom,* I tell the story of Bree Newsome and James Tyson. In June 2015, in an act of civil disobedience, Newsome climbed a flagpole in front of South Carolina's statehouse and removed its Confederate flag. As Newsome scaled the pole, the authorities planned to tase the pole, possibly killing Newsome. Tyson, a White man, waited at the bottom, tightly holding on to the flagpole so that if they tased the pole, they would potentially electrocute him, too. This direct action of resistance seemed like a spontaneous act, but it was premeditated and done in solidarity with a community of activists.

Newsome's actions were about much more than the Confederate flag. They also paid tribute to the victims and survivors of the Mother Emanuel AME massacre, which had occurred ten days prior, as well as served to protest racial injustice broadly. Newsome and Tyson met just days before they took down the flag. Both were from North Carolina, both were veteran activists. They met at a meeting in Charlotte where activists were planning to take down a Confederate flag. Newsome, who volunteered to climb the statehouse flagpole, had no climbing experience, so she had to train. Newsome and Tyson made history the day they took the flagpole down, but the two strangers put their lives on the line for each other. Their commitment to racial justice is an example of solidarity, trust, and the centering of Black women. Tyson was more than Newsome's ally—he was her co-conspirator.

Tyson demonstrated a deep understanding of how privilege works. He knew that the police were far less likely to kill him than they were to kill Newsome. He knew his Whiteness, maleness, and able-bodiedness could shield Newsome. Tyson was willing to use his intersections of privilege and power in support of Newsome and to confront racism.

Much reflection on co-conspiracy, a concept promoted by racial justice movement activists, has increased my understanding of how co-conspirators show up in the world. Over the years, I have come to appreciate that being a co-conspirator is also understanding how we *all* harm people; how, as a society, we are obsessed with punishment, and how we fail to take accountability for the harm we have caused because of shame and fear of loss of community. Being a co-conspirator is not just about the outward work of fighting White supremacy—it is about the inward work of repairing and healing ourselves to do less harm in the world. Co-conspirators actively work, sometimes fumble, and keep pushing to create, in solidarity with Black people, queer people, and people of color, spaces that center healing, rage, trust, connection, safety, joy, accountability, and love.[12]

Historian Robin D. G. Kelley is a prolific thinker and writer who has shaped my understanding of abolition and the level of imagination needed to create justice. I keep a quote from him on my phone as a daily reminder: "Without new visions, we don't know what to build, only what to knock down. We not only end up confused, rudderless, and cynical, but we forget that making a revolution is not a series of clever maneuvers and tactics, but a process that can and must transform us."[13] Healing and accountability are challenging tasks because we live in a world that rewards perfectionism, urgency, defensiveness, binaries, scarcity, individualism, confrontation, and, ironically, a fear of conflict—all qualities of White supremacy culture.[14]

The culture of White supremacy is active in our lives and damages our interpersonal relationships and the movement spaces we want and need to build. I know firsthand how seductive White supremacy culture is and how easily it creeps into Black liberation spaces. I have personally found myself leading and working in communities with mostly Black-organized spaces that still center White supremacy culture. Although this was never our intention, we focused on perfectionism, urgency, individualism, and a fear of conflict that caused our actions—my actions—to do harm. We moved at the speed of Whiteness, sometimes pushing toward completion of a project when we did not have authentic buy-in from our partners or the desire to make something truly reflective of our values, and my community has held me accountable for that harm. I have apologized and experienced my own process of accountability. Equally importantly, we changed policies and institutional structures to address harm structurally.

The social contract isn't concerned with, nor does it even consider, healing, accountability, and reducing harm because its very existence is death and despair. Over the years, I have learned that hurry is the enemy of love, which requires giving your full attention.[15] As I wake up daily trying to be better, not reaching for perfectionism but becoming a more loving, kind, tender human, I recite the words of therapist and political organizer Prentis Hemphill: "We are challenged with growing and building Black movements that can push back the onslaught. How we protect and care for each other along the way and come through connected and stronger on the other end are possibly the most critical and meaningful questions we face."[16] These are the questions of co-conspirators.

Co-conspirators grab the flagpole with one hand and reach toward healing and accountability with the other. We need co-conspirators who are willing to anchor their work of justice in the work of collective healing. To do this, co-conspirators are actively working to break generational trauma and violence through therapy, critical self-reflection, accountability, atoning for harm, and healing, while understanding one will constantly repeat these processes. We need co-conspirators to actively work toward collective healing, reflection, and joy, attempting to love as many humans as they can along their journey.

11

LET US CELEBRATE

Style has a profound meaning to Black Americans. If we can't drive, we will invent walks and the world will envy the dexterity of our feet. If we can't have ham, we will boil chitterlings; if we are given rotten peaches, we will make cobblers; if given scraps, we will make quilts; take away our drums, and we will clap our hands. We prove that the human spirit will prevail. We will take what we have to make what we need. We need confidence in our knowledge of who we are.

—Nikki Giovanni[1]

My Hush Harbor

I love being Black. This love was instilled in me as a child through Black joy. My mother and father loved Black people and wanted nothing more for their children than to enjoy being Black. I did not grow up reading books at home about Black history or celebrating Kwanzaa. My parents did not take me to protests or talk about the civil rights era, and we did not go to church on Sundays, or even on Easter. My Black spirituals on Sunday mornings were the Four Tops, The Gap Band, Patti LaBelle, James Brown,

Marvin Gaye, Luther Vandross, Aretha Franklin, Donna Summer, Stevie Wonder, Donny Hathaway, Minnie Riperton, Roberta Flack, The O'Jays, Betty Wright, Bobby "Blue" Bland, The Whispers, and Bob Marley.

My dad worked at the airport as a skycap, so we always had an influx of new Black people he met and befriended there. My dad's nickname was "Honey." Honey Love—you can imagine how smooth you must be to warrant that nickname as a grown man. Because I was a daddy's girl, my nickname was Lil Love. He took me everywhere and never once said a word about me playing with G.I. Joes instead of Barbies or that I hated to wear dresses. My dad had gold teeth, a belly, and, to everyone's delight, could cook almost any Southern cuisine. He did not watch or play sports—or even own a pair of sneakers. But he loved watching movies with action heroes like Chuck Norris, Bruce Lee, and Charles Bronson.

My parents loved to throw parties. The music was loud, the food was fried, the liquor was brown, and everyone was Black. It was a thrill to sneak downstairs and watch everyone dancing, drinking, and laughing. These gatherings are some of my happiest memories as a child.

I remember the preparation on the day of a party. My mom would start cleaning the house early Saturday morning to Chaka Khan and Anita Baker. My dad and I would go to the farmers' market and sample as much as we bought—he considered that breakfast. My dad did most of the cooking for the party, and my job was easy: stay out of the way and somehow pretend to sleep as music blasted, my uncles yelling over the songs. During the parties, I had the best seat in the house: the top of the stairs. From my perch, I had a full view of the front room that housed the record player—that was all I needed. Friends and family had big smiles on their faces; they were happy to see each other, bodies pressed together, cigarettes hanging from their mouths.

I felt safe in their joy. I felt protected by their smiles. As family and friends arrived before my bedtime, they would call me over; I was the baby, and partygoers knew me. My brother and sister were ten and fourteen years older than I was, living their lives independently. I was the only one left at home. After I answered a few generic questions about school, it was time to get paid. On most party nights, I would make as much as twenty to thirty dollars, handed to me by my parents' friends in crisp one- and five-dollar bills. They were ready to have a good time, and since the food and drinks were free, giving me five dollars seemed like a steal. I happily took their money and watched them dance and laugh all night. Sometimes, I got caught people-watching and ran back into my bedroom; other nights, I fell asleep on the steps and was carried up to my bed. And on rare occasions, I got invited down to dance and steal the show, as only a kid at a grown-up party can do, dancing and singing at the top of my lungs along with James Brown: "Say it loud, I'm Black and I'm proud," or Aretha Franklin's "Respect."

As an adult, I now recognize that my house was more than just the party house on those Saturday nights. It was a sanctuary, a place of refuge, a space that demanded that pain and trauma be left at the door and replaced with Black joy. It told me who I was and gave me confidence in who I could be. It was a space where we could celebrate ourselves. Celebrate our music. Celebrate our community. It was a space where Whiteness was not invited or even acknowledged. It was a modern-day hush harbor filled with Black joy. Black joy is ours; it is our refusal to give Whiteness our emotional, physical, spiritual, and mental lives. Black joy is not resistance; it is refusal. Resistance "enable[s] us to switch positions in the game of recognition"; refusal "is a rejection on the game altogether."[2] Those nights at my house, Whiteness was nowhere to be found; my house was an emancipatory space of Black joy.

Historically, a hush harbor was a hidden sanctuary. As the scholar Vorris Nunley writes, enslaved African and free Black people "utilized camouflaged locations, hidden sites, and enclosed places as emancipatory cells where they [could] come in from the wilderness, untie their tongues, speak the unspoken, and sing their own songs to their own selves in their own communities."[3] Enslaved Africans "stole away" from the cruelties of enslavement into what bell hooks called the "wild places" to worship, mourn, scream, sing, dance, and in those moments find joy and freedom. They would bring pots to the hush harbor to muffle their screams, shouts, and singing.[4] They put holes in the ground to sing to their lord and muffle the sound of their voices.[5] The hush harbor was their space to remember Africa, release pain, love, heal, repair, rage, subvert Whiteness, and move the body in ways that summoned Black joy.

Hidden by the beauty of nature, hush harbors existed in thickly wooded areas, hollows, and gullies filled with "hushed utterances and muffled voices," where Black people "prayed for freedom and relief from physical pain and ailments, found hope, and experienced a degree of comfort, solace and even joy."[6] Even amid the hideous cruelties of enslavement, my ancestors were able to find Black joy. They, like my parents, generations later, loved, healed, and were determined to have Black joy and prevail.

See Us for Who We Are

What Black people have accomplished amid unspeakable violence and oppression should be the road map to America's endless journey toward democracy. We have shown this country—physically, mentally, materially, and spiritually—how to work toward justice with grace and love while refusing to give up our humanity. We stand as America's scapegoat, perpetually sacrificed for the illusion of its supremacy. But our humanity is a stunning testimony to the power of grace, Black joy, and the strength of the human spirit.

Recognizing Black people's humanity is one of the very first steps we all need to take in striving for a more just society. As my good friend Leigh Patel reminds me, "Tina, Blackness is bigger than anti-Blackness." Her words ring in my head daily. Because if you step back, take a deep breath, and humble yourself, you have no choice but to marvel at Blackness. We need to be seen for our greatness. Our history does not start with George Floyd, Breonna Taylor, or enslavement—we must remember them, of course, but we must acknowledge that we are more than the pain that has been inflicted on us.

Time and time again, we choose love, forgiveness, peace, and Black joy because we choose to remember who we are—despite daily attempts by White supremacy to diminish and make invisible our histories, contributions, spiritualities, and lived experiences.[7] Sometimes we forgive without an apology; in my opinion, sometimes we forgive too soon, but we want to heal, so we forgive without demanding repair because we believe in something higher than humankind. Our creative labor and energy are the ingredients of dreams of freedom, and in driving humanity, freedom dreams make the lives of all Americans more courageous, kind, graceful, joyous, and loving. We have also found liberation in rage. Rage has served Black people well as our armor for pain and suffering.[8] Rage that can be "harnessed into cultural and political strategy "and "visionary organizing"[9] is a necessary tool for justice.

To be clear, I do not argue that Black people are perfect; that notion of perfection is rooted in White supremacy. Instead, it is our imperfections, along with our memories, our resistance, our refusal, our rage, and our joy, that constitute our humanity. The ways we resist domination, heal and repair, and dearly hold on to and practice the idea that no one is disposable—we show this nation the possibilities of humanity. In conversation with Maya Angelou, bell hooks said, "For me, forgiveness and compassion are always linked: How do we hold people accountable for wrongdoing and yet at the same time remain in touch with their humanity enough to believe in their capacity to be transformed?"[10] Navigating this fundamental, constant moral tension is what it means to repair, heal, and love: to believe in people's humanity enough to see the good in them beyond their worst moments.

This nation must reckon with the notion of healing, repair, and love—of loving Black people because we are human. We are not superhuman; we cannot stop bullets, but we love, create, heal, and give this world our gifts, and in return, we simply want freedom. We are oftentimes exhausted by our strength; we want and deserve tenderness, softness, support, and ease.[11] How could this nation not see us, not marvel at the beauty of our lives that we have shaped out of, as poet Lucille Clifton eloquently put it, "starshine and clay"?[12] How could you not celebrate us?

This nation needs to know who we are because democracy depends on it. Each day that America's education system omits and erases Black people from curricula, democracy is, in turn, diminished, and we become more divested from love, repair, and healing. Each day we fail to celebrate Black people in America, humanity stays in our rearview mirror. After centuries of our free labor, creativity, art, music, ideas of justice, inventions, intellectual contributions, and the killing of our leaders who inspire the world, we are only mentioned when America wants economic or political gain from momentarily repenting for her sins or commodifying Black History Month with kente cloth on everything. America must celebrate us because the path to humanity is a path we, with comrades of color and queer folx, have devoted our lives to; it is the path of abolition born from the joy of creating systems and institutions that are life-giving.

However, I do not believe we were placed in this nation to fight racism or save America. John Edgar Wideman reminds us, "Our stories, songs, dreams, dances, social forms, style of walk, talk, dressing, cooking, sport, our heroes and heroines provide a record . . . so distinctive and abiding that its origins in culture have been misconstructed as rooted in biology."[13] It is not biological to fight racism. It is not our divine destiny to make White people better. We do what we do to survive and one day thrive in this nation. The swag, grace, and style that Black folx exude, that the entire world consumes, "evolved from a cultural willingness to improvise, from a cultural imperative to adapt, and in reaction to a rule change."[14]

Rules are constantly changing for Black people, and we adjust. If we happen to get a glimpse of the finish line, the so-called American dream, the goalpost will inevitably be moved for Black people, in turn hurting all Americans. Improvisation is a skill. We improvise because we have studied all the ways we have been excluded. So we adjust, we adapt, and we fight. Take voting rights, for example. In the 1700s and 1800s, Black people attempted to exercise their right to vote, but this country told us we were three-fifths of a person. So we adjusted, we adapted, and we fought. By the 1900s, when we again attempted to exercise our right to vote, this country enacted literacy tests and poll taxes to stop us from voting. So we protested, marched, boycotted, took legal action, and sacrificed our lives for voting rights. Today, six decades after the Voting Rights Act of 1965, we are still fighting for voting rights and facing voter suppression on multiple fronts, from strict voter ID laws and reduced voting times to restricted registration rules and purged voter rolls. And we will continue to adjust, adapt, and fight, humanizing America along the way.

If this country truly wants justice, it will celebrate us! Celebrating Black lives means this nation not only understands and finds inspiration in our struggles but acknowledges that this nation is *our* struggle. In doing so, this country will begin the long, beautiful, and contentious road of repair, truth-telling, healing, compensation, and transformation—the road to abolition.

Abolition

Abolitionists seek to build a world "commit[ted] to secure a future of freedom, community, justice, and possibility for all."[15] When abolitionists fight for justice, the word *justice* is expansive to include healing justice, environmental justice, disability justice, health justice, immigrant justice, reproductive justice, economic justice, body justice, gender justice, and LGBTQIA justice. Abolitionists like myself want all human beings to have everything they need to feel whole, supported, cared for, and to live in communities that hold people accountable for harm without creating more harm or violence. Abolitionists understand harm through the framework of "transformative justice," which "connect incidences of violence to the conditions that create and perpetuate them."[16] As abolitionists, we acknowledge that so much of the state-sanctioned violence we experience in our schools and everyday lives is a result of capitalism, poverty, White supremacy, fatphobia, misogyny, ableism, homophobia, transphobia, targeted mass incarceration, displacement, and gender oppression.[17] Abolitionists want to end the conditions that make state-sanctioned violence possible. Transformative justice is trying to prevent future violence and harm by teaching us the tools to break generational cycles of violence in our institutions and personal lives.

This world we envision as abolitionists is not only possible but it is actively being built, right now, by people who are collectively freedom dreaming and healing in real time. Collectivism and community are the strengths of abolition; movements are built on an "ecosystem" of feminist minded, trans, and queer networks and collectives that deepen the work of liberation. The work is never about one individual, it's always the collective.[18] However, the work of the collective is made stronger each time we, as individuals, take accountability for harm, choose to let go of the binaries of good and bad, broken versus unbroken, and guilty versus innocent, and commit to transforming ourselves, while accepting that we will fumble along the way and releasing the shame of those fumbles. Mariame Kaba tells us that abolition is much more than a feeling; it is mutual aid campaigns, movements to shrink police budgets, closing prisons, creating community collectives and hotlines that respond to mental health crises instead of calling the police, and removing police from schools.[19] Each of these acts of love lessens the reach of the prison industrial complex as we build communal systems of care and safety. Our goal is to end the prison industrial complex. And in terms of schools, scholar Monique W. Morris invites us to understand that schools will not be "locations of learning" until they are "locations of healing."[20] I often remind myself of the words of activist and artist Aurora Levins Morales: "In order to build the movement capable of transforming our world, we have to do our best to live with one foot in the world we have not yet created."[21]

Abolition, for me, has been a long but fulfilling journey of discovery. Choosing compassion, love, joy, forgiveness, rage, and accountability has saved my life and marriage and has helped me commit to the work of self-reflection that is required to be an abolitionist. Kaba writes "what happens in our interpersonal relationships is mirrored and reinforced by the larger systems."[22] The way we treat each other every day is reflected in our structures and institutions. When we believe there is only one way to do anything, our lack of imagination will never allow us to "make the impossible possible."[23] Abolition requires us to understand and confront "oppressive systems that live out there—and within us."[24] Therefore, the work is deeply personal and rooted in how we care for each other.

Abolitionist Micah Herskind says abolition is "the dual-pronged project of tearing down and building up, the dismantling of life-sucking systems alongside the construction of life-giving ones."[25] And we must never forget along the way that how we tear down is just as important as what we build. Political scientist Adom Getachew calls the process of tearing down and building a "worldmaking" project deeply concerned with social connection and movement beyond merely criticizing injustice.[26]

To live closer to the world we know is possible, this nation must hold itself accountable for the educational harms placed on the bodies, dreams, and lives of Black children. And how do we repair, restore, acknowledge, compensate, and commit to not repeatedly sacrificing Black children for White America's supremacy? The answer, I believe, is educational reparations.

12

A CALL FOR EDUCATIONAL REPARATIONS

> Federal assistance to black people in any form is not a
> gift but a down payment for centuries of unpaid labor,
> violence, and exploitation. We need not go all the way
> back to slavery to make the case . . . Let us take just
> one example: education.
>
> —Robin D. G. Kelley, *Freedom Dreams:*
> *The Black Radical Imagination*[1]

Making Justice Invisible

Our public school system prior to *Brown v. Board of Education* is legible to the American public as racist. Black children were relegated to dilapidated schoolhouses with outdated books, while White children were given new buildings. As a nation, we understand how racism functioned within education because the country simply did not try to hide it. On the other hand, the insidious nature of education reform lies in the masquerade of seemingly benign and benevolent policies that are, in fact, deeply anti-Black. Because of such policies, there is little national conversation today about the structural overhaul of America's racist school system; cosmetic changes, rooted in anti-Blackness, are now passed off as justice.

As I have shown in these pages, reform removes the possibility of radically overhauling our educational system. Reforms are used to keep Black progress at bay as super predators remove opportunity after opportunity, stripping our communities of public services and investments to strengthen communities and jobs while, at worst, killing and incarcerating us. Reform takes advantage of our hopes of living outside the conditions created for us. We are punished for fighting for justice.

What is owed to Black children and their families who have been educated in a violent system dedicated to their deprivation? How can we end and repair the harm wrought over the past forty years?

The answer is clear: it is time for educational reparations. Many scholars, activists, and authors—among them Kimberlé Crenshaw, William Darity Jr., Dania Francis, A. Kirsten Mullen, Katherine Franke, Darrick Hamilton, Robin D. G. Kelley, Angela Davis, Nikole Hannah-Jones, Robert K. Fullinwider, "Queen Mother" Audley Moore, Clarence Munford, the Black Panthers, the Republic of New Afrika, Judith Lichtenberg, Melvin Oliver, Thomas Shapiro, Boris Bittker, Ta-Nehisi Coates, and Randall Robinson—have called for reparations to help address the exploitation and oppression of Black people over the past four centuries. Few, however, have done so in the field of education.

Reparations

Countless reparations proposals were presented before the Civil War and after the federal government reneged on its promise to give freed Black people forty acres of land. Organizations and Black nationalists like "Queen Mother" Audley Moore, who elevated the concept of reparations for descendants of Africans in the United States after World War II, thought deeply about how reparations could uplift and empower the Black community.

Moore formed the Reparations Committee of Descendants of U.S. Slaves. Her organization demanded $500 trillion from the U.S. government as partial compensation for enslavement and Jim Crow.[2] The money, she said, would be controlled by the community. Moore wanted a "thoroughly democratic structure" in place so that everyday Black folx could decide what to do with the funds.[3]

The Black Panther Party also demanded reparations as restitution for enslaved labor and the mass murder of Black people. In 1969, the Black Manifesto, presented by former Student Nonviolent Coordinating Committee executive secretary James Forman, was released as the "first systematic, fully elaborated plan for reparations to emerge from the black freedom movement."[4] The manifesto asked for $500 million in reparations to be paid by White churches and synagogues for their role in perpetuating and maintaining enslavement and racism. The money would be spent creating a Southern land bank, Black-owned television networks and publishing companies, job-training centers, labor unions, and Black universities. The Black Manifesto inspired subsequent demands for reparations, including a plan put forth in 1987 by the National Coalition of Blacks for Reparations, which advocated for Congress to pay at least $3 billion annually to African Americans.

In their groundbreaking 1995 book, *Black Wealth / White Wealth,* sociologists Thomas Shapiro and Melvin Oliver gave language to what Black folx have known for centuries. Shapiro and Oliver took a nuanced approach by analyzing wealth's role rather than income. Economic disparities are driven by centuries of structural racism, all of which date back to the enslavement of Black people, that persist in housing, banking, health care, education, tech, and discrimination in the labor market. Studying income disparities does not capture the magnitude of wealth that

White America has accumulated and passed down over centuries by benefiting from racism and educational White rage. And experts maintain that the greatest transfer of wealth is happening today.[5] Those in the baby boomer generation have begun to pass down their wealth. Researchers have projected that by 2045, as much as $84 trillion will be transferred to a relatively small pool of heirs and philanthropic organizations; in contrast, 93.6 million Americans will split $59 trillion.[6] In *Repair: Redeeming the Promise of Abolition,* Katherine Franke writes that "the heirs of white baby boomers are poised to inherit sums ranging from nice nest eggs to veritable fortunes from our parents."[7]

As Nikole Hannah-Jones succinctly puts it: "Wealth begets wealth, and White Americans have had centuries of government assistance to accumulate wealth, while the government has for the vast history of this country worked against Black Americans doing the same."[8] William Darity Jr., a leading reparations scholar on the wealth gap, estimates that gap at $11.2 trillion.[9] In a comparison of Black and White wealth in 2019, the "average figure for Black households was $142,500; for white households, $983,400, close to $1 million."[10] "Incremental measures," Darity argues, "will not be sufficient to address the enormous racial wealth disparity."[11]

Another proposal that has gained traction in recent years is baby bonds. A bond would be given to all newborns, regardless of race, in a trust account, the amount of which would be determined by the child's family income. At age eighteen, the bond could be used for wealth-building activities like buying a home or paying for higher education. Eliminating student debt is another popular proposal to address the wealth gap. In 2022, the Biden administration announced a plan to forgive up to $20,000 in federal student loan debt for those who qualify. This type of student loan debt relief is a step in the right direction, but it's not enough. A 2021 report found that erasing $50,000 in student loan debt for all borrowers would increase Black wealth by 40 percent.[12] Although baby bonds and canceling student debt are necessary, they are incremental approaches and fall short of reparations and addressing the structural policies that maintain the wealth gap. More recently, the Movement for Black Lives called for reparations to systemically account for, acknowledge, and repair past and ongoing harm—not solely through monetary compensation but also through ending anti-Black policies.[13]

Each of these perspectives informs my understanding of reparations. But I believe that the field of education provides Black people a clear path toward collectively reaching an agreement that sufficiently addresses harm, structural policies, and redress for educational injustice. I am advocating for reparations from damages caused by education reform over the past forty years. Public education's divestments and policies document our nation's commitment to anti-Blackness, providing a clear and concise road map to understanding how Black children—unlike their White peers—have been under-resourced, over-policed, over-tested, and deprived of educational opportunities with lifelong earning effects. As a nation, we must commit to ending education reform to move public education toward healing and transformation.

But we shouldn't stop with education. I would like to see a calculation of reparations of each major industry in the U.S. What does the banking industry owe Black people? What do the medical, housing, and prison industries owe Black people? What does our violent foster care system owe Black people? Answering these questions thoroughly and honestly allows us to name the harm and move toward repairing, healing, and transforming each industry. Addressing reparations through only one lever—the wealth gap—does not allow people who have been harmed to lead in transforming these industries, which in turn transforms society.

The Fullness of Reparations Is Democracy

Educational reparations are not about creating a better education system that will benefit only Black children. Instead, all children benefit from an abundantly funded public education system. Every child would benefit from the hiring and retaining of an overrepresentation of Black teachers and teachers of color. Schools must center healing and joy, multiple languages, religions, and abilities. Schools must work to sever education's ties to carcerality by replacing cops with counselors, therapists, social workers, and nurses. I am not against tests, but we need to end high-stakes standardized testing and replace it with in-house tests that assist teachers in understanding the areas in which their students need more support. Reparations would fund well-resourced state-of-the-art schools with curricula that honor different cultures and traditions with love and admiration and where neurodivergence is welcomed and celebrated. Schools that function in a thriving democracy don't track their students; they provide curricula to ensure that all students receive rich and engaging learning opportunities. Schools that function in a thriving democracy provide nutritious food and medical, mental, and dental care. They offer robust art, music, dance, and athletic programs. Ultimately, they transform education for all children of all skin colors and economic backgrounds.

Educational reparations *are* the essence of democracy. In their fullness, reparations include the processes of accountability, truth-telling, repair, cessation, compensation, healing, and transformation. Educational reparations would fundamentally move this nation beyond buzzwords that signal justice without action. They would put in place a process of atonement for generations of harm.

By definition, atonement is an "apology plus reparations,"

with no obligation for the people who have been harmed to forgive.[14] The apology must be sincere and come from a place of humanity instead of legality.[15] The objective of the apology is not simply to acknowledge harm but to repair it. To atone is to morally reach beyond the apology to a redemptive act that ends the individual or institutional practice(s) of harm and starts the process of healing and, ultimately, transformation. Only after we take accountability for harm can we enter a conversation about restitution; accountability and restitution are determined by the individual, group, or community that has been harmed. Cessation is also a crucial component of reparations; we cannot move forward with reparations without ending harm.

As a nation, we are long overdue in needing to build the skills to listen to each other, develop the muscles of empathy and vulnerability, deal with the shame of Whiteness and its violence, and celebrate Blackness in all its shades, genders, sexualities, languages, religions, and abilities. I am describing a lengthy process full of fumbles, generative conflicts, and addressing harm, power, and oppression interpersonally and institutionally[16]; this process is necessary to truly transform education and our nation.

For inspiration, we need only look outside the U.S. For example, countries around the world have launched commissions to confront racism, state-sanctioned violence, and systemic injustice. The most well-known is South Africa's Truth and Reconciliation Commission. After the end of apartheid, South Africa entered a formal reconciliation process. In order for Black South African people to know what happened to their loved ones, White nationalists at public hearings revealed the brutal violence they perpetrated—in exchange, they received amnesty from prosecution. Compensation was another part of the commission, but it fell short of any amount required to address economic injustices or redistribute power adequately. Reflecting on the imperfect process in 2020, Pumla Gobodo-Madikizela, a psychologist on the commission and now a leading authority on forgiveness, told *The New York Times*:

> The commission had recommended that one of the things that has to happen is to pay attention to how we rebuild families, how we rebuild communities. And how you do that is ensuring that structures like schools are properly running. What you find today is the brokenness of the culture and the environment where people live. They are places not really suitable for the dignity of human life. People don't feel a sense of worth. They sense that their government doesn't care for them.[17]

The fullness of reparations is not simply compensating individuals for harm but also repairing and transforming society. Dr. King said it best: "You have got to have a reconstruction of the entire society, a revolution of values. . . . We are not interested in being integrated into *this* value structure. Power must be relocated, a radical redistribution of power must take place."[18]

A History of Lost Opportunities

After 250 years of enslavement, 90 years of Jim Crow, 60 years of the separate-but-equal doctrine, 35 years of housing discrimination, and 40 years of education reform, the U.S. government owes a compounded moral and financial debt to Black people.[19] In 2008 and 2009, the House of Representatives and Senate put forth long-overdue resolutions to apologize for enslavement and Jim Crow. They failed, however, to propose any accompanying redemptive actions.[20] This omission is especially glaring when you consider that this country has previously accompanied an official apology with action.

After World War II, the U.S. government created the Indian Claims Commission to compensate any federally recognized tribe for land stolen by the government. The commission paid out roughly $1.3 billion—at the time, less than $1,000 for every Native American.[21] The compensation fell far short of addressing the economic injustices of colonization, and still today, the U.S. government violently takes Indigenous land.

The Civil Liberties Act, signed by Ronald Reagan in 1988, acknowledged the "grave injustice" that Japanese Americans endured during World War II as they were rounded up and held in internment camps. An apology was issued, and more than $1.6 billion in compensation was paid. Survivors and heirs of prisoners—82,219 people in all—received $20,000 each.[22] A smaller group of Japanese American claimants also received $37 million in compensation for lost property in 1948.[23]

In 2013, a $10 million fund was created to compensate over 7,600 people in North Carolina who were sterilized under a decades-long eugenics program.[24] However, many victims, largely poor, disabled, and Black, were "deemed ineligible because they had been sterilized by county welfare offices and not the state eugenics program" or were deceased—the fund did not transfer to survivors or heirs.[25] Similarly, in California, a $7.5 million fund was created for roughly 600 victims of "coerced sterilization, both under the eugenics law and in prison." There, comparable restrictions limited eligibility.[26]

In 2015, the city of Chicago agreed to pay $5.5 million in compensation to fifty-seven victims of police brutality and torture—Black men who were beaten, shocked, and suffocated to extract confessions.[27] The city also established a Torture Justice Center to provide counseling to survivors of police brutality and educate Chicago students about police torture.[28] The nearby city of Evanston, Illinois, agreed to distribute $10 million for the harm of discriminatory housing policies and practices to Black residents who lived in the city between 1919 and 1969 or suffered from such discrimination in later years.[29] In 2022, the city of Asheville, North Carolina, approved the Reparations Commission to repair the "damage caused by public and private systemic racism."[30] Asheville committed $2.1 million to their reparations fund.[31]

In 2019, Georgetown University voted to increase tuition by $27 to compensate descendants of the 272 enslaved Africans who were sold to keep the school open in 1838. Georgetown, a private school with a $1.66 billion endowment, passed the obligation of compensation to its students.[32]

In 2022, Harvard University released a report detailing the school's ties to enslavement. The report disclosed how faculty and staff enslaved Black people from the university's founding in 1636 to when Massachusetts banned enslavement in 1783.[33] Even after enslavement was illegal in the state, Harvard still profited from donors whose money came from the textile industry. "During the first half of the 19th century," the report said, "more than a third of the money donated or promised to Harvard by private individuals came from just five men who made their fortunes from slavery and slave-produced commodities." The university plans to distribute $100 million in compensation to Black and Indigenous students, partner with Historically Black Colleges and Universities, and create an endowment to continue reparations efforts.

In 2021, Congress put forth a bill to study reparations, originally proposed by Representative John Conyers of Michigan in 1989. The bill remains stuck in limbo—Republicans oppose the legislation, and President Biden is not acting on the issue, despite having the power to establish a commission on reparations without Congress. However, one of the most promising and ambitious developments in the fight for reparations is happening in the state of California. In 2020, the Golden State's governor, Gavin Newsom, formed a nine-member task force to start the formal process of examining the best way to administer reparations to Black Californians. In December of 2022, the task force determined that Black Californians were owned $569 billion in reparations, or $223,200 per person, for decades of systemic racism.[34] The task force identified five areas for compensation: housing discrimination, mass incarceration, unjust property seizures, devaluation of Black businesses, and health.[35] Education is missing from the task force report, but I am optimistic because this is the largest examination of reparations since Reconstruction.[36]

The concept of Black reparations is difficult for many Americans to grasp because of the profundity of anti-Blackness and the weight of the truth. And that is precisely why reparations must include transformative measures. The few examples of economic reparations I have cited have not led to repair, healing, or transformation. Compensation is crucial, but transformation, or even an end to oppression, is the goal—otherwise, the cycle will continue. Police brutality in Chicago has not ceased because of compensation to victims of police brutality; it is systemically ingrained in policing. As Robin D. G. Kelley writes, when we envision reparations "as part of a broad strategy to radically transform society—redistributing wealth, creating a democratic and caring public culture, exposing the ways capitalism and slavery produced massive inequality—then the ongoing struggle for reparations holds enormous promise for revitalizing movements for social justice."[37]

I agree with Kelley's holistic reparations argument: "Money and resources are always important, but a new vision and new values cannot be bought. And without at least a rudimentary critique of the capitalist culture that consumes us, even reparations can have disastrous consequences."[38] This is why reformers at the forefront of anti-Black education policies must not be allowed to shape-shift and maneuver to become the leading authorities on educational reparations without atoning, restructuring values, and redistributing power and resources. Reformers and educational entrepreneurs love to reinvent themselves to fit the needs of the communities they have destroyed and put in the position to need the reformers' help.

To put an even finer point on it: the likes of Bill and Melinda Gates cannot lead the movement to repair the harm of the past forty years of educational damage. In addition, we need these powerful reformers to relinquish control and end the damage caused by their reform policies and influence. Finally, we need reparations as compensation for the harm they've caused.

Compensation for the harm of education reform is only the start. Well-funded public schools and communities driven by the people who live there need to center on love, joy, healing, and the emotional well-being of students. This will improve the lives of Black children; it will also improve our nation—and our humanity—as a whole. We must value education beyond job skills and economic productivity as a nation. Education should be a space where children, our greatest gift, learn to love, understand difference, communicate inside of disagreement and conflict, find joy in learning, and have the time and resources to be guided by their imaginations.

A Call to Duty

It is no small task to calculate precisely how the past forty years of education reform have harmed Black people. To do so, I had the help of three experts: Shanyce L. Campbell, a critical quantitative scholar at the University of Pittsburgh who studies how policies influence access to quality learning opportunities for students of color; Hope Wollensack, a senior strategist at the Economic Security Project in Atlanta; and Nzinga H. Broussard, an experienced applied microeconomist.

Together, through the rigorous data collection and analysis detailed below, we determined that Black folx are collectively owed an estimated $56 billion for surviving the past forty years of experimental school reform. Specifically, we (Black folx) are owed $33 billion for years spent in subpar school buildings. We are owed $16 billion for their disparate experience of policing and surveillance in their schools. We are owed $6 billion for educational time lost due to disparate out-of-school suspensions. We are owed $1.1 billion for having been denied rich and engaging curricula. In addition to the above, we are owed between $1.5 trillion and $2.0 trillion for lifetime earnings lost due to school reform. Here's how we arrived at these numbers.

First, we developed a rigorous set of criteria. To calculate reparations, we considered the severest injustices caused by education reforms, focusing on three areas: the physical condition of schools, access to rich and engaging learning, and the carceral inevitability that undergirds schools. We also calculated the cost of Black children being pushed out of school due to the lack of Black teachers and postsecondary earning loss. We drew on existing studies conducted by policy institutions and academic scholars for each area.

To determine what is owed to Black folx due to education reforms, we calculated the economic costs incurred by the cohort of children that entered kindergarten between 1985 and 2005. We chose this twenty-year cohort for our analysis because these are the groups of students who were most influenced by the 1980s and 1990s education reforms and are now in the workforce.

These students are the earliest to have experienced education reform policies that affected all thirteen years of their education.

For example, a Black person who started kindergarten in 2005 would have graduated high school in 2018 and, in 2022, completed college and entered the workforce. At this point, higher education and labor market decisions, which their K–12 education would have influenced, would have been determined. In short, there are little to no education-related factors or resources that policy makers could introduce that would impact this group's lifetime earnings trajectories. Those entering kindergarten after 2005 are still in the decision stage in terms of either educational or labor market decisions. They can be influenced by governmental factors and additional support that may impact their lifetime earnings trajectory.

A cohort model allowed us to group the shared educational experiences of each incoming class of Black students in those twenty years. The cohorts included in our analysis totaled 11,945,000 Black students. The last cohort graduated in 2018. We argue that the past forty years' educational policies directly impacted their K–12 educational outcomes and indirectly on their higher education and labor market decisions and outcomes.

It's important to note that we used conservative fiscal estimates to determine the dollar amounts we believe are owed to Black folx. When ranges were provided in studies, we used the lower amounts in our calculations. The lower-bounded calculations (all reported in 2021 dollars) allow us to understand the *bare minimum owed to us.*

To our knowledge, these are the first calculations of educational reparations with categories of harm. The only other comprehensive work on educational reparations is by Preston C. Green III, Bruce D. Baker, and Joseph O. Oluwole, who also argue for educational reparations, but specifically in terms of school finance. Their work on school finance and reparations is critical to

272 • Punished for Dreaming

understanding just how inadequate racist and anti-Black school funding formulas are in providing educational justice. We hope our calculations expand the imagination of the categories of educational harm, so we fully understand how Black children have been disposed of by our own public education system.[39]

Lastly, we cannot calculate harm fully because some data sets we needed simply don't exist. For example, there are no clear data on how many police officers are in schools every day. Additionally, we lack national or even state-level data across grade levels to fully calculate the number of Black students not enrolled in enriching and engaging courses. Finally, historical data on capital outlay spent across each school in the nation is not readily available to estimate the extent to which school buildings are being neglected. We need better data that capture educational harm to calculate educational reparations fully.

We hope our work stands as a call of duty to start the conversation surrounding educational reparations and move us closer to investing in Black education for America's future.

School Funding and Spending Inequalities

Before we share our data and calculations, we think it's important to address school funding and spending, which would need to be rightsized alongside any forthcoming reparations approach. Looking at school funding and spending, especially on the state and local level, could be a way to determine how fiscal disparities persist for Black students. Unfortunately, this information is poorly documented and difficult to parse. States use a variety of funding formulas. School districts have different demographics and sizes. As such, it's hard to generate a simple statistic on funding disparities by race.

While aggregate data can show what appears to be funding similarities, when the data are disaggregated, disparities between

Black students and White students persist in many districts and states. Furthermore, relatively equal funding does not mean equitable outcomes. For example, Pennsylvania has the most inequitable school funding formula in the U.S.[40] In Pennsylvania, according to *The Washington Post,* "on average, high-poverty districts spend approximately 30 percent less than more affluent districts."[41] Underfunded schools are asked to do more with fewer academic resources, personnel, and continued budget cuts. Pennsylvania is just one example of why communities and children who have experienced aggressive underinvestment and divestment for decades will require additional funding to promote equitable outcomes.

School spending is where Black students are losing the most. As discussed in chapter 5, Biden proposed doubling funding for Title I schools in 2023. The primary purpose of this increase was to combat spending disparities. Although per-pupil spending may appear relatively equal nationally—there are many outliers like Pennsylvania—how those funds are spent by schools serving a majority Black student population varies substantially, thus creating a de facto gap in resources and investment in Black students.

Schools serving a majority Black student population tend to spend a higher portion of their budgets on security equipment, SROs, and building repair and maintenance. These schools, then, spend their money in ways that maintain and uphold anti-Blackness. By contrast, as researchers C. Kirabo Jackson, Rucker C. Johnson, and Claudia Persico have shown, school finance reforms that increase school funding, not anti-Blackness, produce "sizable improvements in measured school quality, including reductions in student-to-teacher ratios, increases in teacher salaries, and longer school years."[42] Their findings show that greater funding can improve learning outcomes. We therefore support the increase in school funding that Biden has proposed as a starting place for a more progressive school-funding model. But we also need an asset-based school-spending approach. Again, money matters, but how we spend it also matters.

K–12 Educational Reparations

SCHOOL BUILDING CONDITIONS

Our communities ask Black children to enter poorly maintained or crumbling school buildings for at least six hours daily. We see this in multiple reports from across the country, from lead that has been found in the water of 98 percent of all schools in Philadelphia to old HVAC systems and windowless classrooms. Black children across the country spend a quarter of their lives at schools with polluted water and air, poor lighting, and sunlight-deprived conditions. This contrast was shockingly evident during the pandemic, when affluent White schools were able to implement COVID-19 prevention strategies to keep their students safe because their schools had windows, space to keep students separated, and money for masks.

Research demonstrates that underinvestment in school buildings directly impacts students' learning and well-being. For example, the poor air quality of many schools directly affects students' health and learning. Childhood asthma linked to poor air exposure results in roughly 13.8 million missed school days yearly.[43] *The Washington Post* reported that "between 1995 and 2004, school districts spent nearly $600 billion in capital expenditures." However, "non-White, non-affluent districts were more likely to spend on basic repairs such as to roofs and windows that failed from years of deferred maintenance, while affluent White districts were more likely to invest in educational enhancements such as science labs or performance arts spaces."[44]

We calculated the total per-pupil capital outlay expenditures for Black and White students in 2018 using the Department of

Education's National Center for Education Statistics, Common Core of Data. Capital outlay expenditures per Black student were $1,298; per White student, the figure was $1,494. For the cohort of 11,945,000 Black students who attended school between 1985 and 2005, we therefore calculated that due to unequal funding in capital outlay expenditures, we were denied roughly **$33 billion.**

Enriching Curriculum

In schools across the country, racialized tracking and ability grouping are practices that continue to deny Black children a rich and expansive learning environment. Studies show that Black students are systematically placed in lower tracks, such as remedial or regular courses.[45] Once students are placed on a track, the opportunities for switching tracks are minimal. While some might suggest that enrollment into advanced courses is based on students' ability, crudely measured by their standardized test scores, their placements are rooted in teachers' and counselors' lower expectations and discriminatory behaviors.[46] These racist practices are highlighted in a study investigating the reasons Black students are less likely than White students to be placed in advanced courses.[47]

To quantify what is owed to the Black community for the loss of opportunities to experience a meaningful, rich, engaging curriculum, we considered the market rate of taking an advanced course. Specifically, we asked how much an Advanced Placement or International Baccalaureate course was worth. Because nearly all colleges and universities award credits for receiving a passing AP and IB exam score, the cost of those high school courses is equivalent to a single college-level course. In 2022, the average cost of a college course for an in-state student at a four-year public university was $1,170.[48]

According to a 2010 report by the Education Trust, about 97,000 Black students were not enrolled but would participate in an AP or IB course at the same rate as their peers if given the opportunity.

For the cohort of 11,945,000 Black students who attended school between 1985 and 2005, we estimated that 4 percent, or 508,857 students, were in high school but not allowed to participate in AP or IB programs due to racist practices. The 4 percent was arrived at by taking the total number of Black high school students who had the opportunity to enroll in advanced courses based on the 2010 report (~97,000 Black students) and dividing them by the total number of Black high school students in the cohort (2,275,238). For having been denied these rich and engaging learning conditions, Black folx are therefore owed **$1.1 billion.**

CARCERAL INEVITABILITY

Suspensions
As I have explained throughout this book, Black students receive significantly more—and worse—disciplinary punishments than their White peers. In the 2019 report, *Beyond Suspensions,* the U.S. Commission on Civil Rights found:

> Students of color as a whole, as well as by individual racial group, do not commit more disciplinable offenses than their white peers—but black students, Latino students, and Native American students in the aggregate receive substantially more school discipline than their white peers and receive harsher and longer punishments than their white peers receive for like offenses.[49]

The Learning Policy Institute and Center for Civil Rights Remedies recently calculated the unjust disparities in out-of-school suspensions. Across the nation in 2016, Black students lost fifty-one more days of school due to out-of-school suspensions than White students. For all these unjustly lost days, some schools continue to receive dollars on the students' behalf. This money is spent on the salaries of administrators, teachers, and school resource officers, yet caregivers bear the financial burden of finding care for their children or forfeiting work when their children are suspended.

Using the 2016 per-pupil expenditure of $12,618, the cost of disparities in suspension was $36 per Black student. For the cohort of 11,945,000 Black students who attended school between 1985 and 2005, we calculated the cost to be **$6 billion.** This amount might appear large, but the figure is a lower-bound estimate if we account for the current underfunding of schools; the estimate also does not consider the inequities from in-school suspensions.

School Resource Officers

The presence of police in schools has mental and physical impacts on Black children, who are surveilled by school staff and administration. As I have detailed, the presence of SROs results in an increase in arrests and referrals to the juvenile justice system. It also disrupts learning. Both have consequences on lifetime earnings.[50] As a nation, we have normalized carceral logic, even in our understanding of safety. As Erica Meiners has written:

> The prevailing contemporary carceral logic recycles the false notion that safety can be achieved through essentially more of the same: more guards, fences, surveillance, suspensions, punishment, etc. Inviting abolition futures pushes us to name how this "more of the same"—building more youth detention centers and prisons, funneling more youth into suspensions or expulsions, placing more police and cameras in schools—will not make schools safer, or our communities stronger. We must reclaim definitions of safety.[51]

Safety must look and feel different, and this nation must compensate for the violence inflicted on Black bodies in the name of safety. To calculate the carceral conditions experienced overwhelmingly by Black students, we used the Department of Education's National Center for Education Statistics' School Survey on Crime and Safety data. The data show that for the 2017–2018 school year, 61.4 percent of public schools had one or more security staff, totaling 60,477 public schools. We used the median salary and benefits data for a senior security guard, which closely mirrors the skills of an SRO, along with the estimated costs for equipment and overhead, to determine the total cost of one SRO in a school: $80,099.[52]

Our argument here is that the presence of SROs has deleteriously impacted Black students. Their salaries can quantify this presence. If SROs were not in schools, these monies could have been spent on resources that positively benefit Black students, such as additional social workers, school nurses, counselors, and so on. For the cohort of 11,945,000 Black students who attended school between 1985 and 2005, the cost of having at least one SRO in each school came to **$16 billion.** This estimate was calculated for schools with only one SRO and does not consider that many Black students attend schools with a higher presence of security personnel.

Over the past forty years, failed education policy reforms have resulted in an educational system where, for decades, Black folx couldn't, and today still can't, thrive. The school buildings we are asked to enter, the suboptimal classes we are made to take, and the carceral logics that undergird schools must be repaired if we are ever to improve the conditions of Black folx and this nation as a whole. For the cohort of 11,945,000 Black students who attended school between 1985 and 2005 and endured thirteen years of this schooling, the sum total owed across the three areas listed above is estimated at **$56 billion.**

Post-Secondary Educational Reparations

EARNINGS LOSS DUE TO BLACK TEACHER DISPLACEMENT AND BLACK STUDENT PUSH-OUT

Black people have suffered a loss in earnings due to policies that displaced Black teachers and contributed to higher dropout rates among Black students. For our 1985–2005 cohorts, we have estimated that 56 percent of them never had a Black teacher during their thirteen years of schooling.[53] Research shows that having at least one Black teacher in grades K–3 increases the likelihood of graduating high school by more than 10 percent.[54] Using those numbers, we found that if the 56 percent of Black students who never had a Black teacher had at least one Black teacher during their thirteen years of schooling, at least 582,000 additional Black students would have graduated high school. Research by Christopher Tamborini, ChangHwan Kim, and Arthur Sakamoto shows that adults with a high school degree earn between $285,000 and $357,000 more in median lifetime earnings than those who did not graduate high school. If the 582,000 additional Black high school graduates earned the extra income that came with a high school degree, the additional income generated over their lifetimes would be between **$209 billion and $262 billion.**

EARNING LOSS DUE TO PREVENTION OF COLLEGE ATTENDANCE

To calculate the loss in earnings due to educational policies over the past forty years that adversely affected Black students, we relied on literature that shows there are significant returns to a college degree compared to a high school degree; the past forty years of anti-Black educational policies, we argue, contributed to Black students being less likely to attain a college degree than their White peers. Using data from the Current Population Survey, we found that since 1980, 10 percent fewer Black students obtained bachelor's degrees than their White peers.

We estimate that if Black students attained college degrees in the same proportion as their White peers, there would have been an additional 1.6 million Black college and university graduates over the past twenty years. Studies show that adults with bachelor's or advanced degrees earn between $587,000 and $840,000 more in median lifetime earnings than high school graduates.[55] If the 1.6 million more Black university graduates earned that additional income from college degrees, the income generated over their lifetimes would be between **$1.2 trillion and $1.7 trillion.**

In total, we estimate that Black folx who endured thirteen years of racist educational policies that were put in place over the past forty years are owed between **$1.5 trillion and $2.0 trillion in lifetime earnings.**

Policies that took a toll on Black students' educational environments, learning outcomes, and educational-attainment decisions affected them not only during their thirteen years of

Educational Reparations for 40 Years of Reform

CURRICULUM
For being excluded from enriching curriculum: $1.1 billion

OFFICERS
For the unnecessary and violent presence of School Resource Officers: $16 billion

EARNINGS LOSS
For losses in earning due reforms: between $1.2 trillion and $1.7 trillion

BLACK FOLX ARE OWED $1.5-$2.0 TRILLION

SUSPENSIONS
For unjust out-of-school suspensions: $6 billion

EARNINGS LOSS - PUSHOUT
For losses in earnings due to being pushed out and never having a Black teacher: between $209 billion and $262 billion

BUILDINGS
For attending dilapidated schools that are detrimental to their well-being: $33 billion

The dollar amounts are based on conservative estimates and should be considered minimum amounts owed to Black folx.

schooling—they also have consequences for lifetime earnings. We estimate that Black households in our cohort are owed between **$1.5 trillion and $2.0 trillion,** about the equivalent of the GDP of Texas. The chart on page 280 is a visual representation of our calculations.

Who Pays?

The federal government perpetrated much of the harm done to Black children by America's public school system. Therefore, a large part of the funding for educational reparations should be paid by the U.S. government. Much of what I understand about how the federal government should fund reparations is detailed in William Darity Jr. and A. Kirsten Mullen's book *From Here to Equality: Reparations for Black Americans in the Twenty-First Century.* As Darity and Mullen wrote, "The invoice for reparations must go to the nation's government. The U.S. government, as the federal authority, bears responsibility for sanctioning, maintaining, and enabling slavery, legal segregation, and continued racial inequality."[56] The authors add that the U.S. Congress should have jurisdiction over Black reparations and that Black reparations should be removed from the judicial system because of "lawsuits brought against corporations, colleges and universities for their participation in slavery are unlikely to succeed because slavery was legal" and the "courts do not have the capacity to implement or enforce any legal mandate they might hand down for black reparations."[57]

Removing Black reparations from the judicial system and putting the decision squarely in the hands of Congress would increase the odds of reparations being approved. However, it would still be a daunting task in the current state of this nation. Regardless, it's the nation's moral duty to right such wrongs. Economic and political journalist Matthew Yglesias reported that

Congress has the authority to direct the Federal Reserve to fund reparations, either fully or partially. Darity and Mullen agree. "The Fed," they write, "certainly could manage an annual outlay of $1 to $1.5 trillion without any difficulty—and this funding mechanism would not have to affect tax rates for any American. Moreover, the Federal Reserve is a *public* bank charged with conducting a public responsibility."[58]

Darity and Mullen suggest that a series of individual payments over several years "would increase the prospect of financing." These payments would be adjusted for inflation over time. In the case of educational reparations, I propose that payments be administered by an educational reparations supervisory board overseen by the Department of Education. Working with the Department of Education, the Federal Reserve would create an in-house educational reparations supervisory board, and payments would go directly to individuals harmed by education reform over the past forty years. These payments do not simply represent compensation for the harm caused by the U.S. education system. They are also an investment in Black futures, Black education, Black self-determination, and democracy. The payments would decrease the wealth gap, but they would not eliminate it, so we must fight for reparations beyond educational settlements. So much harm has been done, but compensation is a movement toward justice and is connected to the larger movements for racial justice in this country. As the Department of Education distributes funds to individuals harmed by its system, philanthropic foundations and corporations must also be held responsible for the harm they inflicted and profited from through education reform.

We need an additional reparations fund of billions, if not trillions, of philanthropic and corporate dollars for the harm they have caused Black lives. This superfund is separate from the federal government's reparation payments. It is needed to support health care and mental health initiatives; home-buying funds; arts programs; job training and job-growth initiatives; community birth centers; programs to address environmental racism, expand internet access, eliminate food deserts, provide rental assistance and financial resources for those incarcerated and formerly incarcerated; and funds to meet community needs. We didn't calculate this fund due to a lack of resources and data. Still, we hope that the amount will be calculated in the future to hold corporations and philanthropic foundations accountable.

Who Is Eligible?

There is a growing debate in the fight for reparations concerning who is eligible to receive them. Some believe that only descendants of enslaved Black folx should receive reparations. Some go even further, arguing that reparations should go to individuals who can trace their lineage to enslaved people held in the United States, thereby excluding children of African or Caribbean descent. I strongly disagree with the exclusion of African and Caribbean people. What we need is a more expansive and inclusive approach to eligibility. I want to be clear that these data sets that label Black students as Black also erase countless Black students who are Indigenous, multiracial, and/or Caribbean. There are multiple racialized experiences that are not captured in the term "Black." No data set can capture the complexity of race and identity that is needed to fully understand Blackness. In our nation's schools, if a child self-identifies as Black or the school labels them Black, they are treated as Black. Education reform has been indiscriminately violent toward Black children regardless of their genealogy. Hence, once you are seen as Black in this country, anti-Blackness follows, making you disposable.

With that said, educational reparations should focus on repairing harm for all children labeled as Black or identifying as

Black who entered schools in the past four decades. The years we have considered in our calculations allow us to look at only a 20-year cohort of the more than 400 years since 1619—when enslavement began in America—making the case for reparations for all Black people. However, I hope that researchers will be inspired to calculate educational reparations dating back to the start of public education.

The National Center for Education Statistics collects, analyzes, and publishes statistics on education and public school district finances from across the country. It defines Black or African Americans as "A person having origins in any of the Black racial groups of Africa." This includes the diaspora. A starting place to determine eligibility would be school district data collected by NCES to determine who is labeled Black by public schools and should therefore receive compensation, but this data set would be just the starting point. Complexity and nuance are needed to be as inclusive as possible to prevent as much Black erasure as possible.

Reparations are fundamentally about repairing harm, improving our democracy, and confronting anti-Blackness; we cannot leave out millions of Black-born Americans and Black immigrants who have also suffered under reform.

Transforming DEI

Freedom is much more than the absence of bondage;
it requires the tools, the capacities, and opportunities
that make independent human action possible.[59]

—Katherine Franke,
Repair: Redeeming the Promise of Abolition

For years, I have had the privilege of working with countless DEI leaders around the country. These school leaders are committed to equity, and they are frustrated. Their job descriptions do not match the realities of their work, nor do they align with the principles of equity and justice. These leaders need the ability to do their jobs, not be positioned as protectors of Whiteness while trying to shield Black students from racism.

The work DEI leaders need to do is a massive undertaking, and it seems impossible in the current state of public education. Uprooting racism, sexism, homophobia, transphobia, and other forms of discrimination; eliminating structural barriers that have historically excluded people of color, queer folx, trans folx, disabled folx, and women; creating school climates where all students, families, and educators feel welcomed, supported, and valued; and ensuring that students from all backgrounds and abilities have what they need to excel while understanding students whose families have survived racism and anti-Blackness for centuries—this will require additional resources. These goals are critical to educational justice and building a nation committed to freedom. As Katherine Franke makes plain, freedom is much more than the absence of captivity—it is living in a nation that supports thriving by providing its people with the tools and opportunities to "make independent human action possible." Public education committed to these goals is the foundation for a nation where all people thrive.

These goals are not achievable under the current structure of DEI work. DEI that doesn't address power, harm, accountability, and repair will remain an insufficient tool for justice. We need something new, and a simple name change won't do. We need a commitment to truth, an end to educational White rage, compensation for harm, and healing that leads to transformation. We need to move past DEI and instead embrace the work of Community and School Reparations Collectives (CSRCs).

In my vision for educational reparations, DEI departments that are already a part of school districts across the country would work with the educational reparations supervisory board and appointed community members, parents, and students to form CSRCs. Not only would CSRCs advise the superfund created by philanthropic and corporate dollars, but they would lead the fullness of reparations within their districts and communities. School districts, reformers, and educational entrepreneurs must atone for the harm they have caused and continue to cause through reform. School districts and state officials must commit to ending the harm of educational White rage and start telling the truth about all the policies they use to dispose of Black children.

CSRCs would lead truth-telling commissions, similar to those in South Africa, but focused on the generational harm that public education has caused. Working with community members, healers, abolitionists, and therapists, CSRCs would start the repair needed to transform public education fully.

The Future

Not just a love for the Harlem Renaissance or the Civil Rights Movement, but love for loud colors and loud voices. Love for sagging pants, hoodies, and corner store candies. Love for gold grills and belly laughs on hot summer porches. Carry it on as a site of struggle—as engaging with the historical and contemporary yearning to be at peace. As forging refuge from the gaze of White supremacy—where Black children dream weightless, unracialized, and human. Where language flows freely and existence is nurtured and resistance is breath. Where the Black educational imagination dances wildly into the night—quenching the thirst of yearning and giving birth to becoming.[60]

—Michael J. Dumas and kihana miraya ross,
"'Be Real Black for Me': Imagining BlackCrit in Education"

I am not naive enough to think that educational reparations and the end of education reform are around the corner. But I do believe it is coming. The work of reparations is already being actively undertaken in communities around the country on local and state levels.

Public education can be different if our values are different. The possibilities are endless when we value love, generosity, accountability, truth, freedom, belonging, and redemption—and when we have a humane approach to the economy, public safety, banking, housing, health care, and, yes, education.

This book is about more than just documenting the harm of reform. I hope it stands as a pathway forward toward the long road of repair, healing, and transformation. My work focuses on the lives of Black people, but I welcome other racialized groups to make the sorely needed case for educational reparations and calculate what is owed. I am in solidarity with you. Ending reform and fighting for educational reparations—this, I believe, is what can deliver genuine freedom for all children. But we need other influential sectors—banking, housing, health care, and tech, to name a few—to do the same, guided by justice.

I end this book where I began it, with my friend Zook. Our paths were shaped by policies intended for us to survive, perhaps, but never thrive. Both of us have been in therapy for years, learning how the conditions made for us by reform profoundly impacted every relationship in our lives. Anger and rage have always been my tools for survival. For Zook, violence proved to be a survival tool. We are still learning how to be vulnerable and demand rest, ease, and comfort. We are trying to live in a way that resists being called *resilient* yet again.

Some might say we are living the American dream. We have great careers, nice homes, and beautiful families. We "made it," so why do we deserve reparations? Our scars might be invisible, but they are still there. The harm we experienced is real. And we can't rely on exceptionalism. We live in a country where Black people must be extraordinary to live less than ordinary lives.

I want to live in a world where Black children do not have to be twice as good to get half of what White people have. The alternative is exhausting, compounded by the daily reality of White terror. Will your grocery store, church, school, community center, or home be the next site of a deadly White supremacist attack?

Repair and transformation are the hope for the future, a future where Black folx are safe and where we *all* thrive together. Repair, healing, and transformation are the only hope for our crumbling democracy. The path to and through repair and transformation is long overdue, but it is possible. Possible if we see a future where "Black children dream weightless, unracialized, and human."[61] This is our dream, a dream that heals this entire nation.

LOVE NOTES

Chels: "You're My Latest, My Greatest Inspiration," Teddy Pendergrass and "Plastic off the Sofa," Beyoncé

Chanson: "As," Stevie Wonder

Lauryn: "I Love Every Little Thing About You," Stevie Wonder

Tanya: "Outstanding," The Gap Band

Brandelyn: "Count On Me," Whitney Houston and CeCe Winans

Elisabeth: "When You Believe," Mariah Carey and Whitney Houston

St. Martin's Press team (Jennifer, Laura, Martin, Gabi, Paul, Ciara, and Jamilah): "Bigger," Beyoncé

Richard: "Simply the Best," Tina Turner

Florie: "Freedom," George Michael

Gumbee: "Don't You Know That," Luther Vandross

Gene: "Can You Feel It?," The Fat Boys

Patty and Honey: "Black Parade," Beyoncé

Mrs. Judy Knight and Mr. Knight: "Whenever You Call," Mariah Carey

Coach Nally and Mary Beth: "Gratitude," Earth Wind & Fire

Natina: "Alien Superstar," Beyoncé

Dani: "Magnificent Sanctuary Band," Donny Hathaway

John: "Wake Up Everybody," Harold Melvin & The Blue Notes

Lara: "I'll Be There," Mariah Carey

ATN Family (Sarah, Farima, Dave, Martha, Chels): "I Gotta Find Peace of Mind," Lauryn Hill

Flylight Creative Team: "I'm Every Woman," Chaka Khan (sang by Whitney Houston)

Dr. Dillard: "Giving You the Best That I Got," Anita Baker

Drina: "Always Be My Baby," Mariah Carey

Cutts: "Savage Remix," Megan Thee Stallion and Beyoncé

Treva: "Ain't No Mountain High Enough," Marvin Gaye and Tammi Terrell

Gholdy: "Golden Lady," Stevie Wonder

Yolie: "Orange Moon," Erykah Badu

Shanyce, Hope, and Nzinga: "Thank You," Kehlani

Billie: "You Got a Friend," Donnie Hathaway

Zook, Eb, Eb Shante, Vic, Ericka, Derrick, and Ray: "Joyful," Dante Bowe

Elita, Tiffany (Snaps), Regina, Joan, Nadia, LaChia, Haywood, Blair, Kelly, Jencie, Elicia, Rich, Marilyn, Roger, LaChia, RogLynn, Andrea, Austin, Torie, Shannon, Leigh, and Ki: "Be Alive," Beyoncé

Diallo: "Black Man," Stevie Wonder

Bruce and Bean: "Count on Me," Bruno Mars

Damaris, Marsha, Jam, Ashira, Alex, Kristen, Elisabeth, Willy, and Yari: "That's How Strong My Love Is," Otis Redding

Stevie/Dr. View: "Summer in the City," Quincy Jones

Dena: "I Say a Little Prayer," Aretha Franklin

Dr. Peat: "Optimistic," August Greene, Brandy, Common, Robert Glasper, and Kareem Riggins

All the people I interviewed: "Someday We'll All Be Free," Donny Hathaway

NOTES

Introduction

1. Farima Pour-Khorshid, "Y(our) Pain Matters: Toward Healing and Abolition," YouTube video, 21:01, posted by TEDx Talks, May 20, 2022, https://www.youtube.com/watch?v=lKWfxMFNZFw.
2. Mariame Kaba, *We Do This 'Til We Free Us: Abolitionist Organizing and Transforming Justice* (Chicago: Haymarket Books, 2021).
3. *Chartered for Profit: The Hidden World of Charter Schools Operated for Financial Gain,* Network for Public Education, January 23, 2022, https://networkforpubliceducation.org/chartered-for-profit/.
4. Mariame Kaba and Andrea Ritchie, *No More Police: A Case for Abolition* (New York: New Press, 2022).

1. Setting the Stage: Educational White Rage

1. Carol Anderson, *White Rage: The Unspoken Truth of Our Racial Divide* (New York: Bloomsbury, 2016).
2. Anderson, *White Rage.*
3. Anderson, *White Rage.*
4. Tomiko Brown-Nagin, *Courage to Dissent: Atlanta and the Long History of the Civil Rights Movement* (New York: Oxford University Press, 2011), 95–96, 445.
5. Brown-Nagin, *Courage to Dissent,* 68.
6. Jon Hale, *The Choice We Face: How Segregation, Race, and Power Have Shaped America's Most Controversial Education Reform Movement* (Boston: Beacon Press, 2021).
7. Richard Rothstein, *The Color of Law: A Forgotten History of How Our Government Segregated America* (New York: Liveright, 2017).
8. Equal Justice Initiative, "On This Day–Dec 18, 1952: Georgia Governor Proposes Abolition of Public School System to Avoid Integration," A History of Racial Injustice, accessed September 7, 2022, https://calendar.eji.org/racial-injustice/dec/18.
9. Equal Justice Initiative, "On This Day–Dec 18, 1952."
10. Equal Justice Initiative, "'Segregation Forever': Leaders of White Supremacy,"

Segregation in America, 2018, https://segregationinamerica.eji.org/report/segregation-forever-leaders.html.

11. Anderson, *White Rage,* 72.

12. Max Blau and Todd Michney, "Terror in the City Too Busy to Hate: How the English Avenue School Bombing Challenged Atlanta's Popular Myth of Racial Progress," *Atlanta Studies* (December 2020), https://doi.org/10.18737/atls20201212.

13. Anderson, *White Rage,* 80.

14. Anderson, *White Rage,* 80.

15. Anderson, *White Rage.*

16. Anderson, *White Rage.*

17. Anderson, *White Rage.*

18. Vanessa Siddle Walker, *Their Highest Potential: An African American School Community in the Segregated South* (Chapel Hill: University of North Carolina Press, 1996), 3.

19. bell hooks, *Teaching to Transgress: Education as the Practice of Freedom* (New York: Routledge, 1994), 1.

20. hooks, *Teaching to Transgress,* 1.

21. hooks, *Teaching to Transgress,* 2.

22. Mildred J. Hudson and Barbara J. Holmes, "Missing Teachers, Impaired Communities: The Unanticipated Consequences of *Brown v. Board of Education* on the African American Teaching Force at the Precollegiate Level," *Journal of Negro Education* 63, no. 3 (1994), https://doi.org/10.2307/2967189.

23. Hudson and Holmes, "Missing Teachers, Impaired Communities."

24. Lisa Trei, "Black Children Might Have Been Better Off Without *Brown v. Board,* Bell Says," *Stanford Report,* April 21, 2004.

25. W. E. Burghardt Du Bois, "Does the Negro Need Separate Schools?," *Journal of Negro Education* 4, no. 3 (1935), https://doi.org/10.2307/2291871.

26. Katie Gleason, "Black Gender Gap in Education: Historical Trends and Racial Comparisons," Journalist's Resource, October 4, 2011, https://journalistsresource.org/economics/black-gender-gap-college/.

27. Leslie T. Fenwick, *Jim Crow's Pink Slip: The Untold Story of Black Principal and Teacher Leadership* (Cambridge, MA: Harvard Education Press, 2022).

28. Fenwick, *Jim Crow's Pink Slip.*

29. Madeline Will, "65 Years After 'Brown v. Board,' Where Are All the Black Educators?," *Education Week,* May 14, 2019, https://www.edweek.org/policy-politics/65-years-after-brown-v-board-where-are-all-the-black-educators/2019/05.

30. Linda C. Tillman, "(Un)Intended Consequences? The Impact of the *Brown v. Board of Education* Decision on the Employment Status of Black Educators," *Education and Urban Society* 36, no. 3 (1994), https://doi.org/10.1177%2F0013124504264360.

31. Hudson and Holmes, "Missing Teachers, Impaired Communities."

32. Vanessa Siddle Walker, *Hello Professor: A Black Principal and Professional Leadership in the Segregated South* (Chapel Hill: University of North Carolina Press, 2009).

33. Jon Hale, "'The Development of Power Is the Main Business of the School': The Agency of Southern Black Teacher Associations from Jim Crow Through Deseg-

regation," *Journal of Negro Education* 87, no. 4 (2018), https://doi.org/10.7709/jnegroeducation.87.4.0444.

34. Justin Murphy, *Your Children Are Very Greatly in Danger: School Segregation in Rochester, New York* (Ithaca, NY: Cornell University Press, 2022).

35. Justin Murphy, "How Rochester's Growing City and Suburbs Excluded Black Residents," *Rochester Democrat and Chronicle,* February 5, 2020, https://www.democratandchronicle.com/in-depth/news/2020/02/05/rochester-ny-kept-black-residents-out-suburbs-decades/2750049001/.

36. City Roots Community Land Trust and the Yale Environmental Protection Clinic, *Confronting Racial Covenants: How They Segregated Monroe County and What to Do About Them* (Rochester, NY: City Roots Community Land Trust, 2020), accessed September 7, 2022, https://law.yale.edu/sites/default/files/area/clinic/document/2020.7.31_-_confronting_racial_covenants_-_yale.city_roots_guide.pdf.

37. Justin Murphy, "50 Years Ago Rochester Tried an Experiment with Desegregation. It Lasted Less Than 2 Months," *Rochester Democrat and Chronicle,* February 22, 2022, https://www.democratandchronicle.com/in-depth/news/education/2022/02/22/rochester-new-york-school-integration-effort-50-years-ago/9142502002/.

38. James Baldwin, *Giovanni's Room* (New York: Vintage International, 1956).

39. Murphy, *Your Children.*

40. Alex Love, "Nearly Half of Children in Rochester Live in Poverty, Second-Highest Rate in the Nation," *Rochester First,* March 29, 2022, https://www.rochesterfirst.com/news/local-news/nearly-half-of-all-children-in-rochester-live-in-poverty-second-highest-in-the-nation/.

41. Jacob Schermerhorn, "Rochester's Homicide Surge," *Rochester Beacon,* February 3, 2022, https://rochesterbeacon.com/2022/02/03/rochesters-homicide-surge/.

42. Schermerhorn, "Rochester's Homicide Surge."

43. Justin Murphy, "Stanford University Study: Rochester Schools Last in U.S. in Growth," *Rochester Democrat and Chronicle,* December 5, 2017, https://www.democratandchronicle.com/story/news/2017/12/05/stanford-cepa-rochester-academic-growth-reardon/922583001/.

44. Nancy MacLean, *Democracy in Chains: The Deep History of the Radical Right's Stealth Plan for America* (New York: Viking Penguin, 2017).

45. MacLean, *Democracy in Chains.*

46. MacLean, *Democracy in Chains.*

47. Michael Chwe, "The Beliefs of Economist James Buchanan Conflict with Basic Democratic Norms. Here's Why," *Washington Post,* July 25, 2017, https://www.washingtonpost.com/news/monkey-cage/wp/2017/07/25/the-beliefs-of-economist-james-buchanan-conflict-with-basic-democratic-norms-heres-why/.

48. Carlon Howard, "A Brief History of School Choice: 1955 to Now," Medium, December 4, 2017, https://medium.com/the-new-leader/a-brief-history-of-school-choice-1955-to-now-3f7dc4a3cb93.

49. Hale, *The Choice We Face.*

50. Milton Friedman, *Capitalism and Freedom* (Chicago: University of Chicago Press, 1962).

51. Friedman, *Capitalism and Freedom.*

52. Friedman, *Capitalism and Freedom.*
53. Binyamin Appelbaum, foreword to *Capitalism and Freedom,* by Milton Friedman (Chicago: University of Chicago Press, 2020).
54. "Milton Friedman—Should Higher Education Be Subsidized?," YouTube video, 12:58, posted by LibertyPen, August 14, 2013, https://www.youtube.com/watch?v=w3-_r_t7AZU.
55. Gary K. Clabaugh, "The Educational Legacy of Ronald Reagan," *Educational Horizons* 82, no. 4 (2004).
56. Mehrsa Baradaran, *The Color of Money: Black Banks and the Racial Wealth Gap* (Cambridge, MA: Harvard University Press, 2017), 5.
57. George Monbiot, "Neoliberalism: The Ideology at the Root of All Our Problems," *Guardian,* April 15, 2016, https://www.theguardian.com/books/2016/apr/15/neoliberalism-ideology-problem-george-monbiot.
58. MacLean, *Democracy in Chains.*
59. Jane Mayer, *Dark Money: The Hidden History of the Billionaires Behind the Rise of the Radical Right* (New York: Anchor Books, 2017).
60. John Nichols, "How ALEC Took Florida's 'License to Kill' Law National," *Nation,* March 22, 2012, https://www.thenation.com/article/archive/how-alec-took-floridas-license-kill-law-national/.
61. John Ganz, "The Forgotten Man: On Murray Rothbard, Philosophical Harbinger of Trump and the Alt-Right," *Baffler,* December 15, 2017, https://thebaffler.com/latest/the-forgotten-man-ganz.

2. Black Children at Risk

1. Saidiya Hartman, *Lose Your Mother: A Journey Along the Atlantic Slave Route* (New York: Farrar, Straus and Giroux, 2008).
2. Olivia B. Waxman, "Here's How Stop-and-Frisk Laws Got Their Start," *Time,* September 21, 2016, https://time.com/4503412/donald-trump-stop-frisk-history/.
3. Mariame Kaba, *We Do This 'Til We Free Us: Abolitionist Organizing and Transforming Justice* (Chicago: Haymarket Books, 2021).
4. Rosie Blunt, "Rikers Island: Tales from Inside New York's Notorious Jail," BBC, October 20, 2019, https://www.bbc.com/news/world-us-canada-50114468.
5. Michelle Alexander, *The New Jim Crow: Mass Incarceration in the Age of Colorblindness* (New York: New Press, 2010).
6. Elissa Nadworny and Cory Turner, "This Supreme Court Case Made School District Lines a Tool for Segregation," NPR, July 25, 2019, https://www.npr.org/2019/07/25/739493839/this-supreme-court-case-made-school-district-lines-a-tool-for-segregation.
7. Tom Lobianco, "Report: Aide Says Nixon's War on Drugs Targeted Blacks, Hippies," CNN, March 24, 2016, https://www.cnn.com/2016/03/23/politics/john-ehrlichman-richard-nixon-drug-war-blacks-hippie/index.html.
8. Mehrsa Baradaran, *The Color of Money: Black Banks and the Racial Wealth Gap* (Cambridge, MA: Harvard University Press, 2017).
9. Baradaran, *The Color of Money,* 3.
10. Baradaran, *The Color of Money,* 166.
11. Nadworny and Turner, "This Supreme Court Case."

12. George Roumell Jr. and Kristi Bowman, "Brown at 60 and Milliken at 40," *Ed.*, Summer 2014, https://www.gse.harvard.edu/news/ed/14/06/brown-60-milliken-40.

13. Noliwe M. Rooks, *Cutting School: Privatization, Segregation, and the End of Public Education* (New York: New Press, 2017).

14. Rucker C. Johnson, *Children of the Dream: Why School Integration Works* (New York: Basic Books, 2019), 54.

15. Katherine E. Ryan and Lorrie A. Shepard, eds., *The Future of Test-Based Educational Accountability* (New York: Routledge, 2008).

16. Ryan and Shepard, *The Future.*

17. Maris A. Vinovskis, *From a Nation at Risk to No Child Left Behind: National Education Goals and the Creation of Federal Education Policy* (New York: Teachers College Press, 2009), 11.

18. Jean Anyon, *Radical Possibilities: Public Policy, Urban Education, and a New Social Movement* (New York: Routledge, 2005), 3.

19. Binyamin Appelbaum, foreword to *Capitalism and Freedom,* by Milton Friedman (Chicago: University of Chicago Press, 2020), xv.

20. Diane Ravitch, *Slaying Goliath: The Passionate Resistance to Privatization and the Fight to Save America's Public Schools* (New York: Knopf, 2020).

21. Michelle Alexander, *The New Jim Crow: Mass Incarceration in the Age of Colorblindness* (New York, New Press, 2012).

22. Michelle Alexander, *The New Jim Crow,* 8.

23. James Cullen, "The History of Mass Incarceration," Brennen Center for Justice, July 20, 2018, https://www.brennancenter.org/our-work/analysis-opinion/history-mass-incarceration.

24. Cullen, "Mass Incarceration."

25. Nikole Hannah-Jones, "Choosing a School for My Daughter in a Segregated City," *New York Times,* June 9, 2016, https://www.nytimes.com/2016/06/12/magazine/choosing-a-school-for-my-daughter-in-a-segregated-city.html.

26. Lance Williams, "W. Glenn Campbell, Confidant of Reagan," SFGate, November 27, 2001, https://www.sfgate.com/news/article/W-Glenn-Campbell-confidant-of-Reagan-2851204.php.

27. David C. Berliner and Bruce J. Biddle, *The Manufactured Crisis: Myths, Fraud, and the Attack on America's Public Schools* (New York: Basic Books, 1995), 135.

28. Berliner and Biddle, *The Manufactured Crisis,* 16.

29. Zachary A. Goldfarb, "These Four Charts Show the SAT Favors Rich, Educated Families," *Washington Post,* March 5, 2014, https://www.washingtonpost.com/news/wonk/wp/2014/03/05/these-four-charts-show-how-the-sat-favors-the-rich-educated-families/.

30. Sarah Reckhow, *Follow the Money: How Foundation Dollars Change Public School Politics* (New York: Oxford University Press, 2013).

31. National Commission on Excellence in Education, *A Nation at Risk: The Imperative for Educational Reform* (Washington, D.C.: Government Publishing Office, 1983).

32. Ravitch, *Slaying Goliath,* 17.

33. National Commission on Excellence in Education, *A Nation at Risk.*

34. Reckhow, *Follow the Money.*

35. Reckhow, *Follow the Money,* 134.

36. Berliner and Biddle, *The Manufactured Crisis,* 140.
37. Ravitch, *Slaying Goliath.*
38. Maris Vinovskis, "The Road to Charlottesville: The 1989 Education Summit," Department of History, Institute for Social Research and School of Public Policy University of Michigan, https://govinfo.library.unt.edu/negp/reports/negp30 .pdf.
39. William L. Boyd, "President Reagan's School-Reform Agenda," *Education Week,* March 18, 1987, https://www.edweek.org/education/president-reagans-school -reform-agenda/1987/03.
40. Steven R. Weisman, "Reagan Urges More Discipline in Schools," *New York Times,* December 9, 1983, https://www.nytimes.com/1983/12/09/us/reagan -urges-more-discipline-in-schools.html.
41. Weisman, "Reagan Urges."
42. Weisman, "Reagan Urges."
43. Rick Perlstein, "Exclusive: Lee Atwater's Infamous 1981 Interview on the Southern Strategy," *Nation,* November 13, 2012, https://www.thenation.com/article /archive/exclusive-lee-atwaters-infamous-1981-interview-southern-strategy/.
44. Tracy Thompson, "D.C. Student Is Given Ten Years in Drug Case," *Washington Post,* November 2, 1990, https://www.washingtonpost.com/archive/local/1990 /11/01/dc-student-is-given-10-years-in-drug-case/2384c4eb-8871–4d28-a4f0 -a3919335c311/.
45. "Testimony of Jesselyn McCurdy, ACLU Legislative Counsel, at a United States Sentencing Commission Hearing on Cocaine and Sentencing Policy," American Civil Liberties Union, accessed September 18, 2021, https://www.aclu.org/other /testimony-jesselyn-mccurdy-aclu-legislative-counsel-united-states-sentencing -commission.
46. Jack Schneider, "George H.W. Bush Laid the Foundation for Education Reform," *Conversation,* December 3, 2018, https://theconversation.com/george-h-w-bush -laid-the-foundation-for-education-reform-108018.
47. Vinovskis, *From a Nation.*
48. Rooks, *Cutting School,* 31.
49. Claudio Sanchez, "From a Single Charter School, a Movement Grows," National Public Radio, August 31, 2012, https://www.npr.org/2012/09/02/160409742 /from-a-single-charter-school-a-movement-grows.
50. Marc Lamont Hill, *Nobody: Casualties of America's War on the Vulnerable, from Ferguson to Flint and Beyond* (New York: Atria, 2016), 79.
51. Manning Marable, *How Capitalism Underdeveloped Black America: Problems in Race, Political Economy, and Society* (Chicago: Haymarket Books, 2015), 2.

3. Scraps

1. Audre Lorde, *Sister Outsider* (New York: Penguin Books, 2020), 63.
2. "Our Mission," Urban-Suburban Interdistrict Transfer Program, accessed October 25, 2022, https://www.monroe.edu/Page/933.
3. Julianne Hing, "Kelley Williams-Bolar's Long, Winding Fight to Educate Her Daughters," Colorlines, May 16, 2012, https://www.colorlines.com/articles /kelley-williams-bolars-long-winding-fight-educate-her-daughters.
4. Daniel Tepfer, "Tanya McDowell Sentenced to 5 Years in Prison," *Connecticut*

Post, March 27, 2012, https://www.ctpost.com/news/article/Tanya-McDowell -sentenced-to-5-years-in-prison-3437974.php.

5. Bill Richards, "Historic Topeka School Case Reopened," *Washington Post,* November 30, 1979, https://www.washingtonpost.com/archive/politics/1979 /11/30/historic-topeka-school-case-reopened/e0908531–1c09–4419–88c8 -b94d890d0896/.

6. Justin Murphy, "Rochester's Poverty Rates Worse in New Census Data," *Rochester Democrat & Chronicle,* December 31, 2018, https://www.democratandchronicle .com/story/news/2018/12/31/rochesters-poverty-rates-worsen-new-census -data/2449077002/.

7. Justin Murphy and Gary Stern, "RCSD Graduation Rate Rises to 68%, Highest in Years, Brockport and Greece Also Make Gains," *Rochester Democrat & Chronicle,* January 14, 2021, https://www.democratandchronicle.com/story /news/education/2021/01/14/rcsd-graduation-rate-2020–68-regents-local /4157954001/.

8. "District Profile," Rochester City School District, October 22, 2021, https://www .rcsdk12.org/domain/8.

9. Justin Murphy, "RCSD's Budget Gap Is Big—but How Big?," *Rochester Democrat & Chronicle,* October 21, 2020, https://www.democratandchronicle.com/story /news/education/2020/10/21/rcsd-budget-gap-carleen-pierce-shelley-jallow -rochester/6003328002/.

10. Thomas P. DiNapoli, *Special Report: Finger Lakes Region Economic Profile* (Albany, NY: Office of the New York State Comptroller, August 2017).

11. Justin Murphy, "'I Am Horrified.' RCSD Teachers Placed on Leave After Offensive Text Messages Uncovered," *Rochester Democrat & Chronicle,* May 27, 2022, https://www.democratandchronicle.com/story/news/2022/05/27/rcsd -teachers-placed-on-leave-after-offensive-text-messages-uncovered-rochester -ny-schools/9959535002/.

12. Olivia Marcucci and Rowhea N. Elmesky, "Coded Racialized Discourse Among Educators: Implications For Social-Emotional Outcomes and Cultures of Antiblackness at an Urban School," *Urban Education* (2022), https://doi.org/10 .1177/00420859221119115.

13. "Demographics," Cobb County Government, September 12, 2022, https://www .cobbcounty.org/economic-development/why-cobb/demographics.

14. Ellen Eldridge, "Parents Angry at Cobb School About Civil War Dress-Up Day," *Atlanta Journal-Constitution,* October 10, 2017, https://www.ajc .com/news/local/parents-angry-cobb-school-about-civil-war-dress-day /ipbVYjyBVNq15bfZqYaopL/.

15. Marlon A. Walker, "Cobb Student Threatens Black People in Racist Online Rant," *Atlanta Journal-Constitution,* March 9, 2017, https://www.ajc.com/news /local-education/online-rant-cobb-county-student-uses-word-wants-slavery -return/ElKDxM9jAUuhYYftdpcBVP/.

16. Rayshawn Ray and Alexandra Gibbons, "Why Are States Banning Critical Race Theory?," Brookings Institution, November 2021, https://www.brookings.edu /blog/fixgov/2021/07/02/why-are-states-banning-critical-race-theory/.

17. Rebecca Gaunt, "Voting Rights Organizations File Lawsuit Over Cobb Schools Redistricting," *Cobb County Courier,* June 10, 2022, https://cobbcountycourier

.com/2022/06/voting-rights-organizations-file-lawsuit-over-cobb-schools
-redistricting/.

18. Charles M. Blow, "Black Dads Are Doing Best of All," *New York Times,* June 8,
2015, https://www.nytimes.com/2015/06/08/opinion/charles-blow-black-dads
-are-doing-the-best-of-all.html.

19. Ife Floyd, LaDonna Pavetti, Laura Meyer, Ali Safawi, Liz Schott, Evelyn Bellew,
and Abigail Magnus, *TANF Policies Reflect Racist Legacy of Cash Assistance*
(Washington, D.C.: Center on Budget and Policy Priorities, August 4, 2021).

20. Alma Carten, "The Racist Roots of Welfare Reform," *New Republic,* August 22,
2016, https://newrepublic.com/article/136200/racist-roots-welfare-reform.

21. Rayshawn Ray et al., "Homeownership, Racial Segregation, and Policy Solutions
to Racial Wealth Equity," Brookings Institution, September 1, 2012, https://
www.brookings.edu/essay/homeownership-racial-segregation-and-policies-for
-racial-wealth-equity/.

22. Ray et al., "Homeownership."

23. Diane Ravitch, *Reign of Error: The Hoax of the Privatization Movement and the
Danger to America's Public Schools* (New York: Alfred A. Knopf, 2013), 19–20.

24. Alan Singer, "Why Hedge Funds Love Charter Schools," *Washington Post,* June
4, 2014, https://www.washingtonpost.com/news/answer-sheet/wp/2014/06/04
/why-hedge-funds-love-charter-schools/.

25. Singer, "Hedge Funds Love."

26. Joey Garrison, "Andre Agassi Embraces Investor-Led Approach to Schools,"
The Tennessean, September 14, 2014, https://www.usatoday.com/story/news
/nation/2014/09/17/andre-agassi-embraces-investor-led-approach-to-schools
/15758357/.

27. Michael Powell, "A Star-Powered School Sputters," *New York Times,* August
9, 2014, https://www.nytimes.com/2014/08/10/sports/prime-prep-academy
-founded-by-deion-sanders-comes-under-scrutiny.html.

28. Powell, "A Star-Powered School."

29. Vanessa De La Torre and Matthew Kauffman, "Acclaimed Capital Prep Magnet
School Bypassed Normal Lottery Process for Athletes, Other Students," *Hartford
Courant,* May 3, 2017, https://www.courant.com/news/connecticut/hc-capital
-prep-lottery-investigation-20170503-story.html.

30. Network for Public Education, *Asleep at the Wheel: How the Federal Charter
Schools Program Recklessly Takes Taxpayers and Students for a Ride* (New York:
Network for Public Education, May 3, 2019); Network for Public Education,
*Still Asleep at the Wheel: How the Federal Charter Schools Program Results in a
Pileup of Waste and Fraud* (New York: Network for Public Education, December
6, 2019).

31. Network for Public Education, *Asleep at the Wheel.*

32. Network for Public Education, *Still Asleep.*

33. Network for Public Education, *Still Asleep.*

34. Network for Public Education, *Still Asleep.*

35. Network for Public Education, *Asleep at the Wheel.*

36. Network for Public Education, *Still Asleep.*

37. *Akron Beacon Journal,* "David Brennan | 1932–2018: Akron Businessman
Promoted Charter Schools in Ohio," *Columbus Dispatch,* October 15, 2018,

https://www.dispatch.com/story/news/education/2018/10/15/david-brennan
-1931–2018-akron/9544175007/.

38. *Akron Beacon Journal*, "David Brennan."

39. Kathleen Maloney, "Court Decides Charter School Case," Court News Ohio, September 15, 2015, https://www.courtnewsohio.gov/cases/2015/SCO/0915 /132050.asp#.YyE3FCHMK3I.

40. Diane Ravitch, "Jeff Bryant: How For-Profit Charters Corrupt Education and Other Once-Public Services," *Diane Ravitch's Blog*, October 21, 2021, https: //dianeravitch.net/2021/10/21/jeff-bryant-how-for-profit-charters-corrupt -education/.

41. "Our Schools," Accel Schools, September 12, 2022, https://accelschools.com/our -schools/.

42. Ravitch, "Jeff Bryant."

43. Dan Glaister, "Abort All Black Babies and Cut Crime, Says Republican," *Guardian*, October 1, 2005, https://www.theguardian.com/world/2005/oct/01/usa .danglaister.

44. Samuel Eli Abrams, "521 Fifth Avenue: The Corporate Makeover of Education and Its Limits" (dissertation, Columbia University, New York, NY, 2018), https: //academiccommons.columbia.edu/doi/10.7916/D89G748J.

45. Diane Ravitch, "Which CEO Made $5 Million Stealing Your Kid's Lunch Money?," *Diane Ravitch's Blog*, July 21, 2012, https://dianeravitch.net/2012/07 /21/which-ceo-made-5-million-stealing-your-kids-lunch-money/.

46. Rhea R. Borja, "Bennett Quits K12 Inc. Under Fire," *Education Week*, October 11, 2005, https://www.edweek.org/leadership/bennett-quits-k12-inc-under-fire /2005/10.

47. "Market Capitalization of K12 (LRN)," Companies Market Cap, September 12, 2022, https://companiesmarketcap.com/k12/marketcap/.

48. Lee Fang, "How Online Learning Companies Bought America's Schools," *Nation*, November 18, 2011, https://www.thenation.com/article/archive/how -online-learning-companies-bought-americas-schools/.

49. "Virtual Public Schools Act," ALEC, January 1, 2005, https://alec.org/model -policy/the-virtual-public-schools-act/.

50. Indigo Oliver, "A Virtual Charter School Company Says Covid-19 Is the 'Tailwind' It's Been Waiting For," *In These Times*, June 18, 2020, https://inthesetimes .com/article/charter-schools-coronavirus-betsy-devos-mckinsey-corporate -education-reform.

51. Oliver, "Virtual Charter School Company."

52. Oliver, "Virtual Charter School Company."

53. Noliwe M. Rooks, *Cutting School: Privatization, Segregation, and the End of Public Education* (New York: New Press, 2017).

54. Stephanie Saul, "Profits and Questions at Online Charter Schools," *New York Times*, December 12, 2011, https://www.nytimes.com/2011/12/13/education /online-schools-score-better-on-wall-street-than-in-classrooms.html.

55. Saul, "Profits and Questions."

56. Saul, "Profits and Questions."

57. Saul, "Profits and Questions."

58. Oliver, "Virtual Charter School Company."

59. Oliver, "Virtual Charter School Company."
60. Rooks, *Cutting School,* 146.
61. Rooks, *Cutting School,* 146.
62. *Chartered for Profit: The Hidden World of Charter Schools Operated for Financial Gain* (New York: Network for Public Education, January 23, 2022).
63. Gloria Ladson-Billings, "From the Achievement Gap to the Education Debt: Understanding Achievement in U.S. Schools," *American Educational Research Journal* 35, no. 7 (2006): 3–12, http://www.jstor.org/stable/3876731.
64. Preston Green et al., "Are We Heading Toward a Charter School 'Bubble'? Lessons from the Subprime Mortgage Crisis," *University of Richmond Law Review* 50: 783–808, https://papers.ssrn.com/sol3/papers.cfm?abstract_id=2704305.
65. Green et al., "A Charter School 'Bubble'?"
66. Green et al., "A Charter School 'Bubble'?"

4. No Entrepreneur Left Behind

1. Noliwe M. Rooks, *Cutting School: Privatization, Segregation, and the End of Public Education* (New York: New Press, 2017).
2. Linda Darling-Hammond, "Research and Rhetoric on Teacher Certification: A Response to 'Teacher Certification Reconsidered,'" *Education Policy Analysis Archive* 10, no. 36 (2002), retrieved September 11, 2022, http://epaa.asu.edu/epaa/v10n36.html.
3. Matthew J. Brouillette, "Must Teachers Be Certified to Be Qualified?," Viewpoints, February 1, 1999, https://www.mackinac.org/V1999-07.
4. Diane Ravitch, *The Death and Life of the Great American School System: How Testing and Choice Are Undermining Education* (New York: Basic Books, 2010).
5. Bettina L. Love, *We Want to Do More Than Survive: Abolitionist Teaching and the Pursuit of Educational Freedom* (Boston: Beacon Press, 2019).
6. Morgaen L. Donaldson, Susan Moore Johnson, and Phi Delta Kappan, "TFA Teachers: How Long Do They Teach? Why Do They Leave?," *Education Week,* October 4, 2011, https://www.edweek.org/teaching-learning/opinion-tfa-teachers-how-long-do-they-teach-why-do-they-leave/2011/10.
7. David Osborne and Ted Gaebler, *Reinventing Government: How the Entrepreneurial Spirit Is Transforming the Public Sector* (New York: Basic Books, 1992), xix.
8. Ravitch, *Death and Life,* 9.
9. Frederick M. Hess and Michael Q. McShane, *Educational Entrepreneurship Today,* Educational Innovations Series (Cambridge, MA: Harvard Education Press, 2016), 208.
10. "Our History," Teach for America, 2020, https://www.teachforamerica.org/what-we-do/our-history.
11. Susan Brenna, "Classroom Experiment," *Newsday,* September 26, 1990.
12. Jonathan Schorr, "Class Action: What Clinton's National Service Program Could Learn from 'Teach for America,'" *Phi Delta Kappan* 75, no. 4 (December 1993): 315–318.
13. Gary K. Clabaugh, "Teach for America?," *Educational Horizons* 70, no. 3 (Spring 1992): 101–103; Linda Darling-Hammond, "Who Will Speak for the Children? How 'Teach for America' Hurts Urban Schools and Students," *Phi Delta Kappan* 76, no. 1 (September 1994): 21–34.

14. Ravitch, *Death and Life.*
15. Ravitch, *Death and Life.*
16. TFA Editorial Team, "Are Teach for America Teachers Effective?," Teach for America, March 6, 2018, https://www.teachforamerica.org/stories/are-teach-for -america-teachers-effective.
17. Annie Waldman, "How Teach for America Evolved into an Arm of the Charter School Movement," ProPublica, June 18, 2019, https://www.propublica.org /article/how-teach-for-america-evolved-into-an-arm-of-the-charter-school -movement.
18. Waldman, "Teach for America Evolved."
19. Waldman, "Teach for America Evolved."
20. Waldman, "Teach for America Evolved."
21. Waldman, "Teach for America Evolved."
22. Donaldson, Johnson, and Phi Delta Kappan, "TFA Teachers."
23. Rachel M. Cohen, "The True Cost of Teach for America's Impact on Urban Schools," *American Prospect,* January 5, 2015, https://prospect.org/civil-rights /true-cost-teach-america-s-impact-urban-schools/.
24. Donaldson, Johnson, and Phi Delta Kappan, "TFA Teachers."
25. Alison Damast, "Q&A: Teach for America's Wendy Kopp," Bloomberg, March 26, 2012, https://www.bloomberg.com/news/articles/2012–03–26/q-and-a -teach-for-americas-wendy-kopp.
26. Talia Richman, "Texas' Largest Teacher Prep Company Is on Probation, Board Decides," *Dallas Morning News,* July 22, 2022, https://www.dallasnews.com /news/education/2022/07/22/can-texas-largest-teacher-prep-company-prove -its-improved/.
27. Richman, "Texas' Largest Teacher Prep."
28. Talia Richman, "1 In 5 New Texas Teachers Were Hired Without Certification Last Year," *Dallas Morning News,* September 22, 2022, https://www.dallasnews .com/news/education/2022/09/22/1-in-5-new-texas-teachers-werent-certified -last-year/
29. Julie Rowland Woods, *Mitigating Teacher Shortages: Alternative Teacher Certification* (Denver, CO: Education Commission of the States, 2016).
30. Woods, *Mitigating Teacher Shortages.*
31. Woods, *Mitigating Teacher Shortages.*
32. Ravitch, *Death and Life.*
33. William Jefferson Clinton, "State of the Union Address" (speech, Washington, D.C., January 23, 1996), https://clintonwhitehouse4.archives.gov/WH/New /other/sotu.html.
34. Elaine C. Kamarck, *How Change Happens—or Doesn't: The Politics of US Public Policy* (Boulder, CO: Lynne Rienner, 2013).
35. Maris A. Vinovskis, *From a Nation at Risk to No Child Left Behind: National Education Goals and the Creation of Federal Education Policy* (New York: Teachers College Press, 2009).
36. Robert Archer, *The Education of Richard Riley: A Case Study Business Involvement in Education* (Bloomington, IN: AuthorHouse 2013).
37. Susan Chira, "Lessons of South Carolina: What Secretary May Try for U.S. Schools," *New York Times,* March 24, 1993, https://www.nytimes.com/1993

/03/24/education/lessons-of-south-carolina-what-secretary-may-try-for-us
-schools.html.

38. "Clinton Promotes Stricter School Discipline," CNN, July 20, 1998, https://www
.cnn.com/ALLPOLITICS/1998/07/20/clinton.education.

39. "Clinton Promotes," CNN.

40. Vanessa Williams, "1994 Crime Bill Haunts Clinton and Sanders as Criminal
Justice Reform Rises to Top in Democratic Contest," *Washington Post,* February
12, 2016, https://www.washingtonpost.com/news/post-politics/wp/2016/02/12
/1994-crime-bill-haunts-clinton-and-sanders-as-criminal-justice-reform-rises
-to-top-in-democratic-contest/.

41. Rooks, *Cutting School.*

42. *Chartered for Profit: The Hidden World of Charter Schools Operated for Financial
Gain* (New York: Network for Public Education, January 23, 2022).

43. *Chartered for Profit.*

44. *Chartered for Profit.*

45. *Chartered for Profit.*

46. Mario Loyola, "Almost a Miracle," *City Journal,* 2016, https://www.city-journal
.org/html/almost-miracle-14734.html.

47. Loyola, "Almost a Miracle."

48. Rebecca Leung, "The Texas Miracle," *60 Minutes,* August 23, 2004, https://www
.cbsnews.com/news/the-texas-miracle-637913/.

49. Walt Haney, "The Myth of the Texas Miracle in Education," *Education Policy
Analysis Archive* 8, no. 41 (August 19, 2000), https://epaa.asu.edu/index.php
/epaa/article/view/432/828.

50. Jason Stanford, "Mute the Messenger," *Texas Observer,* September 3, 2014, https:
//www.texasobserver.org/walter-stroup-standardized-testing-pearson/; Vinh
Huy Pham, "Computer Modeling of the Instructionally Insensitive Nature of
the Texas Assessment of Knowledge and Skills (TAKS) Exam" (dissertation,
University of Texas at Austin, 2009), https://repositories.lib.utexas.edu/handle
/2152/10602.

51. Haney, "The Myth."

52. Alec MacGillis, "Testing Time: Jeb Bush's Educational Experiment," *New Yorker,*
January 19, 2015, https://www.newyorker.com/magazine/2015/01/26/testing-time.

53. MacGillis, "Testing Time."

54. MacGillis, "Testing Time."

55. MacGillis, "Testing Time."

56. MacGillis, "Testing Time."

57. MacGillis, "Testing Time."

58. MacGillis, "Testing Time."

59. Jeb Bush and Brian Yablonski, *Profiles in Character* (Tallahassee: Foundation for
Florida's Future, 1995).

60. Elizabeth A. Gershoff and Sarah A. Font, "Corporal Punishment in U.S. Public Schools: Prevalence, Disparities in Use, and Status in State and Federal Policy," *Social Policy Report* 30, no. 1, https://www.ncbi.nlm.nih.gov/pmc/articles
/PMC5766273/.

61. Michael Barbaro, "For Jeb Bush, Evolving Views Over 2 Decades," *New York*

Times, January 10, 2015, https://www.nytimes.com/2015/01/11/us/politics/for
-jeb-bush-evolving-views-over-2-decades.html.

62. Alice Miranda Ollstein, "Jeb Bush Hires Worst Possible Person to Be Adviser on
Inequality," ThinkProgress, April 1, 2015, https://archive.thinkprogress.org/jeb
-bush-hires-worst-possible-person-to-be-adviser-on-inequality-7323dce42720/.

63. Ollstein, "Jeb Bush Hires Worst."

64. Ollstein, "Jeb Bush Hires Worst."

65. Ollstein, "Jeb Bush Hires Worst."

66. Lee Fang, "America's Online Learning Curve," National Public Radio, November 18, 2011, https://www.npr.org/2011/11/18/142498808/the-nation-americas
-online-learning-curve.

67. Fang, "America's Online Learning Curve."

68. Fang, "America's Online Learning Curve."

69. Lindsey Layton, "Jeb Bush Education Foundation Played Leading Role in Mixing
Politics, Policy," *Washington Post,* January 6, 2015, https://www.washingtonpost
.com/local/education/jeb-bush-education-foundation-played-leading-role-in
-mixing-politics-policy/2015/01/06/db1db176-903b-11e4-a900-9960214d4cd7
_story.html.

70. Layton, "Jeb Bush Education Foundation."

71. George W. Bush, "George W. Bush's Speech to the NAACP" (speech, Baltimore, MD, July 10, 2000), https://www.washingtonpost.com/wp-srv/onpolitics
/elections/bushtext071000.htm.

72. Bettina L. Love, *We Want to Do More Than Survive: Abolitionist Teaching and the
Pursuit of Educational Freedom* (Boston: Beacon Press, 2019).

73. Thomas Lickona, "The Return of Character Education," *Educational Leadership*
51, no. 3 (November 1993): 6–11.

74. Lickona, "Character Education."

75. Susan Black, "The Character Conundrum," *American School Board Journal* 183,
no. 12 (December 1996): 29–31.

76. Melissa McEwan, "George Bush's Sex Education Failure," *Guardian,* July 20,
2009, https://www.theguardian.com/commentisfree/cifamerica/2009/jul/20
/george-bush-teen-pregnancy-abstinence.

77. Jessica Grose, "Most Parents Don't Favor Abstinence-Only Sex Ed. Why Is the
Government Still Funding It?," *New York Times,* October 26, 2022, https://www
.nytimes.com/2022/10/26/opinion/abstinence-only.html.

78. Grose, "Most Parents Don't Favor."

79. Ravitch, *Death and Life.*

80. John Rosales, "Closing Schools: Privatization Disguised as 'Accountability,'"
National Education Association, December 15, 2015, https://www.nea.org
/advocating-for-change/new-from-nea/closing-schools-privatization-disguised
-accountability.

81. Rosales, "Closing Schools."

82. Dara Shifrer and Rachel Fish, "A Multilevel Investigation into Contextual Reli-
ability in the Designation of Cognitive Health Conditions Among U.S. Children,"
Society and Mental Health 10, no. 2 (May 10, 2019): 180–197, https://journals
.sagepub.com/doi/10.1177/2156869319847243.

83. Shifrer and Fish, "A Multilevel Investigation."

84. Christina A. Samuels, "Special Education Is Broken," *Education Week,* January 8, 2019, https://www.edweek.org/teaching-learning/special-education-is-broken /2019/01.

85. Julian Vasquez Heilig and Linda Darling-Hammond, "Accountability Texas-Style: The Progress and Learning of Urban Minority Students in a High-Stakes Testing Context," *Educational Evaluation and Policy Analysis* 30, no. 2 (2008): 75–110, https://doi.org/10.3102/0162373708317689.

86. Radley Balko, *Rise of the Warrior Cop: The Militarization of America's Police Forces* (New York: Public Affairs, 2013).

87. Milton Friedman, "The Promise of Vouchers," *Wall Street Journal,* December 5, 2005, https://www.wsj.com/articles/SB113374845791113764.

88. Naomi Klein, *The Shock Doctrine: The Rise of Disaster Capitalism* (New York: Henry Holt, 2007).

89. Klein, *The Shock Doctrine,* 4.

90. Klein, *The Shock Doctrine,* 6.

91. Emmanuel Felton, "What Happens When a City of Teachers, Most of Them Black, Was Fired," *Washington Monthly,* May 31, 2017, https://washingtonmonthly .com/2017/05/31/what-happened-when-a-city-full-of-teachers-most-of-them -black-was-fired/.

92. Beth Sondel and Joseph L. Boselovic, "'No Excuses' in New Orleans," *Jacobin,* July 24, 2014, https://jacobinmag.com/2014/07/no-excuses-in-new-orleans.

93. Louisiana Department of Education, *Recovery School District,* https://www .louisianabelieves.com/docs/default-source/katrina/final-louisana-believes-v8 -recovery-school-district.pdf?sfvrsn=2.

94. Felton, "What Happens When."

95. Klein, *The Shock Doctrine,* 6.

96. Andrea Gabor, *After the Education Wars: How Smart Schools Upend the Business of Reform* (New York: New Press, 2018).

97. Klein, *The Shock Doctrine.*

98. Adrienne D. Dixson, Kristen L. Buras, and Elizabeth K. Jeffers, "The Color of Reform: Race, Education Reform, and Charter Schools in Post-Katrina New Orleans," *Qualitative Inquiry* 21, no. 3 (2015): 288–299, https://doi.org/10.1177 /1077800414557826.

99. Jitu Brown, Eric Gutstein, and Pauline Lipman, "Arne Duncan and the Chicago Success Story: Myth or Reality," *Rethinking Schools* 23, no. 3 (2009): 10–14.

100. Ravitch, *Death and Life.*

101. Fred Hiatt, "How Bill Gates Would Repair the Nation's Schools," *Seattle Times,* March 30, 2009, https://www.seattletimes.com/opinion/how-bill-gates-would -repair-the-nations-schools/.

102. Megan E. Tompkins-Stange, *Policy Patrons: Philanthropy, Education Reform, and the Politics of Influence* (Cambridge, MA: Harvard Education Press, 2016).

103. Tompkins-Stange, *Policy Patrons.*

104. Ravitch, *Death and Life,* 172.

105. Ravitch, *Death and Life,* 61.

106. Ravitch, *Death and Life.*

107. Shani Robinson and Anna Simonton, *None of the Above: The Untold Story of the*

Atlanta Public Schools Cheating Scandal, Corporate Greed, and the Criminalization of Educators (Boston: Beacon Press, 2018).

108. Robinson and Simonton, *None of the Above,* 13.

109. Robinson and Simonton, *None of the Above,* 18.

110. Robinson and Simonton, *None of the Above.*

111. Robinson and Simonton, *None of the Above,* 58.

112. Mark Niesse, "Atlanta Teacher Bonus Payments Revealed," *Atlanta Journal-Constitution,* May 1, 2013, https://www.ajc.com/news/local/atlanta-teacher-bonus-payments-revealed/iFKsav7KNFVf1cDYnpYALI/.

113. Robinson and Simonton, *None of the Above,* 79.

114. Anna Simonton, "Time to Put Atlanta Cheating Scandal to Rest," *Atlanta Journal-Constitution,* August 18, 2020, https://www.ajc.com/education/get-schooled-blog/opinion-time-to-put-atlanta-cheating-scandal-to-rest/PGPGHZH2KVFEXKWOXG47M5NMNE/.

115. Robinson and Simonton, *None of the Above.*

116. Rhonda Cook, "Update: New Mother Gets Prison, Former Principal Jail in APS Case," *Atlanta Journal-Constitution,* September 1, 2015, https://www.ajc.com/news/crime—law/update-new-mother-gets-prison-former-principal-jail-aps-case/nmqSLZUeoZPEhMlmK67sAO/.

117. Robinson and Simonton, *None of the Above,* 79.

118. Mariame Kaba, *We Do This 'Til We Free Us: Abolitionist Organizing and Transforming Justice* (Chicago: Haymarket Books, 2021).

119. Maureen Downey, "Race to the Top: Did the $400 Million Federal Grant Pay Off for Georgia?," *Atlanta Journal-Constitution,* December 17, 2014, https://www.ajc.com/blog/get-schooled/race-the-top-did-the-400-million-federal-grant-pay-off-for-georgia/AKPuPNlML9TAAmSe7omqiI/.

120. Julianne Hing, "Cheating Atlanta Schools Received $500k in Bonuses. What Now?," Colorlines, August 15, 2011, https://www.colorlines.com/articles/cheating-atlanta-schools-received-500k-bonuses-what-now.

121. Dana Goldstein, "How High-Stakes Testing Led to the Atlanta Cheating Scandal," Slate, July 21, 2011, https://slate.com/human-interest/2011/07/atlanta-cheating-scandal-how-the-teacher-incentives-in-high-stakes-testing-situations-lead-to-cheating-outbreaks.html.

122. Goldstein, "How High-Stakes Testing."

5. Erasure

1. Abolitionist Teaching Network, *Guide for Racial Justice & Social and Emotional Learning* (Cincinnati, OH: Abolitionist Teaching Network, August 2020).

2. Abolitionist Teaching Network, *Guide.*

3. Jennifer Psaki, press briefing, Washington D.C., July 21, 2021.

4. Audre Lorde, "A Litany for Survival," in *The Collected Poems of Audre Lorde* (New York: W. W. Norton, 1997), 255–256.

5. "1776 Commission Takes Historic and Scholarly Step to Restore Understanding of the Greatness of the American Founding," White House, January 18, 2021, https://trumpwhitehouse.archives.gov/briefings-statements/1776-commission-takes-historic-scholarly-step-restore-understanding-greatness-american-founding/.

6. Benjamin Wallace-Wells, "Conservative Activist Invented the Conflict Over Critical Race Theory," *New Yorker*, June 18, 2021, https://www.newyorker.com /news/annals-of-inquiry/how-a-conservative-activist-invented-the-conflict -over-critical-race-theory.

7. "Executive Order on Combating Race and Sex Stereotyping," White House, September 22, 2020, https://trumpwhitehouse.archives.gov/presidential-actions /executive-order-combating-race-sex-stereotyping/.

8. Jack Brewster, "Trump Says Critical Race Theory Borders on 'Psychological Abuse,'" *Forbes*, June 18, 2021, https://www.forbes.com/sites/jackbrewster/2021 /06/18/trump-says-critical-race-theory-borders-on-psychological-abuse/?sh =61f54565450e.

9. Thomas B. Edsall, "Republicans Are Once Again Heating Up the Culture Wars," *New York Times*, November 10, 2021, https://www.nytimes.com/2021/11/10 /opinion/republicans-democrats-crt.html/.

10. Nicholas Reimann, "Georgia Gov. Brian Kemp Slams Critical Race Theory as 'Dangerous Ideology,' Says It Shouldn't Be Taught," *Forbes*, May 20, 2021, https: //www.forbes.com/sites/nicholasreimann/2021/05/20/georgia-gov-brian-kemp -slams-critical-race-theory-as-dangerous-ideology-says-it-shouldnt-be-taught /?sh=68326d8454eb.

11. Tyler Kingkade, Brandy Zadrozny, and Ben Collins, "Critical Race Theory Battle Invades School Boards—with Help from Conservative Groups," NBC News, June 15, 2021, https://www.nbcnews.com/news/us-news/critical-race-theory -invades-school-boards-help-conservative-groups-n1270794?cid=sm_npd_ms _tw_ma.

12. Laura Meckler, "Teachers Union Sues New Hampshire Over Law Barring Certain Race Lessons," *Washington Post*, December 13, 2021, https://www .washingtonpost.com/education/2021/12/13/new-hampshire-critical-race -theory-lawsuit/.

13. Alex Bollinger, "Moms for Liberty Activists Wants LGBTQ Students Separated into Separate Classes," LGBTQ Nation, August 18, 2022, https://www .lgbtqnation.com/2022/08/moms-liberty-activist-wants-lgbtq-students -separated-special-classes/.

14. Marc Ramirez and Kathryn Varn, "'We Are War Moms': Moms for Liberty Dominates School Board Politics Across US," *USA Today*, August 16, 2022, https://www.usatoday.com/story/news/nation/2022/08/16/conservative-moms -liberty-takes-school-boards-across-us/10255129002/?gnt-cfr=1.

15. Katie Reilly, "Florida's Governor Just Signed the 'Stop Woke Act.' Here's What It Means for Schools and Businesses," *Time*, April 22, 2022, https://time.com /6168753/florida-stop-woke-law/.

16. Andrew Atterbury, "Federal Judge Temporarily Blocks DeSantis' 'Stop-WOKE' Law," Politico, August 18, 2022, https://www.politico.com/news/2022/08/18 /federal-judge-temporarily-blocks-desantis-stop-woke-law-00052768.

17. Eesha Pendharkar, "Bills Targeting Classroom Talk on Race and Gender Identity Ballooned This Year," *Education Week*, August 18, 2022, https://www.edweek .org/leadership/bills-targeting-classroom-talk-on-race-and-gender-identity -ballooned-this-year/2022/08.

18. Denise Taliaferro Baszile, "National Days of Teaching Truth," YouTube video, 7:10, posted by The Brainwaves Video Anthology, May 6, 2022, https://www.youtube.com/watch?v=eSFxUksFfOE.

19. Brian Lopez, "State Education Board Members Push Back on Proposal to Use 'Involuntary Relocation' to Describe Slavery," *Texas Tribune,* June 30, 2022, https://www.texastribune.org/2022/06/30/texas-slavery-involuntary-relocation/.

20. Barbara VanDenburgh, "Book Bans Are on the Rise. What Are the Most Banned Books and Why?," *USA Today,* June 29, 2022, https://www.usatoday.com/story/entertainment/books/2022/06/29/banned-books-explained/7772046001/.

21. VanDenburgh, "Book Bans."

22. Kalyn Belsha, "Chilling Effect: 1 in 4 Teachers Told to Limit Class Talk on Hot-Button Issues," Chalkbeat, August 10, 2022, https://www.chalkbeat.org/2022/8/10/23299007/teachers-limit-classroom-conversations-racism-sexism-survey.

23. Nicole Carr, "White Parents Rallied to Chase a Black Educator Out of Town. Then, They Followed Her to the Next One," ProPublica, June 16, 2022, https://www.propublica.org/article/georgia-dei-crt-schools-parents.

24. Carr, "White Parents Rallied."

25. Carr, "White Parents Rallied."

26. Carr, "White Parents Rallied."

27. Carr, "White Parents Rallied."

28. Carr, "White Parents Rallied."

29. Carr, "White Parents Rallied."

30. Carr, "White Parents Rallied."

31. Lawrence Ross, "Brittney Cooper's Truth-Telling Is Too Much for the Cowardly Right-Wing Mob," HuffPost, November 8, 2021, https://www.huffpost.com/entry/brittney-cooper-racist-right-wing-mob_n_61887ea0e4b055e47d7c0af0.

32. Stephen Henderson, "Betsy DeVos and the Twilight of Public Education," *Detroit Free Press,* December 3, 2016, https://www.freep.com/story/opinion/columnists/stephen-henderson/2016/12/03/betsy-devos-education-donald-trump/94728574/.

33. Valerie Strauss, "New Book: Obama's Education Department and Gates Foundation Were Closer Than You Thought," *Washington Post,* August 25, 2016, https://www.washingtonpost.com/news/answer-sheet/wp/2016/08/25/new-book-obamas-education-department-and-gates-foundation-were-closer-than-you-thought/.

34. Anya Kamenetz, "What 'A Nation at Risk' Got Wrong, and Right, About U.S. Schools," NPR, April 29, 2018, https://www.npr.org/sections/ed/2018/04/29/604986823/what-a-nation-at-risk-got-wrong-and-right-about-u-s-schools.

35. Strauss, "New Book."

36. Stephen Henderson, "DeVos Family Showers GOP with Contributions After DPS Vote," *Detroit Free Press,* September 3, 2016, https://www.freep.com/story/opinion/columnists/stephen-henderson/2016/09/03/charter-devos-money-michigan/89774760/.

37. Henderson, "Betsy DeVos."

38. Henderson, "Betsy DeVos."

39. Henderson, "Betsy DeVos."

40. Yongmei Ni, "The Impact of Charter Schools on the Efficiency of Traditional Public Schools: Evidence from Michigan," *Economics of Education Review* 28 (2009): 571–584, https://doi.org/10.1016/j.econedurev.2009.01.003.

41. Anya Kamenetz, "DeVos Family Money Is All Over the News Right Now," NPR, August 2, 2018, https://wamu.org/story/18/08/02/devos-family-money-is-all -over-the-news-right-now/.

42. Andrew Ujifusa, "COVID-19 May Energize Push for School Choice in States. Where That Leads Us Is Unclear," *Education Week,* January 27, 2021, https: //www.edweek.org/policy-politics/covid-19-may-energize-push-for-school -choice-in-states-where-that-leads-is-unclear/2021/01.

43. Anya Kamenetz, "DeVos to Rescind Obama-Era Guidance on School Discipline," NPR, December 18, 2018, https://www.npr.org/2018/12/18/675556455 /devos-to-rescind-obama-era-guidance-on-school-discipline.

44. Valerie Strauss, "Betsy DeVos's Controversial New Rule on Campus Sexual Assault Goes into Effect," *Washington Post,* August 14, 2020, https://www .washingtonpost.com/education/2020/08/14/betsy-devoss-controversial-new -rule-campus-sexual-assault-goes-into-effect/.

45. Strauss, "Controversial New Rule."

46. Samantha Schmidt, Emily Wax-Thibodeaux, and Moriah Balingit, "Biden Calls For LGBTQ Protections in Day 1 Executive Order, Angering Conservatives," *Washington Post,* January 21, 2021, https://www.washingtonpost.com/dc-md-va /2021/01/21/biden-executive-order-transgender-lgbtq/.

47. Cleve R. Wootson Jr. and Tracy Jan, "Biden Signs Orders on Racial Equity, and Civil Rights Groups Press for More," *Washington Post,* January 26, 2021, https:// www.washingtonpost.com/politics/biden-to-sign-executive-actions-on-equity /2021/01/26/3ffbcff6-5f8e-11eb-9430-e7c77b5b0297_story.html.

48. Dustin Jones, "Biden's Title IX Reforms Would Roll Back Trump-Era Rules, Expand Victim Protections," NPR, June 23, 2022, https://www.npr.org/2022/06/23 /1107045291/title-ix-9-biden-expand-victim-protections-discrimination.

49. Juan Perez Jr., "Biden Administration's Push for Standardized Tests Irks Teachers Unions, State Leaders," Politico, March 2, 2021, https://www.politico.com/news /2021/03/02/biden-standardized-tests-teachers-unions-472831J.

50. Perez Jr., "Biden Administration's Push."

51. Dana Goldstein, "Does It Hurt Children to Measure Pandemic Learning Loss?," *New York Times,* May 8, 2021, https://www.nytimes.com/2021/04/08/us/school -testing-education-covid.html.

52. Erica L. Green, "New Twist in Pandemic's Impact on Schools: Substitutes in Camouflage," *New York Times,* February 20, 2022, https://www.nytimes.com /2022/02/20/us/politics/substitute-teachers-national-guard-new-mexico.html.

53. Shelby Montgomery, "Moore Police Receive Support, Backlash After Substituting in Schools," KOCO News, January 19, 2022, https://www.koco.com/article /moore-police-support-backlash-substituting-schools/38821587.

54. Jill Tucker, "S.F. Teacher Payroll Fiasco: District Declares State of Emergency," *San Francisco Chronicle,* November 7, 2022, https://www.sfchronicle.com /bayarea/article/S-F-teacher-payroll-fiasco-District-declares-17564951.php.

55. Jill Tucker, "S.F. Teacher Got Paid $0 in April. So Her Principal Loaned Her $4,500 for Rent Amid SFUSD Payroll Debacle," *San Francisco Chronicle*, May 4, 2022, https://www.sfchronicle.com/sf/article/This-S-F-teacher-got-paid-0-in -April-Her-17148841.php,

56. Tala Hadavi, "2020 Has Shown a Light on the Importance of Good Teachers, But Many Are Paid Less Than a Living Wage in the U.S.," CNBC, December 11, 2020, https://www.cnbc.com/2020/12/11/why-teachers-salaries-are-so-low-in -the-us.html.

57. Kathryn Dill, "School's Out for Summer and Many Teachers Are Calling It Quits," *The Wall Street Journal*, June 20, 2022, https://www.wsj.com /articles/schools-out-for-summer-and-many-teachers-are-calling-it-quits -11655732689.

58. Libby Stanford, "U.S. Education Secretary Cardona: How To Fix Teacher Shortages, Create Safe Schools," *Education Week*, August 23, 2022, https:// www.edweek.org/policy-politics/u-s-education-secretary-cardona-how-to-fix -teacher-shortages-create-safe-schools/2022/08.

59. Madeline Will, "States Crack Open the Door to Teachers Without College Degrees," *Education Week*, August 2, 2022, https://www.edweek.org/teaching -learning/states-crack-open-the-door-to-teachers-without-college-degrees /2022/08.

60. Carolyn Jones, "Biden Budget Includes 15.6% Boost in Education Spending," *EdSource*, March 28, 2022, https://edsource.org/updates/biden-budget-includes -15–6-boost-in-education-spending#:~:text=In%20his%202023%20fiscal%20 year,15.6%25%20over%20last%20year's%20spending.

61. Mark Lieberman, "Biden Budget Seeks Big Funding Increases for High-Need Schools, Student Mental Health," *EdWeek*, March 28, 2022, https://www.edweek .org/policy-politics/biden-budget-seeks-big-funding-increases-for-high-need -schools-student-mental-health/2022/03.

62. Lieberman, "Biden Budget."

63. Kalyn Belsha and Matt Barnum, "$100 Million and Many Open Questions: Here's How Biden Is Approaching School Integration," *Chalkbeat*, June 22, 2021, https://www.chalkbeat.org/2021/6/22/22545227/biden-cardona-school -integration-desegregation-diversity.

64. Lieberman, "Biden Budget."

65. Amanda Menas, "6 Reasons We Must Address Our Nation's Crumbling School Buildings," *NEA*, April 6, 2020, https://www.nea.org/advocating-for-change /new-from-nea/why-we-must-address-crumbling-school-buildings.

66. Menas, "6 Reasons."

67. *2019 State of the States*. San Francisco, CA: EducationSuperHighway.

68. Menas, "6 Reasons," para.12.

69. Lauren Camera, "Democrats Quietly Nix Biden's $100B for School Modernization from Infrastructure Package," *U.S. News and World Report*, November 5, 2021, https://www.usnews.com/news/education-news/articles/2021–11–05 /democrats-quietly-nix-bidens-100b-for-school-modernization-from -infrastructure-package.

70. Lieberman, "Biden Budget."

6. Carceral Inevitability

1. Chesa Boudin and Rachel Marshall, "Redemptive Justice with Bryan Stevenson," *Chasing Justice* (podcast), May 11, 2021, https://www.chasingjusticepodcast .com/episodes/season-2-episode-1-redemptive-justice-with-bryan-stevenson.
2. Carl Suddler, *Presumed Criminal: Black Youth and the Justice System in Postwar New York* (New York: New York University Press, 2019).
3. Monique W. Morris, *Pushout: The Criminalization of Black Girls in Schools* (New York: New Press, 2016).
4. Rebecca Epstein, Jamilia Blake, and Thalia González, *Girlhood Interrupted: The Erasure of Black Girls' Childhood* (Washington, D.C.: Georgetown Law Center on Poverty and Inequality, June 2017).
5. Epstein, Blake, and González, *Girlhood Interrupted.*
6. Monique W. Morris, *Pushout: The Criminalization of Black Girls in Schools* (New York: New Press, 2016).
7. Jesse Hagopian, "Making Black Lives Matter at School: The National Movement Has Four Key Demands to Eliminate Racism in Education," *Progressive,* December 1, 2020, https://progressive.org/magazine/making-black-lives-matter -hagopian/.
8. Hagopian, "Making Black Lives Matter."
9. Chelsea Connery, *The Prevalence and the Price of Police in Schools* (Storrs, CT: Center for Education Policy Analysis, October 27, 2020), https://education .uconn.edu/2020/10/27/the-prevalence-and-the-price-of-police-in-schools/#.
10. Connery, *Police in Schools.*
11. Michelle Morton et al., *The Cost of School Policing: What Florida's Students Have Paid for a Pretense of Security* (Miami: ACLU of Florida, 2020), https://www .aclufl.org/en/publications/cost-school-policing.
12. Morton et al., *School Policing.*
13. Morton et al., *School Policing.*
14. Morton et al., *School Policing.*
15. Char Adams, "More Police Isn't The Answer After Texas Shooting, Experts Say," *NBCNews,* May 31, 2022, https://www.nbcnews.com/news/nbcblk/police-arent -answer-texas-shooting-experts-say-rcna30763.
16. Simone Browne, *Dark Matters: On the Surveillance of Blackness* (Durham, NC: Duke University Press, 2015).
17. Joel Handley, "The Poverty of School Reform," *In These Times,* December 19, 2011, https://inthesetimes.com/article/the-poverty-of-school-reform.
18. Maya Dukmasova, "Rahm's Police Academy Plan Met with Youth-Led Backlash from #NoCopAcademy Campaign," *Chicago Reader,* October 13, 2017, https: //chicagoreader.com/blogs/rahms-police-academy-plan-met-with-youth-led -backlash-from-nocopacademy-campaign/; Kiran Misra, "#NoCopAcademy and the Movement to Defund the Police," Belt Magazine, July 31, 2020, https: //beltmag.com/no-cop-academy-movement-defund-police-chicago/.
19. Tony Fabelo et al., *Breaking Schools' Rules: A Statewide Study of How School Discipline Relates to Students' Success and Juvenile Justice Involvement* (New York: Council of State Governments Justice Center, 2011), https://csgjusticecenter.org /publications/breaking-schools-rules/.
20. Fabelo et al., *Breaking Schools' Rules.*

21. Fabelo et al., *Breaking Schools' Rules.*

22. Max Marchitello, "Congress Takes on the School-to-Prison Pipeline," Civil Rights, December 17, 2012, https://civilrights.org/edfund/resource/congress -takes-on-the-school-to-prison-pipeline/.

23. Brittney McNamara, "Florida Sheriff Says New School Discipline Policy Will Be 'Disruptive' Students' 'Worst Nightmare,'" *Teen Vogue,* December 1, 2022, https: //www.teenvogue.com/story/florida-sheriff-school-discipline-policy.

24. Molly Redden, "The Human Cost of Kamala Harris' War on Truancy," Huff-Post, March 27, 2019, https://www.huffpost.com/entry/kamala-harris-truancy -arrests-2020-progressive-prosecutor_n_5c995789e4b0f7bfa1b57d2e.

25. Redden, "The Human Cost."

26. Annette Fuentes, "The Truancy Trap," *Atlantic,* September 5, 2012, https://www .theatlantic.com/national/archive/2012/09/the-truancy-trap/261937/.

27. Fuentes, "The Truancy Trap."

28. Jamie Stengle, "Texas Turns Away from Criminal Truancy Courts for Students," Al Jazeera America, June 20, 2015, http://america.aljazeera.com/articles/2015/6 /20/texas-turns-away-from-criminal-truancy-courts-for-students.html.

29. John Luciew, "No Charges in Case of Pa. Mom Who Died in Jail Over Truancy Fines: Justice?," Penn Live, January 5, 2019, https://www.pennlive.com/midstate /2014/09/no_charges_in_case_of_pa_mom_w.html.

30. Joseph Shapiro, "In Ferguson, Court Fines and Fees Fuel Anger," NPR, August 25, 2014, https://www.npr.org/2014/08/25/343143937/in-ferguson-court-fines -and-fees-fuel-anger.

31. Shapiro, "In Ferguson."

32. Shapiro, "In Ferguson."

33. Erica Meiners, *For the Children?: Protecting Innocence in a Carceral State* (Minneapolis: University of Minnesota Press, 2016).

34. Ameer Hasan Loggins, "We're All Living in a Future Created by Slavery," Medium, October 16, 2020, https://level.medium.com/were-all-living-in-a-future -created-by-slavery-d20199979a72.

35. Keri Blakinger, "Do Texas Prison Conditions Violate Human Rights Standards? One Scottish Court Says Yes," Marshall Project, March 17, 2022, https://www .themarshallproject.org/2022/03/17/do-texas-prison-conditions-violate-human -rights-standards-one-scottish-court-says-yes.

36. Damien M. Sojoyner, "Black Radicals Make for Bad Citizens: Undoing the Myth of the School to Prison Pipeline," *Berkeley Review of Education* 4, no. 2 (2013): 241–263, https://doi.org/10.5070/B84110021.

37. Bettina L. Love, *We Want to Do More Than Survive: Abolitionist Teaching and the Pursuit of Educational Freedom* (Boston: Beacon Press, 2019).

38. Sabina E. Vaught, *Compulsory: Education and the Dispossession of Youth in a Prison School* (Minneapolis: University of Minnesota Press, 2017).

39. Vaught, *Compulsory*; Meiners, *For the Children?*

40. Elaine Woo and Eric Malnic, "Controversial LAPD Chief," *Los Angeles Times,* April 17, 2010, https://www.latimes.com/archives/la-xpm-2010-apr-17-la-me -daryl-gates17-2010apr17-story.html.

41. Dennis P. Rosenbaum and Gordon S. Hanson, "Assessing the Effects of School-Based Drug Education: A Six-Year Multilevel Analysis of Project D.A.R.E.,"

Journal of Research in Crime and Delinquency 35, no. 4 (1998): 381–412, https://doi.org/10.1177/0022427898035004002.

42. Steven L. West and Keri K O'Neal. "Project D.A.R.E. Outcome Effectiveness Revisited," *American Journal of Public Health* 94, no. 6 (2004): 1027–1029, https://doi.org/10.2105/AJPH.94.6.1027.

43. Angela Y. Davis, *Abolition Democracy: Beyond Prisons, Torture, and Empire* (New York: Open Media, 2005), 41.

44. Rebecca Kavanaugh, "The DARE Program Is Back in Some School Districts—Here's What to Know," *Teen Vogue,* August 11, 2022, https://www.teenvogue.com/story/dare-program-back-schools.

45. Kavanaugh, "The DARE Program."

46. Dorothy Roberts and Nia T. Evans, "The 'Benevolent Terror' of the Child Welfare System," *Boston Review,* March 31, 2022, https://www.bostonreview.net/articles/the-benevolent-terror-of-the-child-welfare-system/.

47. Mariame Kaba, *We Do This 'Til We Free Us: Abolitionist Organizing and Transforming Justice* (Chicago: Haymarket Books, 2021).

48. Kaba, *We Do This,* 9.

49. Kathleen M. Cerrone, "The Gun-Free Schools Act of 1994: Zero Tolerance Takes Aim at Procedural Due Process," *Pace Law Review* 20, no. 1 (1999): 131–188, https://digitalcommons.pace.edu/cgi/viewcontent.cgi?referer=&httpsredir=1&article=1265&context=plr.

50. Maya Lindberg, "False Sense of Security: Police Make Schools Safer, Right?," *Learning for Justice,* Spring 2015, https://www.learningforjustice.org/sites/default/files/general/False%20Sense%20of%20Security%20-%20TT50.pdf.

51. Mariame Kaba and Erica R. Meiners, "Arresting the Carceral State," *Jacobin,* February 24, 2014, https://jacobin.com/2014/02/arresting-the-carceral-state/.

52. Kaba and Meiners, "Arresting the Carceral State."

53. Ranya Shannon, "3 Ways the 1994 Crime Bill Continues to Hurt Communities of Color," *Center for American Progress,* May 10, 2019, https://www.americanprogress.org/article/3-ways-1994-crime-bill-continues-hurt-communities-color/.

54. Lindberg, "False Sense of Security."

55. Lindberg, "False Sense of Security."

56. Vanessa Hernandez, *Students Not Suspects: The Need to Reform School Policing in Washington State* (Seattle, WA: American Civil Liberties Union of Washington, April 18, 2017), 4, https://www.aclu-wa.org/docs/students-not-suspects-need-reform-school-policing-washington-state.

57. Lisa H. Thurau and Johanna Wald, "Controlling Partners: When Law Enforcement Meets Discipline in Public Schools," *New York Law School Law Review* 54, no. 10 (2009): 1004.

58. Yi-Jin Yu, "School Resource Officers: What Are They and Are They Necessary?," *Today,* June 19, 2020, https://www.today.com/tmrw/what-school-resource-officer-t184614.

59. Jodi S. Cohen and Jennifer Smith Richards, "The Price Kids Pay: Schools and Police Punish Students with Costly Tickets for Minor Misbehavior," ProPublica, April 28, 2022, https://www.propublica.org/article/illinois-school-police-tickets-fines.

60. Cohen and Richards, "The Price Kids Pay."

61. Jennifer Smith Richards et al., "The Price Kids Pay: Black Students Far More Likely to Be Ticketed by Police for School Behavior," *Chicago Tribune*, May 6, 2022, https://www.chicagotribune.com/investigations/ct-illinois-schools-discipline-tickets-racial-disparities-20220506-2e5yzeouungaxgolusvwp26ljy-htmlstory.html.

62. Richards et al., "The Price Kids Pay."

63. Richards et al., "The Price Kids Pay."

64. Jennifer Smith Richards and Jodi S. Cohen, "A Teen Was Ticketed at Naperville North for Theft. 30 Months Later, She's Still Fighting to Clear Her Name," *Chicago Tribune*, June 16, 2022, https://www.chicagotribune.com/investigations/ct-illinois-school-ticketing-naperville-case-20220616-jt3dbqqajjglvlo5g7rvb5fklu-htmlstory.html.

65. Cohen and Richards, "The Price Kids Pay."

66. kihana miraya ross, "Call It What It Is: Anti-Blackness," *New York Times*, June 4, 2020, https://www.nytimes.com/2020/06/04/opinion/george-floyd-anti-blackness.html.

67. Dan Losen et al., *The Striking Outlier: The Persistent, Painful and Problematic Practice of Corporal Punishment in Schools* (Montgomery, AL: Southern Poverty Law Center and the Center for Civil Rights Remedies, June 11, 2019).

68. Angela Y. Davis, *Are Prisons Obsolete?* (New York: Seven Stories Press, 2003), 85.

69. Savannah Shange, *Progressive Dystopia: Abolition, Antiblackness, and Schooling in San Francisco* (Durham, NC: Duke University Press, 2019).

70. Ruth Wilson Gilmore, *Golden Gulag: Prisons, Surplus, Crisis, and Opposition in Globalizing California* (Berkeley: University of California Press, 2007).

71. Kayln Womack, "Why Do Black Women Go to Jail for Self-Defense?," New York Minute Mag, October 9, 2020, https://www.newyorkminutemag.com/why-do-black-women-go-to-jail-for-self-defense/.

72. Tamar Kraft-Stolar et al., *From Protection to Punishment: Post-Conviction Barriers to Justice for Domestic Violence Survivor-Defendants in New York State* (Ithaca, NY: Avon Global Center for Women and Justice and Dorothea S. Clarke Program in Feminist Jurisprudence, 2011); Angela Browne, Brenda Miller, and Eugene Maguin, "Prevalence and Severity of Lifetime Physical and Sexual Victimization Among Incarcerated Women," *International Journal of Law and Psychiatry* 22, no. 3–4 (1999): 301–322; Shannon M. Lynch et al., "Women's Pathways to Jail: Examining Mental Health, Trauma, and Substance Use," Bureau of Justice Assistance Policy Brief, NCJ241045, 2013.

73. Lauren E. Glaze and Laura M. Maruschak, *Parents in Prison and Their Minor Children* (Washington, D.C.: Bureau of Justice Statistics, March 30, 2010).

74. David Murphey and P. Mae Cooper, *Parents Behind Bars: What Happens to Their Children?* (Washington, D.C.: Child Trends, October 27, 2015), https://www.childtrends.org/publications/parents-behind-bars-what-happens-to-their-children.

75. Glaze and Maruschak, *Parents in Prison*.

76. Gilmore, *Golden Gulag*, 22.

77. Trevariana Mason, "Extreme Sentences Disproportionately Impact and Harm Black Women," National Black Women's Justice Institute, September 23, 2021, https://www.nbwji.org/post/extreme-sentences-disproportionately-impact-and-harm-black-women

78. Ryan King, Marc Mauer, and Tracy Huling, *Big Prisons, Small Towns: Prison Economics in Rural America* (Washington, D.C.: Sentencing Project, February 1,

2003), https://www.sentencingproject.org/publications/big-prisons-small-towns-prison-economics-in-rural-america/.

79. Kristy N. Kamarck, *Defense Primer: Junior Reserve Officers' Training Corps (JROTC)* (Washington, D.C.: Congressional Research Service, June 15, 2022), https://sgp.fas.org/crs/natsec/IF11313.pdf.

80. Sylvia McGauley, "The Military Invasion of my High School: The Role of JROTC," *Rethinking Schools*, Fall 2014, https://rethinkingschools.org/articles/the-military-invasion-of-my-high-school/.

81. Charles A. Goldman et al., *Geographic and Demographic Representativeness of the Junior Reserve Officers' Training Corps* (Santa Monica, CA: Rand Corporation), https://www.rand.org/pubs/research_reports/RR1712.html.

82. Nick Martin, "The Military Views Kids as Fodder for Its Forever Wars," *New Republic*, January 7, 2020, https://newrepublic.com/article/156131/military-views-poor-kids-fodder-forever-wars.

83. Catherine Lutz and Lesley Bartlett, *Making Soldiers in the Public Schools: An Analysis of the Army JROTC Curriculum* (Philadelphia, PA: American Friends Service Committee, 1995), 8.

84. Morley Musick, "Meet the Boy Scouts of the Border Patrol," *Nation*, January 21, 2020, https://www.thenation.com/article/politics/scouts-border-immigration-trump/.

85. Musick, "Meet the Boy Scouts."

86. Vanessa Serna, "Sheriff's Deputy Accidentally Shoots and Injures Indiana High School Student During 'Bad Guy Drill,'" *Daily Mail*, November 17, 2022, https://www.dailymail.co.uk/news/article-11441635/Sheriffs-deputy-accidentally-SHOOTS-injures-Indiana-high-school-student-bad-guy-drill.html.

87. Serna, "Sheriff's Deputy Accidentally Shoots."

88. "Police Academy Magnet Schools," LAPD Cadets, accessed September 18, 2022, https://lapdcadets.com/police-academy-magnet-school/.

89. "Police Academy Magnet Schools," 2022.

7. Standardizing Carcerality

1. Phillip Atiba Goff et al., "The Essence of Innocence: Consequences of Dehumanizing Black Children," *Journal of Personality and Social Psychology* 106, no. 4 (2014): 526–545, https://www.apa.org/pubs/journals/releases/psp-a0035663.pdf.

2. Goff et al., "The Essence of Innocence," 532.

3. National Center for Education Statistics, *Characteristics of Public School Teachers* (Washington, DC: U.S. Department of Education, May 2021), https://nces.ed.gov/programs/coe/indicator/clr.

4. Monique W. Morris, *Pushout: The Criminalization of Black Girls in Schools* (New York: New Press, 2016).

5. Seth Gershenson et al., "The Long-Run Impacts of Same-Race Teachers" (NBER Working Paper 25254, National Bureau of Economic Research, Cambridge, MA, February 2021).

6. Gershenson et al., "The Long-Run Impacts of Same-Race Teachers."

7. Morris, *Pushout*, 8–9.

8. Khalil Gibran Muhammad, *The Condemnation of Blackness: Race, Crime, and the Making of Modern Urban America* (Boston: Harvard University Press, 2011), 6.

9. Muhammad, *The Condemnation of Blackness*, 6–7.

10. Muhammad, *The Condemnation of Blackness*, 7.
11. Albert Murray, *The Omni-Americans: Some Alternatives to the Folklore of White Supremacy* (New York: Library of America, 2020), 37.
12. Murray, *The Omni-Americans*, 37.
13. John Rosales and Tim Walker, "The Racist Beginnings of Standardized Testing," NEA, March 20, 2021, https://www.nea.org/advocating-for-change/new-from-nea/racist-beginnings-standardized-testing.
14. "A Brief History of the SAT," *Frontline*, https://www.pbs.org/wgbh/pages/frontline/shows/sats/where/history.html.
15. Rosales and Walker, "The Racist Beginnings."
16. Rosales and Walker, "The Racist Beginnings."
17. W. E. B. Du Bois, *Dusk of Dawn: An Essay Toward an Autobiography of a Race Concept* (New York: Oxford University Press, 2007), 50.
18. Isabel Wilkerson, *Caste: The Origins of Our Discontents* (New York: Random House, 2020), 79.
19. Edwin Black, *War Against the Weak: Eugenics and America's Campaign to Create a Master Race* (London: Basic Books, 2004), 276.
20. Daniel Patrick Moynihan, *The Negro Family: The Case for National Action* (Washington, D.C.: Department of Labor, 1965), 29.
21. James T. Patterson, "Moynihan and the Single-Parent Family," *Education Next*, December 12, 2014, https://www.educationnext.org/moynihan-and-the-single-parent-family/.
22. James S. Coleman, "Equal Education Opportunity: A Definition," *Oxford Review of Education* 1, no. 1 (1975), https://doi.org/10.1080/0305498750010104.
23. Bettina L. Love, *We Want to Do More Than Survive: Abolitionist Teaching and the Pursuit of Educational Freedom* (Boston: Beacon Press, 2019).
24. Ladson-Billings, Gloria. "From the Achievement Gap to the Education Debt: Understanding Achievement in U.S. Schools." *Educational Researcher* 35, no. 7 (2006): 3–12. http://www.jstor.org/stable/3876731.
25. Valerie Strauss, "Confirmed: Standardized Testing Has Taken Over Our Schools. But Who's To Blame?," *Washington Post*, October 24, 2015, https://www.washingtonpost.com/news/answer-sheet/wp/2015/10/24/confirmed-standardized-testing-has-taken-over-our-schools-but-whos-to-blame/.
26. Strauss, "Confirmed."
27. Strauss, "Confirmed."
28. "Test Punish, Push-Out: How 'Zero Tolerance' and High Stakes Testing Funnel Youth into the School-to-Prison Pipeline," Advancement Project, March 2010, https://www.justice4all.org/wp-content/uploads/2016/04/Test-Punish-Push-Out.pdf.
29. Olesya Baker and Kevin Lang, "The Effect of High School Exit Exams on Graduation, Employment, Wages and Incarceration" (NBER Working Paper 19182, National Bureau of Economic Research, Cambridge, MA, June 2013).
30. Sam Dillon, "Study Finds High Rate of Imprisonment Among Dropouts," *New York Times*, October 8, 2009, https://www.nytimes.com/2009/10/09/education/09dropout.html.
31. Donald J. Hernandez, *How Third-Grade Reading Skills and Poverty Influence High School Graduation* (New York: Annie E. Casey Foundation, 2012). https://assets.aecf.org/m/resourcedoc/AECF-DoubleJeopardy-2012-Full.pdf.

32. Hernandez, *Third-Grade Reading.*
33. "Testing and Educational Support Industry in the US: Market Research Report," IBISWorld, July 6, 2022, https://www.ibisworld.com/united-states/market-research-reports/testing-educational-support-industry/.
34. "Client Profile: S&P Global," OpenSecrets, https://www.opensecrets.org/federal-lobbying/clients/summary?cycle=2021&id=D000035733; "Client Profile: Educational Testing Service," OpenSecrets, https://www.opensecrets.org/federal-lobbying/clients/summary?cycle=2021&id=D000050420; "Client Profiles: Pearson PLC," OpenSecrets, https://www.opensecrets.org/federal-lobbying/clients/summary?cycle=2021&id=D000068157; "Client Profiles: Houghton Mifflin Harcourt," OpenSecrets, https://www.opensecrets.org/federal-lobbying/clients/summary?cycle=2021&id=D000018389.
35. Murray N. Rothbard, "Race! That Murray Book," *Rothbard-Rockwell Report,* December 1994: 3.
36. Andrew S. Winston, "Neoliberalism and IQ: Naturalizing Economic and Racial Inequality," *Theory and Psychology* 28, no. 5 (2018): 611, https://doi.org/10.1177/0959354318798160.
37. Wayne Au, *Unequal by Design: High-Stakes Testing and the Standardization of Inequality,* 2nd ed. (New York: Routledge, 2023), 22 (preprint).
38. Au, *Unequal by Design,* 22.
39. Marilyn Rhames, "Will Little Sally Go to Yale or Jail? There's an Algorithm for That," *Education Week,* March 19, 2014, https://www.edweek.org/education/opinion-will-little-sally-go-to-yale-or-to-jail-theres-an-algorithm-for-that/2014/03
40. Rhames, "Yale or Jail?"
41. Will Douglas Heaven, "Predictive Policing Algorithms Are Racist. They Need to Be Dismantled," *MIT Technology Review,* July 17, 2020, https://www.technologyreview.com/2020/07/17/1005396/predictive-policing-algorithms-racist-dismantled-machine-learning-bias-criminal-justice/.

8. White Philanthropy

1. Eric W. Robelen, "Teacher Who Inspired KIPP Schools Dies in Houston," *Education Week,* February 10, 2011, https://www.edweek.org/teaching-learning/teacher-who-inspired-kipp-schools-dies-in-houston/2011/02.
2. Jay Mathews, *Work Hard. Be Nice.: How Two Inspired Teachers Created the Most Promising Schools in America* (Chapel Hill, NC: Algonquin Books of Chapel Hill, 2009), 74.
3. Daniel J. Losen et al., *Charter Schools, Civil Rights, and School Discipline: A Comprehensive Review* (Los Angeles: Civil Rights Project / Proyecto Derechos Civiles, March 2016), https://civilrightsproject.ucla.edu/resources/projects/center-for-civil-rights-remedies/school-to-prison-folder/federal-reports/charter-schools-civil-rights-and-school-discipline-a-comprehensive-review/losen-et-al-charter-school-discipline-review-2016.pdf.
4. Losen et al., *Charter Schools.*
5. Jay Mathews, "'No-Excuse Schools' Make No Excuse for Updating Their Approach," *Washington Post,* August 2, 2019, https://www.washingtonpost.com

/local/education/no-excuses-schools-make-no-excuse-for-updating-their
-approach/2019/08/01/7a3e9052-b31b-11e9–8f6c-7828e68cb15f_story.html.

6. Mathews, *Work Hard. Be Nice.*, 163.

7. Dave Levin, "Dave Levin: On His Magical Mentor, Harriet Ball," YouTube video, 10:27, posted by The 74, May 20, 2022, https://youtu.be/XSJQeoDbQWc.

8. Levin, "On His Magical Mentor."

9. Levin, "On His Magical Mentor."

10. Jim Horn, *Work Hard, Be Hard: Journeys Through No Excuses Teaching* (Lanham, MD: Rowman & Littlefield, 2016).

11. Joel Warner, "Reed Hastings: Netflix CEO Goes Nuclear on Public Schools," Capital & Main, November 1, 2018, https://capitalandmain.com/reed-hastings
-the-disrupter-1101.

12. Warner, "Reed Hastings."

13. Richard Whitmire, *On the Rocketship: How Top Charter Schools Are Pushing the Envelope* (Hoboken, NJ: Wiley, 2014).

14. Jeff Bryant, "How the Cutthroat Walmart Business Model Is Reshaping American Public Education," AlterNet, March 13, 2016, https://www.alternet.org
/2016/03/how-cutthroat-walmart-business-model-reshaping-american-public
-education/.

15. Diane Ravitch, *The Death and Life of the Great American School System: How Testing and Choice Are Undermining Education* (New York: Basic Books, 2010).

16. Bryant, "Cutthroat Walmart Business Model."

17. Bryant, "Cutthroat Walmart Business Model."

18. Bryant, "Cutthroat Walmart Business Model."

19. Megan E. Tompkins-Stange, *Policy Patrons: Philanthropy, Education Reform, and the Politics of Influence* (Cambridge, MA: Harvard Education Press, 2016).

20. Thomas M. Philip et al., "Making Justice Peripheral by Constructing Practice as 'Core': How the Increasing Prominence of Core Practices Challenges Teacher Education," *Journal of Teacher Education* 70, no. 3 (2019): 251–264.

21. Philip et al., "Making Justice Peripheral."

22. Joanne Barkan, "Got Dough? How Billionaires Rule Our Schools," *Dissent*, Winter 2011, https://www.dissentmagazine.org/article/got-dough-how-billionaires
-rule-our-schools.

23. On December 13, 2022, I called KIPP Foundation's Vice President of Communications. We spoke about the nature of my book. I told her that a section of my book discussed Harriett Ball. I sent the questions below:

    1. Was Harriett Ball ever compensated by KIPP? If so, how much?

    2. Was Harriett Ball ever compensated for her songs or chants?

    3. Did Harriett Ball ever sign any release forms that granted KIPP the use of her songs and/or chants?

    4. Did she physically appear on the Oprah Show with David and Mike?

    5. If she didn't physically appear on the Oprah Show, did David and Mike invite her?

    6. Was she ever offered a top leadership position at KIPP's headquarters?

On January 5, 2023, KIPP sent me an official statement from the KIPP Foundation. That statement in its entirety appears in the book.

24. William H. Watkins, *The White Architects of Black Education: Ideology and Power in America, 1865–1954* (New York: Teachers College Press, 2001), 21.
25. Watkins, *The White Architects.*
26. Watkins, *The White Architects,* 20.
27. Edward H. Berman, *The Influence of the Carnegie, Ford, and Rockefeller Foundations on American Foreign Policy: The Ideology of Philanthropy* (Albany: State University of New York Press, 1983), 15–16.
28. Robert F. Arnove, *Philanthropy and Cultural Imperialism: The Foundations at Home and Abroad* (Boston: G. K. Hall, 1980).
29. Watkins, *The White Architects,* 6.
30. Watkins, *The White Architects,* 6.
31. Noliwe M. Rooks, *Cutting School: Privatization, Segregation, and the End of Public Education* (New York: New Press, 2017).
32. Rooks, *Cutting School.*
33. Rooks, *Cutting School.*
34. Rooks, *Cutting School,* 55.
35. Watkins, *The White Architects.*
36. Rooks, *Cutting School,* 60.
37. Rooks, *Cutting School,* 50.
38. Watkins, *The White Architects,* 47.
39. Rooks, *Cutting School,* 65.
40. Watkins, *The White Architects.*
41. Waldemar A. Nielsen, *The Big Foundations* (New York: Columbia University Press, 1972), 358.
42. Richard McKenzie, "Decade of Grief?," NPR, June 10, 2004, https://www.nationalreview.com/2004/06/decade-greed-richard-mckenzie/.
43. Michael Grasso, "Champagne Wishes and Caviar Dreams," *Jacobin,* May 27, 2021, https://jacobinmag.com/2021/04/champagne-wishes-and-caviar-dreams.
44. Reynold Levy, *Give and Take: A Candid Account of Corporate Philanthropy* (Boston: Harvard Business School Press, 1999), xix–xx.
45. Michael Harriot, "Millions of Students Are Quietly Being Taught the Koch Brothers' Whitewashed Version of Black History," Root, March 14, 2018, https://www.theroot.com/millions-of-students-are-quietly-being-taught-the-koch-1823742091.
46. Harriot, "Millions of Students."
47. Casey Parks, "The Rise of Black Homeschooling," *New Yorker,* June 14, 2021, https://www.newyorker.com/magazine/2021/06/21/the-rise-of-black-homeschooling.
48. Parks, "Black Homeschooling."
49. Parks, "Black Homeschooling."
50. Rob Larson, *Bit Tyrants: The Political Economy of Silicon Valley* (Chicago: Haymarket Books, 2020).
51. Sharon Pian Chan, "Long Antitrust Saga Ends for Microsoft," *Seattle Times,* May 11, 2011, https://www.seattletimes.com/business/microsoft/long-antitrust-saga-ends-for-microsoft/.
52. Larson, *Bit Tyrants.*
53. Marta P. Baltodano, "The Power Brokers of Neoliberalism: Philanthrocapitalists and Public Education," *Policy Futures in Education* 15, no. 2 (2017): 141–156.

54. Baltodano, "Power Brokers of Neoliberalism."
55. Baltodano, "Power Brokers of Neoliberalism."
56. Valerie Strauss, "Bill and Melinda Gates Have Spent Billions to Shape Education Policy. Now, They Say, They're 'Skeptical' of 'Billionaires' Trying to Do Just That," *Washington Post,* February 10, 2020, https://www.washingtonpost.com/education /2020/02/10/bill-melinda-gates-have-spent-billions-dollars-shape-education -policy-now-they-say-theyre-skeptical-billionaires-trying-do-just-that/.
57. Lyndsey Layton, "How Bill Gates Pulled Off the Swift Common Core Revolution," *Washington Post,* June 7, 2014, https://www.washingtonpost.com/politics /how-bill-gates-pulled-off-the-swift-common-core-revolution/2014/06/07 /a830e32e-ec34–11e3–9f5c-9075d5508f0a_story.html.
58. Layton, "How Bill Gates."
59. Layton, "How Bill Gates."
60. Layton, "How Bill Gates."
61. Layton, "How Bill Gates."
62. Katie Schoolov, "Google Is Winning in Education, but Apple and Microsoft Are Battling for Market Share," CNBC, March 20, 2019, https://www.cnbc.com/2019 /03/20/apple-google-microsoft-are-battling-for-dominance-in-education.html.
63. Jonathan Martin, "Republicans See Political Wedge in Common Core," *New York Times,* April 20, 2014, https://www.nytimes.com/2014/04/20/us/politics /republicans-see-political-wedge-in-common-core.html.
64. Layton, "How Bill Gates."
65. Layton, "How Bill Gates."
66. Bill Gates, "Annual Letter 2009," Bill & Melinda Gates Foundation, January 2009, https://www.gatesfoundation.org/ideas/annual-letters/annual-letter-2009.
67. Strauss, "Bill and Melinda Gates."
68. Alex Park, "Is the Gates Foundation Still Investing in Private Prisons?," *Mother Jones,* December 8, 2014, https://www.motherjones.com/politics/2014/12/gates -foundation-still-investing-private-prisons/.
69. Park, "Gates Foundation."
70. "Gates Millennium Scholars Program," Gates Millennium Scholars, accessed October 9, 2021, http://www.gmsp.org/.
71. Judith Scott-Clayton and Jing Li, *Black-White Disparity in Student Loans Debt More Than Triples After Graduation* (Washington, D.C.: Brookings Institution, October 20, 2016), https://www.brookings.edu/research/black-white-disparity -in-student-loan-debt-more-than-triples-after-graduation/.
72. "Indicator 22: Financial Aid," National Center for Education Statistics, February 2019, https://nces.ed.gov/programs/raceindicators/indicator_rec.asp.
73. Peter Granville, *Parent PLUS Borrowers: The Hidden Casualties of the Student Debt Crisis* (New York: Century Foundation, May 31, 2022).
74. Tressie McMillan Cottom, "The Coded Language of For-Profit Colleges," *Atlantic,* February 22, 2017, https://www.theatlantic.com/education/archive/2017/02 /the-coded-language-of-for-profit-colleges/516810/.
75. Tom Winter and Dartunorro Clark, "Federal Court Approves $25 Million Trump University Settlement," NBC News, February 6, 2018, https://www .nbcnews.com/politics/white-house/federal-court-approves-25-million-trump -university-settlement-n845181.

76. Emma Kerr and Sarah Wood, "The Real Cost of For-Profit Colleges," *U.S. News,* January 20, 2022, https://www.usnews.com/education/best-colleges/paying-for -college/articles/the-real-cost-of-for-profit-colleges.

77. Donald E. Heller and Patricia Marin, eds., *State Merit Scholarship Programs and Racial Inequality* (Cambridge, MA: Civil Rights Project at Harvard University, 2004), 15.

78. Michel Martin, "Scholarships: Who Gets Them and Why?," NPR, March 17, 2011, https://www.npr.org/templates/story/story.php?storyId=134623124.

79. "As Districts Face Teacher Shortages, Black and Latino Students Are More Likely to Have Novice Teachers Than Their White Peers," Education Trust, December 12, 2021, https://edtrust.org/press-release/as-districts-face-teacher-shortages -black-and-latino-students-are-more-likely-to-have-novice-teachers-than -their-white-peers/.

80. Donald E. Heller, "Merit Aid and College Access" (paper presented at the Symposium on the Consequences of Merit-Based Student Aid, University of Wisconsin, Madison, March 2006), 3.

81. Strauss, "Bill and Melinda Gates."

9. The Trap of Diversity, Equity, and Inclusion

1. Saidiya Hartman, "Saidiya Hartman on Insurgent Histories and the Abolitionist Imaginary," *Artforum,* July 14, 2020, https://www.artforum.com/interviews /saidiya-hartman-83579.

2. Bettina L. Love, "How to Make Anti-Racism More Than a Performance," *Education Week,* January 12, 2021, https://www.edweek.org/leadership/opinion -empty-promises-of-equity/2021/01.

3. Martin Luther King Jr., "Martin Luther King Jr. at Rec Hall on Jan. 21, 1965" (speech, State College, PA, January 21, 1965), https://www.psu.edu/news /campus-life/story/martin-luther-king-jr-rec-hall-jan-21-1965/.

4. William A. Darity and A. Kirsten Mullen, *From Here to Equality: Reparations for Black Americans in the Twenty-First Century* (Chapel Hill: University of North Carolina Press, 2020), 3.

5. Sara Ahmed, *Living a Feminist Life* (Durham, NC: Duke University Press, 2017), 90.

6. Ahmed, *Living a Feminist Life,* 72.

7. Joseph P. Williams, "A Year After George Floyd's Killing, White Allyship Fades," *U.S. News,* May 25, 2021, https://www.usnews.com/news/national-news/articles /2021-05-25/a-year-after-george-floyds-killing-white-support-for-black-lives -matter-fades.

8. Williams, "White Allyship Fades."

9. Williams, "White Allyship Fades."

10. Cheryl Teh, "Black Students Outed Their Private School Teachers for Racist Behavior via an Explosive Instagram Account," Insider, April 28, 2021, https: //www.insider.com/black-students-outed-private-school-teachers-instagram -racist-behavior-2021-4.

11. Teh, "Black Students Outed."

12. Caitlin O'Kane and Olivia Wilson, "A Long Time Coming: Black Students Turn to Social Media to Expose Racism at Private Schools," CBS News, September

14, 2020, https://www.cbsnews.com/news/black-at-instagram-students-private
-school-racism-social-media/.

13. Charles Bethea (@charlesbethea), "I just read the scorching 5-page letter recently
'written on behalf of thousands of parents, alumnae, community supporters &
financial donors of Westminster,' the most elite of Atlanta's . . ." Twitter, April 14,
2021, 4:00 p.m., https://twitter.com/charlesbethea/status/1382423565266530312
?lang=en.

14. Bethea, "I just read."

15. Bethea, "I just read."

16. Harmeet Kaur, "The Coronavirus Pandemic Is Hitting Black and Brown Americans Especially Hard on All Fronts," CNN, May 8, 2020, https://www.cnn.com
/2020/05/08/us/coronavirus-pandemic-race-impact-trnd/index.html.

17. Sheryll Cashin, *White Space, Black Hood: Opportunity Hoarding and Segregation
in the Age of Inequality* (Boston: Beacon Press, 2021).

18. Joseph Ax, "New York City School Segregation Perpetuates Racism, Lawsuit
Contends," Reuters, March 9, 2021, https://www.reuters.com/article/us-new
-york-schools-racism/new-york-city-school-segregation-perpetuates-racism
-lawsuit-contends-idUSKBN2B11WI.

19. Cashin, *White Space, Black Hood.*

20. Cashin, *White Space, Black Hood,* 128.

21. Eliza Shapiro, "Segregation Has Been the Story of New York City's Schools for 50
Years," *New York Times,* March 26, 2019, https://www.nytimes.com/2019/03/26
/nyregion/school-segregation-new-york.html.

22. Shapiro, "Segregation Has Been."

23. Shapiro, "Segregation Has Been."

24. Eliza Shapiro and K. K. Rebecca Lai, "How New York's Elite Public Schools
Lost Their Black and Hispanic Students," *New York Times,* June 3, 2019, https://
www.nytimes.com/interactive/2019/06/03/nyregion/nyc-public-schools-black
-hispanic-students.html.

25. Eliza Shapiro, "Only 7 Black Students Got into Stuyvesant, N.Y.'s Most Selective
High School, Out of 895 Spots," *New York Times,* March 18, 2019, https://www
.nytimes.com/2019/03/18/nyregion/black-students-nyc-high-schools.html.

26. Eliza Shapiro, "Only 8 Black Students Are Admitted to Stuyvesant High School,"
New York Times, April 29, 2021, https://www.nytimes.com/2021/04/29/nyregion
/stuyvestant-black-students.html.

27. Shapiro and Lai, "New York's Elite."

28. Shapiro and Lai, "New York's Elite."

29. Shapiro, "Only 8 Black Students."

30. Eliza Shapiro, "A Perk for N.Y.'s Richest Areas: First Dibs on Top Public Schools,"
New York Times, August 27, 2020, https://www.nytimes.com/2020/08/27/nyregion
/nyc-public-high-school-admissions.html.

31. Shapiro, "A Perk."

32. Dianna Douglas, "Are Private Schools Immoral?," *Atlantic,* December 14, 2017,
https://www.theatlantic.com/education/archive/2017/12/progressives-are
-undermining-public-schools/548084/.

33. Emily Lie, "How Segregated Schools Built Segregated Cities," Bloomberg, February

2, 2017, https://www.bloomberg.com/news/articles/2017–02–02/the-roots-of -america-s-apartheid-schools.

34. George Orfield and Jongyeon Ee, *Our Segregated Capital: A Increasingly Diverse City with Polarized Schools* (Los Angeles: Civil Rights Project / Proyecto Derechos Civiles, February 9, 2017), https://www.civilrightsproject.ucla.edu /research/k-12-education/integration-and-diversity/our-segregated-capital-an -increasingly-diverse-city-with-racially-polarized-schools/POSTVERSION _DC_020117.pdf.

35. Douglas, "Are Private Schools Immoral?"

36. Eliza Shapiro, "How White Progressives Undermine School Integration," *New York Times,* August 21, 2020, https://www.nytimes.com/2020/08/21/nyregion /school-integration-progressives.html.

37. Allison Roda and Amy Stuart Wells, "School Choice Policies and Racial Segregation: Where White Parent's Good Intentions, Anxiety, and Privilege Collide," *American Journal of Education* 119, no. 2 (2013): 261–293.

38. Douglas, "Are Private Schools Immoral?"

39. Laura Meckler and Hannah Natanson, "Schools, Caught by Pandemic and Confronting Racism, Jettison Testing for Admissions," *Washington Post,* December 18, 2020, https://www.washingtonpost.com/education/nyc-schools-admissions -change-segregation/2020/12/18/6dd18590–4163–11eb-8db8–395dedaaa036 _story.html.

40. Shapiro, "Segregation Has Been."

41. Shapiro, "Segregation Has Been."

42. Jim Dwyer, "Decades Ago, New York Dug a Moat Around Its Specialized Schools," *New York Times,* June 8, 2018, https://www.nytimes.com/2018/06/08 /nyregion/about-shsat-specialized-high-schools-test.html.

43. Eliza Shapiro, "De Blasio to Phase Out N.Y.C. Gifted and Talented Program," *New York Times,* October 8, 2021, https://www.nytimes.com/2021/10/08 /nyregion/gifted-talented-nyc-schools.html.

44. Shapiro, "De Blasio to Phase Out."

45. Erin Einhorn, "A Fight over Gifted Education in New York Is Escalating a National Debate over Segregated Schools," NBC News, August 31, 2019, https: //www.nbcnews.com/news/education/fight-over-gifted-education-new-york -escalating-national-debate-over-n1048516.

46. Shapiro, "De Blasio to Phase Out."

47. Lola Fadulu, "New York City to Expand Gifted and Talented Program but Scrap Test," *New York Times,* April 14, 2022, https://www.nytimes.com/2022/04/14 /nyregion/nyc-gifted-talented.html.

48. Michael Elsen-Rooney, "24 Principals in Manhattan's District 3 Sign Petition Against Middle School Admissions Screens," Chalkbeat New York, October 17, 2022, https://ny.chalkbeat.org/2022/10/17/23409777/district-3-principals -oppose-middle-school-screens-manhattan.

49. Bessel A. van der Kolk, *The Body Keeps the Score: Brain, Mind, and Body in the Healing of Trauma* (New York: Penguin Books, 2014).

50. Nina Martin and Renee Montagne, "Black Mothers Keep Dying After Giving Birth. Shalon Irving's Story Explains Why," NPR, December 7, 2017, https://

www.npr.org/2017/12/07/568948782/black-mothers-keep-dying-after-giving
-birth-shalon-irvings-story-explains-why.

51. Martin and Montagne, "Black Mothers Keep Dying."

52. Linda Villarose, "Why America's Black Mothers and Babies Are in a Life-or-Death Crisis," *New York Times,* April 11, 2018, https://www.nytimes.com/2018/04/11/magazine/black-mothers-babies-death-maternal-mortality.html.

53. Villarose, "Black Mothers and Babies."

54. Villarose, "Black Mothers and Babies."

55. Villarose, "Black Mothers and Babies."

56. Gwen Aviles, "Police Killings Are the Sixth Leading Cause of Death Among Young Men, Study Shows," NBC News, August 13, 2019, https://www.nbcnews.com/news/nbcblk/police-killings-are-sixth-leading-cause-death-among-young-men-n1041526.

57. Lindsey Cook, "Why Black Americans Die Younger," *U.S. News,* January 5, 2015, https://www.usnews.com/news/blogs/data-mine/2015/01/05/black-americans-have-fewer-years-to-live-heres-why.

58. Cassie Owens, "What Racism Does to Your Heart and Health," *Philadelphia Inquirer,* July 15, 2020, https://www.inquirer.com/news/racism-health-disparities-coronavirus-pandemic-protests-microaggressions-wellness-advice-20200715.html.

59. Rachel White, "The Body's Real-Time Response to Racism," *Life & Letters,* June 15, 2021, https://lifeandletters.la.utexas.edu/2021/06/the-bodys-real-time-response-to-racism/.

60. Van der Kolk, *The Body Keeps,* 550.

61. Van der Kolk, *The Body Keeps,* 53.

62. Beata Mostafavi, "Understanding Racial Disparities for Women with Uterine Fibroids," Michigan Health Lab, August 12, 2020, https://labblog.uofmhealth.org/rounds/understanding-racial-disparities-for-women-uterine-fibroids.

63. Amy Stuart Wells, *Seeing Past the "Colorblind" Myth: Why Education Policymakers Should Address Racial and Ethnic Inequality and Support Culturally Diverse Schools* (Boulder, CO: National Education Policy Center, March 2014), retrieved October 26, 2021, http://nepc.colorado.edu/publication/seeing-past-the-colorblind-myth.

64. Nikole Hannah-Jones, "What Is Owed," *New York Times Magazine,* June 30, 2020, https://www.nytimes.com/interactive/2020/06/24/magazine/reparations-slavery.html.

10. White People: Save Yourselves

1. Justin Kirkland, "Toni Morrison Broke Down the Truth About White Supremacy in a Powerful 1993 PBS Interview," *Esquire,* August 6, 2019, https://www.esquire.com/entertainment/books/a28621535/toni-morrison-white-supremacy-charlie-rose-interview-racism/.

2. Joanna Slater, "Alex Jones Ordered to Pay Nearly $1 Billion to Sandy Hook Families," *Washington Post,* October 12, 2022, https://www.washingtonpost.com/nation/2022/10/12/alex-jones-sandy-hook-verdict/.

3. Slater, "Alex Jones Ordered."

4. "Alex Jones Concedes That the Sandy Hook Attack Was '100% Real,'" NPR, August 3, 2022, https://www.npr.org/2022/08/03/1115414563/alex-jones-sandy-hook-case.

5. Charles Mills, *The Racial Contract* (Ithaca, NY: Cornell University Press, 1997), 73.

6. Lindsey Norward, "The Day Philadelphia Bombed Its Own People," Vox, August 15, 2019, https://www.vox.com/the-highlight/2019/8/8/20747198/philadelphia-bombing-1985-move.

7. Norward, "Philadelphia Bombed."

8. James Baldwin, *The Price of the Ticket: Collected Nonfiction: 1948–1985* (Boston: Beacon Press, 1985), 169.

9. Adam Serwer, "The Coronavirus Was an Emergency Until Trump Found Out Who Was Dying," *Atlantic*, May 8, 2020, https://www.theatlantic.com/ideas/archive/2020/05/americas-racial-contract-showing/611389/.

10. Mariame Kaba, *We Do This 'Til We Free Us: Abolitionist Organizing and Transforming Justice* (Chicago: Haymarket Books, 2021), 59.

11. Kaba, *We Do This*, 59.

12. Mia Mingus, *Leaving Evidence* (blog), https://leavingevidence.wordpress.com/.

13. Robin D. G. Kelley, *Freedom Dreams: The Black Radical Imagination* (Boston: Beacon Press, 2002).

14. Kenneth Jones and Tema Okun, *Dismantling Racism: A Workbook for Social Change Groups* (n.p.: Changeworks, 2001), https://www.dismantlingracism.org/white-supremacy-culture.html.

15. "Steve Biddulph," HarperCollins Publishers, https://www.harpercollins.com/blogs/authors/steve-biddulph.

16. Prentis Hemphill, "Healing Justice Is How We Can Sustain Black Lives," Huff-Post, February 7, 2017, https://www.huffpost.com/entry/healing-justice_b_5899e8ade4b0c1284f282ffe.

11. Let Us Celebrate

1. Nikki Giovanni, *Racism 101* (New York: William Morrow, 1995), 154–155.

2. Lindsey Stewart, *The Politics of Black Joy: Zora Neale Hurston and Neo-Abolitionism* (Evanston: Northwestern University Press, 2021).

3. Elaine B. Richardson and Ricard L. Jackson, *African American Rhetoric(s): Interdisciplinary Perspectives* (Carbondale: Southern Illinois University Press, 2004), 223.

4. Freddi Williams Evans, *Hush Harbor: Praying in Secret* (Minneapolis, MN: Carolrhoda Books, 2008).

5. Evans, *Hush Harbor*.

6. Evans, *Hush Harbor*.

7. Cynthia B. Dillard, *The Spirit of Our Work: Black Women Teachers (Re)member* (Boston: Beacon Press, 2021).

8. Lama Rod Owens, *Love and Rage: The Path of Liberation Through Anger* (Berkeley, CA: North Atlantic Books, 2020).

9. adrienne maree brown, "exciting lessons from yes on 2," *adrienne maree brown* (blog), November 5, 2021, https://adriennemareebrown.net/2021/11/05/exciting-lessons-from-yes-on-2/.

10. Melvin McLeod, "Angelou," *Shambhala Sun*, January 1998, http://www.hartford-hwp.com/archives/45a/249.html.

11. zandashe l'orelia brown (@zandashe), "I dream of never being called resilient again in my life. I'm exhausted by strength. I want support. I want softness. I want ears. I want to be amongst kin. Not patted on the back for how well I take a hit," Twitter, May 18, 2021, 7:02 p.m., https://twitter.com/zandashe/status/1394805726825099279?s=27.

12. Lucille Clifton, *The Book of Light* (Port Townsend, WA: Copper Canyon Press, 1993), 25.

13. Gena Dagel Caponi, *Signifyin(g), Sanctifiyin' & Slam Dunking: A Reader in African American Expressive Culture* (Amherst: University of Massachusetts Press, 1999), 7.

14. Caponi, *Signifyin(g), Sanctifiyin' & Slam Dunking.*

15. Derecka Purnell, *Becoming Abolitionists: Police, Protests, and Pursuit of Freedom* (New York: Astra House, 2021).

16. Mia Mingus, "Transformative Justice: A Brief Description," *TransformHarm*, January 11, 2019, https://transformharm.org/tj_resource/transformative-justice-a-brief-description/.

17. Mingus, "Transformative Justice."

18. Angela Y. Davis, Gina Dent, Erica Meiners, and Beth Richie, *Abolition. Feminism. Now.* (Chicago: Haymarket Books, 2022).

19. Farima Pour-Khorshid, in discussion with the author, December 22, 2022.

20. Monique M. Morris, *Sing a Rhythm, Dance a Blues: Education for Liberation of Black and Brown Girls* (New York: The New Press, 2019), 7.

21. Aurora Levins Morales, *Medicine Stories: Essays for Radicals* (Durham, NC: Duke University Press, 2019).

22. Mariame Kaba, *We Do This 'Til We Free Us: Abolitionist Organizing and Transforming Justice* (Chicago: Haymarket Books, 2021), 149.

23. Erica Meiners, quoted in Mariame Kaba, "A Jailbreak of the Imagination: Seeing Prisons for What They Are and Demanding Transformation," Truthout, May 3, 2018, https://truthout.org/articles/a-jailbreak-of-the-imagination-seeing-prisons-for-what-they-are-and-demanding-transformation/.

24. Kaba, *'Til We Free Us*, xix.

25. Micah Herskind, "Some Reflections on Prison Abolition," Medium, December 7, 2019, https://micahherskind.medium.com/some-reflections-on-prison-abolition-after-mumi-5197a4c3cf98.

26. Adom Getachew, *Worldmaking After Empire: The Rise and Fall of Self-Determination* (Princeton, NJ: Princeton University Press, 2019).

12. A Call for Educational Reparations

1. Robin D. G. Kelley, *Freedom Dreams: The Black Radical Imagination* (Boston: Beacon Press, 2002), 276.

2. Kelley, *Freedom Dreams.*

3. Kelley, *Freedom Dreams.*

4. Kelley, *Freedom Dreams*, 120.

5. John J. Havens and Paul G. Schervish, *A Golden Age of Philanthropy Still Beck-*

ons: National Wealth Transfer and Potential for Philanthropy Technical Report (Boston: Boston College, 2014).

6. Havens and Schervish, *A Golden Age of Philanthropy.*

7. Katherine Franke, *Repair: Redeeming the Promise of Abolition* (Chicago: Haymarket Books, 2019), 136.

8. Nikole Hannah-Jones, "From the Magazine: 'It Is Time for Reparations,'" *New York Times,* June 24, 2020, https://www.nytimes.com/interactive/2020/06/24/magazine/reparations-slavery.html.

9. William Darity Jr., "The True Cost of Closing the Racial Wealth Gap," *New York Times,* April 30, 2021, https://www.nytimes.com/2021/04/30/business/racial-wealth-gap.html.

10. Darity Jr., "The True Cost."

11. Darity Jr., "The True Cost."

12. Ella Ceron, "Black Wealth Could Get 40% Boost If Biden Heeds Calls to Cancel Student Debt," Bloomberg, December 20, 2021, https://www.bloomberg.com/news/articles/2021-12-20/calls-for-biden-to-cancel-50-000-student-debt-could-boost-black-wealth-by-40.

13. Andrea Ritchie et al., *Reparation Now Toolkit* (n.p.: Movement 4 Black Lives, May 23, 2022), https://m4bl.org/wp-content/uploads/2020/05/Reparations-Now-Toolkit-FINAL.pdf.

14. Roy L. Brooks, *Atonement and Forgiveness: A New Model for Black Reparations* (Berkeley: University of California Press, 2004), 143.

15. Brooks, *Atonement and Forgiveness.*

16. Farima Pour-Khorshid, "Personal and Relational Needs" (presentation, Abolitionist Teaching Network Board Retreat, Atlanta, GA, December 12, 2022).

17. David Marchese, "What Can America Learn from South Africa About National Healing?," *New York Times,* December 14, 2020, https://www.nytimes.com/interactive/2020/12/14/magazine/pumla-gobodo-madikizela-interview.html.

18. Marshall Frady, *Martin Luther King, Jr.: A Life* (New York: Penguin Books, 2005), 192.

19. Ta-Nehisi Coates, "The Case for Reparations," *Atlantic,* February 10, 2022, https://www.theatlantic.com/magazine/archive/2014/06/the-case-for-reparations/361631/.

20. Coates, "The Case for Reparations."

21. Adeel Hassan and Jack Healy, "America Has Tried Reparations Before. Here Is How It Went," *New York Times,* June 19, 2019, https://www.nytimes.com/2019/06/19/us/reparations-slavery.html.

22. Hassan and Healy, "America Has Tried Reparations."

23. Hassan and Healy, "America Has Tried Reparations."

24. Kimberly Johnson, "Righting a Wrong: NC to Pay Victims of Forced Sterilization," Al Jazeera America, August 23, 2013, http://america.aljazeera.com/articles/2013/8/23/righting-a-wrongnctopayvictimsofforcedsterilization.html.

25. Hassan and Healy, "America Has Tried Reparations."

26. Amanda Morris, "'You Just Feel Like Nothing': California to Pay Sterilization Victims," *New York Times,* July 11, 2021, https://www.nytimes.com/2021/07/11/us/california-reparations-eugenics.html.

27. Morris, "California to Pay Sterilization Victims."
28. Morris, "California to Pay Sterilization Victims."
29. Char Adams, "Evanston Is the First U.S. City to Issue Slavery Reparations. Experts Say It's a Noble Start," NBC News, March 26, 2021, https://www.nbcnews.com/news/nbcblk/evanston-s-reparations-plan-noble-start-complicated-process-experts-say-n1262096.
30. "Community Reparations Commission," *The City of Asheville*, December 10, 2022, https://www.ashevillenc.gov/department/city-clerk/boards-and-commissions/reparations-commission/.
31. Kurtis Lee, "California Panel Sizes Up Reparations for Black Citizens," *New York Times*, December 1, 2022, https://www.nytimes.com/2022/12/01/business/economy/california-black-reparations.html.
32. Abigail Johnson Hess, "Georgetown Students Vote to Raise Tuition by $27 Per Semester to Pay Slavery Reparations," CNBC, April 12, 2019, https://www.cnbc.com/2019/04/12/georgetown-votes-to-raise-tuition-by-27-to-pay-for-reparations.html.
33. Ayana Archie, "Harvard Releases Report Detailing Its Ties to Slavery, Plans to Issue Reparations," WUNC, April 27, 2022, https://www.wunc.org/2022-04-27/harvard-releases-report-detailing-its-ties-to-slavery-plans-to-issue-reparations.
34. Alcynna Lloyd, "Black Californians Could Get $223,000 Each in Reparations—And It Could Even Help Close the State's Homeownership Gap," *Business Insider*, December 11, 2022, https://www.businessinsider.com/black-californians-could-use-reparations-funds-to-help-pay-for-housing-2022-12.
35. Lloyd, "Black Californians."
36. Lee, "California Panel."
37. Kelley, *Freedom Dreams*, 129.
38. Kelley, *Freedom Dreams*, 133.
39. Preston C. Green III, Bruce D. Baker, and Joseph O. Oluwole, "School Finance, Race, and Reparations," 27 Wash. & Lee J. Civ. Rts. & Soc. Just. 483 (2021). https://scholarlycommons.law.wlu.edu/crsj/vol27/iss2/7
40. Erika M. Kitzmiller and Akira Drake Rodriguez, "Perspective: The Link Between Educational Inequality and Infrastructure," *Washington Post*, August 6, 2021, https://www.washingtonpost.com/outlook/2021/08/06/school-buildings-black-neighborhoods-are-health-hazards-bad-learning/.
41. Kitzmiller and Rodriguez, "Educational Inequality and Infrastructure."
42. C. Kirabo Jackson, Rucker C. Johnson, and Claudia Persico, "The Effects of School Spending on Educational and Economic Outcomes: Evidence from School Finance Reforms" (NBER Working Paper 20847, National Bureau of Economic Research, Cambridge, MA, January 2015), https://www.nber.org/system/files/working_papers/w20847/w20847.pdf.
43. John B. King, Randi Weingarten, and George Miller, "Our Schools Are in Poor Condition. Here's How to Give Kids a Better Learning Environment," *Wichita Falls Times Record News*, June 27, 2021, https://www.timesrecordnews.com/story/opinion/2021/06/27/our-schools-poor-condition-heres-how-give-kids-better-learning-environment/7779969002/.
44. Kitzmiller and Rodriguez, "Educational Inequality and Infrastructure."

45. Sonali Kohli and Quartz, "Modern-Day Segregation in Public Schools," *Atlantic*, November 18, 2014, https://www.theatlantic.com/education/archive/2014/11/modern-day-segregation-in-public-schools/382846/.

46. Harriet R. Tenenbaum and Martin D. Ruck, "Are Teachers Expectations Different for Racial Minority Than for European American Students? A Meta-Analysis," *Journal of Educational Psychology* 99, no. 2 (2007): 253–273, https://doi.org/10.1037/0022–0663.99.2.253; Kristin Klopfenstein, "Advanced Placement: Do Minorities Have Equal Opportunity?," *Economics of Education Review* 23, no. 2 (2004): 115–131, https://doi.org/10.1016/s0272–7757(03)00076–1; Dania V. Francis and William A. Darity Jr., "Separate and Unequal Under One Roof: How the Legacy of Racialized Tracking Perpetuates Within-School Segregation," *RSF: The Russell Sage Foundation Journal of the Social Sciences* 7, no. 1 (February 2021): 187–202, https://www.jstor.org/stable/10.7758/rsf.2021.7.1.11.

47. Klopfenstein, "Advanced Placement."

48. Melanie Hanson, "Cost of a College Class [2022]: Analysis per Credit Hour," Education Data Initiative, March 31, 2022, https://educationdata.org/cost-of-a-college-class-or-credit-hour.

49. Katherine Culliton-González, Marik Xavier-Brier, and LaShonda Brenson, *Beyond Suspensions-USCCR: United States Commission on Civil Rights* (Washington, D.C.: Department of Education Office of Civil Rights, July 23, 2019), 161, https://www.usccr.gov/files/pubs/2019/07–23-Beyond-Suspensions.pdf.

50. *Education Under Arrest: The Case Against Police in Schools* (Washington, D.C.: Justice Policy Institute, November 2011), https://justicepolicy.org/wp-content/uploads/2022/02/educationunderarrest_fullreport.pdf.

51. Erica R. Meiners, "Ending the School-to-Prison Pipeline/Building Abolition Futures," *Urban Review* 43, no. 4 (2011): 547–565, https://doi.org/10.1007/s11256-011-0187–9.

52. "Security Guard-Armed Salary in the United States," Salary.com, retrieved April 26, 2022, https://www.salary.com/research/salary/benchmark/security-guard-armed-salary.

53. Seth Gershenson, Michael Hansen, and Constance A. Lindsay, *Teacher Diversity and Student Success: Why Racial Representation Matters in the Classroom* (Cambridge, MA: Harvard Education Press: 2021).

54. Gershenson, Hansen, and Lindsay, *Teacher Diversity.*

55. Christopher R. Tamborini, ChangHwan Kim, and Arthur Sakamoto, "Education and Lifetime Earnings in the United States," *Demography* 52, no. 4 (2015):1383–1407, doi:10.1007/s13524-015-0407–0.

56. William A. Darity Jr. and A. Kirsten Mullen, *From Here to Equality: Reparations for Black Americans in the Twenty-First Century* (Chapel Hill: University of North Carolina Press, 2020).

57. Darity Jr. and Mullen, *From Here to Equality,* 257.

58. Darity Jr. and Mullen, *From Here to Equality,* 266.

59. Franke, *Repair,* 136.

60. Michael J. Dumas and kihana miraya ross, "'Be Real Black for Me,'" *Urban Education* 51, no. 4 (2016): 415–442, https://doi.org/10.1177/0042085916628611.

61. Dumas and ross, "'Be Real Black.'"

INDEX

Brown v. Board of Education II, 18,
    67–68
Bryant, Ja'Niah, 142–43
Bryant, Ma'Khia, 142–43, 151
Buchanan, James, 34
Buckle, Dwayne, 162–63
Bush, Columba, 100
Bush, George H. W., 1, 40, 57–61, 154
    anti-Black education reform, 59–61,
        77, 88, 89, 97
    election of 1988, 57–58
Bush, George W., 40, 60, 97–99, 102–9,
    120
    No Child Left Behind, 60, 96, 103–9,
        167
Bush, John Ellis "Jeb," 40, 60, 98–103
Byers, Brook, 93
Byrnes, James, 18

Calandra, John D., 230
California
    education funding, 36
    forced sterilizations, 266
    reparations, 268
    truancy laws, 149
Campbell, Shanyce L., 269–72
Campbell, W. Glenn, 52–53
Canada, Geoffrey, 121
Capital Preparatory Harlem Charter
    School, 80
Caputo-Pearl, Alex, 93
carceral inevitability, 12–13, 139–71,
    276–78
    D.A.R.E., 153–56
    Johnnie's story, 161–66
    Kia's story, 139–44
    loss of childhood, 156–61
    "no fear" and recruitment efforts,
        166–71
    sapping Black children's spirits,
        152–53
    suspensions and truancy laws,
        146–51
    zero-tolerance policies, 52, 150–51,
        157–60, 186
carcerality
    big data and, 182–83

Bush and, 101
Clinton and, 97, 157–58
manufactured crises of the 1980s,
    50–52
Reagan and, 50–51
Roc's story, 43–46
standardizing. *See* standardizing
    carcerality
carceral logic, 8–10
Cardona, Miguel, 136
Carlisle, Kimberly, 80
Carranza, Richard, 135
Cashin, Sheryll, 225–26
Cato Institute, 37–38
celebrating Black lives, 248–55
Chan, Priscilla, 40
character education, 11, 104–5, 189
Charleston church shooting, 143,
    245
charter schools, 8, 78–84
    in Atlanta, 75–77
    Bush and, 60–61
    Bush brothers and, 98–102, 107
    in Chicago, 112–13, 145
    DeVos and, 132–33
    Gates and, 201, 204
    KIPP, 185–90, 192–94
    in New Orleans after Hurricane
        Katrina, 109–12
    "no excuses" discipline approach, 52,
        116, 187
    TFA expansion and, 92
    virtual public, 81–84
Charter Schools USA, 99–100
Chauvin, Derek, 214
Chicago, police brutality in, 182–83,
    266–67, 268
Chicago Public Schools, 106, 112–13,
    145, 203
Chicago School of Economics,
    34–35
Children's Defense Fund, 105
Christie, Chris, 79
Civil Liberties Act of 1988, 266
Civil War, 194, 195
Clark, Ed, 50
Clifton, Lucille, 253